WHAT WORKS

HAMISH McRAE is the principal economic commentator of *The Independent* and the *Independent on Sunday* and associate editor of *The Independent*. He is also the author of the acclaimed work on the future *The World in 2020: Power, Culture and Prosperity*, first published in 1994 and translated into more than a dozen languages. He was awarded the Communicator of the Year at the 2007 Business Journalist Awards, Business and Finance Journalist of the Year in the 2006 British Press Awards and is the winner of the 2005 David Watt Prize for outstanding political journalism. He is a visiting professor at the School of Management at Lancaster University and a council member of the Royal Economic Society. He was educated at Fettes College, Edinburgh and Trinity College, Dublin. He is married to Frances Cairncross, Rector of Exeter College, Oxford, and they have two grown-up daughters.

Praise for *What Works*
'Optimistic yet realistic, humane yet incisive, Hamish McRae's inspiring and wide-ranging book is essential reading for anyone who wants to understand what works, what doesn't, and why.'   TIM HARFORD

Praise for *The World in 2020*
'I read Hamish McRae's book with great pleasure and benefit. Vividly written without any jargon or clichés, it is ideal for anyone who needs to think clearly about the world's future.'   ANTHONY SAMPSON

HAMISH McRAE

What Works

Success in Stressful Times

Harper
Press

Harper*Press*
An imprint of HarperCollins*Publishers*
77–85 Fulham Palace Road
Hammersmith, London W6 8JB
www.harpercollins.co.uk

Visit our authors' blog: www.fifthestate.co.uk
Love this book? www.bookarmy.com

First published in Great Britain by Harper*Press* in 2010

1

Copyright © Hamish McRae 2010
Illustrations © Anna Morrison

Hamish McRae asserts the moral right to
be identified as the author of this work

A catalogue record for this book
is available from the British Library

ISBN 978-0-00-720377-2

Typeset in Garamond and Bodoni by
G&M Designs Limited, Raunds, Northamptonshire

Printed and bound in Great Britain by Clays Ltd, St Ives plc

All rights reserved. No part of this publication may be
reproduced, stored in a retrieval system, or transmitted,
in any form or by any means, electronic, mechanical,
photocopying, recording or otherwise, without the prior
written permission of the publishers.

Mixed Sources
Product group from well-managed
forests and other controlled sources
www.fsc.org Cert no. SW-COC-1806
© 1996 Forest Stewardship Council
FSC

FSC is a non-profit international organization established to promote the
responsible management of the world's forests. Products carrying the FSC
label are independently certified to assure consumers that they come
from forests that are managed to meet the social, economic and
ecological needs of present or future generations.

Find out more about HarperCollins and the environment at
www.harpercollins.co.uk/green

To Frances, Izzy and Alex

List of Contents

Introduction

1. HOW THIS BOOK HAPPENED –
AND HOW IT HAS CHANGED
DURING THE WRITING

This is a book about success. It is about success in good times and bad. Its twenty examples come from every corner of the planet. It encompasses organizations and communities as diverse as the world's best university and the world's best slum. Of course, none of these stories is a tale of perfection and each example has flaws. But they are examples of collective human endeavour that I have found both humbling and inspiring and which I believe have powerful common messages for all of us. By understanding what works, we can make other things work better – the aspects of our daily life that we can improve. By any rational calculation the world is better placed now to make good choices about the future of our species and our planet. We are better educated than ever before; have better health and better information; technology continues to leap forward; and, of course, we are – notwithstanding the odd bump – richer than ever before. But if we are to face the many challenges we have to try to learn from each other. We all have to do it. It is the millions of acts by ordinary people that will eventually make a difference. In a modest way, it is to help us make a difference that I have tried to tell the stories in this book.

What Works has been more than a decade in gestation. In 1994–5 I published a book on the future of the global economy, *The World in 2020*. I then spent a huge amount of time travelling the world, talking about the future I had sketched with companies, academic institutions, management schools, professional bodies – and writing columns for *The Independent* newspaper in London all the while. The more I travelled, the more I began to marvel at the range of things I came across in every part of the globe that worked really well – success stories that deserved a wider audience.

So this book started as a desire to report, to share stories. But, of course, there have been many studies of success, particularly business books promoting apparently successful forms of organization, usually with an ideology attached. This study differs from those in that it does not aim to sell a theory – the notion that if companies or governments adopt this or that form of management theory or organization then they, too, will succeed. Actually they seldom do. You cannot, for example, transport the American corporate model to, say, India and expect every firm there to prosper. Besides, the shelf life of apparently

---

THE LESSONS

1. Optimism, balanced by realism: pessimism paralyses
2. Excellence, tempered by decency: if you neglect your wider responsibilities, you're liable to end up in trouble when you meet headwinds
3. Community works, if it is allowed to: look at things from the ground level up and mobilize community
4. Government works too: compare like with like
5. Become a true magnet for talent: put out the welcome mat
6. Be honest about failure: keep learning, keep making mistakes
7. The need for humility: be as sensitive to success as you are to failure
8. Be nimble: make sure you are quick to adapt
9. Listen to the market: remember, it's about more than money
10. Have a sense of mission: keep the long game in view and do right by those who share your objectives

great ideas is short indeed. Companies universally admired by one generation as models of managerial excellence are reviled by the next as failures. Government initiatives launched by one generation of ambitious politicians are quietly abandoned by the next. And economic principles embraced by one generation of academics are disputed by the next. After all, if financial markets were really as efficient as economic theory suggests, they would not have created two classic bubbles in the past decade: the internet craze and the dot-com crash; and the sub-prime boom and bust.

So what does work? Instead of finding case studies to promote a theory, I worked from the other end. I observed success and tried to draw lessons from that. But the more I travelled, the more I became aware of different examples of successful organization, in different countries, on different continents, on different scales, and in a mixture of the public, private and voluntary sectors. The problem was not how to find case studies offering practical insights into what works – plenty of friends with whom I discussed the project offered candidates of their own – but how on earth to whittle them down to a manageable number.

More about this selection process in a moment. What became clear pretty early on was that for organizations to work really well, they needed to combine two features, the final two are noted opposite.

1. They had to have a deep-seated sense of mission – a vision, drive and commitment to do something that is worth doing even better. This sense of purpose could initially come from an individual but frequently it sprang from a group of like-minded people. Or it could develop from a general ethos accumulated over many years, so that no one could quite identify just who picked up the baton in the first place and who carried it forward at any particular time.
2. They had to be acutely sensitive to the market. They worked because they went with the grain of the market, listening to its signals and being guided by them, and applying its disciplines and adapting to whatever these required.

One without the other does not work. A plan or project that operates with a mission but fails to listen to the market may carry on for a while on a tide of early enthusiasm. But it cannot be sustained.

Pure market-driven endeavours can carry on for much longer. Most good businesses perform the essential task of seeking to fulfil people's needs and desires, and if they do that competently, they make a solid contribution to the material world. However, they cannot change it. Market without mission can certainly help us get richer, improve our living standards and lead a materially better life. But add the sense of mission and you get something much more: a success that can be replicated and scaled.

Each case study in this book is a mix of these two attributes and each is tackled in the same sequence. First, I tell the story, explaining how I came to include this example and trying to capture and explain its special features. Then I seek to draw out some general lessons. Then, because nothing progresses in a straight line, I have to acknowledge what may go wrong and, in some instances, has already gone wrong.

Two other points emerged during the research and writing. One was that there has been a host of 'near misses' – things that ought to work very well but have in some way fallen short. I considered trying to capture this because failure can sometimes carry more messages than success. History is littered with examples of clever and thought-ful people making huge errors, and of plans hatched by apparently very competent organizations resulting in disasters. The 'best and the brightest' get things wrong. In the end I rejected this approach because there were many different reasons for failure. There are common features to the successes but each failure failed in its own particular way. To give a flavour of this, I have sketched some of these near misses in the next part of this introduction.

The other point that became clear is that what happens in a global economic downturn is more interesting than what happens in the good times. Many of these case studies were researched and written in the boom years, with the result that the 'what could go wrong' section of some chapters has become more a tale of 'what has gone wrong'.

I am not at all discouraged by this; indeed I am rather relieved. We are all in some measure prisoners of the moment, and while I was very conscious of the danger of writing a bull-market book, it was hard to lean against the prevailing wind. But a bear-market book, intoning that all is disaster, is not much use either. *What Works* has been completed during the downturn but it does, I hope, retain both its optimism and its perspective. If something does not work in tough times as well as easy ones, what is the point of examining it?

I have tried to look through the current difficulties evident in several of the case studies and make a judgement about the future. If I had not been confident, I would have dumped the example and chosen another. As it has turned out, I have not had to do this in any instance, for what seem to me to be sound reasons that I try to explain. Of course, I face the charge of being an eternal optimist, but I would rather answer to that than be a Dr Doom.

And so to those case studies. These are grouped geographically, partly for clarity but also because to look at the world this way emphasizes the message that really interesting things are happening in all corners of the planet. Some wider themes are drawn out in the final chapter.

It is a personal selection, of course, and it might be helpful next to describe quite how these choices came about.

2. WHY THESE CASE STUDIES WERE CHOSEN — AND A WORD ABOUT THE ONES THAT WERE LEFT OUT

Picking examples from the UK and Ireland was easy, for this is territory I know well. There are three, one each from England, Scotland and Ireland – apologies to Wales, though the country is host to administrative offices of another example, the International Baccalaureate. The English example, the financial services industry of the City of London, was almost too obvious because not only is commenting on it part of my day job, but I co-authored a book about it. Writing about the Irish economy, too, was easy: I know the story as I was brought up there and, as I acknowledge, I greatly admire the achievement. The question in both cases was whether – in the light of the economic downturn and the errors, individual and collective – they should stay in. Actually it was an easy decision, for the achievements have been far greater than the setbacks.

The reverses to the City are small in the context of the difficulties it has faced over the past century: after each of the two world wars its business was destroyed, and during the 1970s it was savaged by political and industrial strife in Britain as well as the greatest outbreak of global inflation the world has ever known.

As for Ireland, the clinching argument was put to me by one of its most senior bankers at a Trinity College Dublin meeting. 'Look,' he said. 'We will go down 10 per cent, maybe a bit more, and that is dreadful. But in the previous fifteen or so years, we added 100 per cent to our GDP. And we will recover.'

One of the first examples I chose, though, was Scottish – and in particular what is by far the world's largest collection of arts events, the Edinburgh Festival. Indeed its combination of a sense of collective mission over several generations and its status as a supreme marketplace for talent actually helped define the nature of the book. Is it particularly Scottish? Well, yes, in the sense that it could not happen without the support of Edinburgh's citizens, who belie their reputation for being strait-laced in the way they relish the edgy stuff that is set out before them. But no in the sense that I am not trying to illustrate or praise national characteristics as such – simply to show what others can learn from undoubted success stories.

For continental Europe, the choices were harder. There are only four examples in this book and I wish I had more. A couple are stories I have wanted to tell for a long time. I have been an admirer of the German Mittelstand, the country's collection of medium-sized companies, since my childhood, for reasons I explain in the text. And ever since I first went there, I have wanted to tell the story of how Copenhagen's taming of the motor car has come to offer a lesson to the world. The other two were harder choices.

The only commercial company in the book is Sweden's Ikea, chosen not because I am handy bolting together its flatpacked furniture or because it is particularly customer-friendly; quite the reverse – it is one of those companies that people love to hate. No, it was because its success goes beyond commerce in that it illustrates the sense of mission very well and also has something essentially Scandinavian about its ethos – a mix of style and equality – that was worth trying to bring to a wider audience.

The fourth European example is the drug-rehabilitation programme introduced in Zurich, and more specifically the rehabilitation of heroin users. I have to acknowledge that this scheme is not perfect; it just seems to have been more effective than any other. This study came about because Frances Cairncross, my spouse, visited its clinics when writing about drugs for *The Economist* magazine, and while the scheme has been imitated elsewhere and there have been some success stories, these have not been as numerous as I would have hoped. I think that is mostly because politics have got in the way, so if telling this tale helps push politics aside then it will have been a worthwhile exercise.

I am just as concerned, though, about the other stories that I would love to have included but have not. One huge success has been Finland's primary and secondary education. According to an OECD study, the performance of Finnish students is quite outstanding. Would the Finnish ideas travel? Well, among the former Eastern bloc countries, Estonia has the best education outcomes. Why so? Officials there explained to me that they had adopted the Finnish model. Estonia is culturally very close to Finland so it is hard to gauge the potential reach of the ideas, but evidently they do have a bit of mileage in them.

There is nothing from France or Italy and, of course, there should be, for each has areas of outstanding excellence. The problem with France was finding examples capable of being replicated elsewhere. For example, the country leads the world in the proportion of its electricity generated by nuclear power stations. Those plants are reliable, efficient and, as far as one can judge, cost-effective. But it would not be easy to transplant a policy and a technology. In any case, a new plant in Finland, being built by a French company, has run into serious difficulties and is behind schedule and over budget.

Another example would be French healthcare, one of my original choices. It is still on balance one of the best systems in the world, if an expensive one, but it failed in the heatwave of August 2003. France had up to 20,000 more deaths than normal as a result of the soaring temperatures. Why? One reason seems to have been that August is the month-long holiday season there and most French doctors and other medical staff were off-duty.

One obvious Italian quality is its design talent, but that is hard to transfer to other countries. An example of excellence that has been imitated elsewhere is Italy's 'slow food' movement – the emphasis on quality rather than quantity in food – which is a philosophy that encompasses other aspects of the Italian way. It would have been good to have included that as a means of examining how the country has managed to sustain one of the most-admired quality-of-life environments anywhere in the world. However, while other parts of the world have tried to copy some of these qualities, I felt the movement is so rooted in the history and culture of Italy that the lessons are limited.

One other European gap is Russia, where a candidate was the country's technical education. This was clearly exceptional, though maybe less so now than a decade or more ago. Another potential case study was the vibrancy of Russian writing, also exceptional. But it was hard to bolt down excellence that could be transferred and so sadly the gap remains.

In North America the choices were extremely tough. I know and like America and have sought to understand it over many years, but choosing key messages for the world was difficult. An obvious area of excellence is in the business community and one of the original examples was General Electric, though I was more interested in it as a school for executives who then worked in other companies, rather than as a business itself. But this is a very well-travelled route and I was not sure I could add much value. I wanted to write about excellence in US healthcare, which at its best delivers a wonderful service. There have been many social initiatives, for example Milwaukee's welfare reforms, which deserve a wider audience. I spent many hours researching, discussing and rejecting.

In the end I went back to a place that I knew and loved. Small towns in America have long fascinated me and having family in Montana has given me what I hope is a special insight into one medium-sized and successful town there, Billings.

Philanthropic New York was another choice, brought about by my affection for the city ever since my first visit in 1964, but also by a growing respect for the generosity of American people. The third US example, Harvard, was originally included not so much as a university but as a fund-management group. That was a bit too quirky and I had gone back to thinking about Harvard's basic message of educational excellence even before the financial meltdown of late 2007 rather destroyed any idea about its special insights into fund management. My perspective has been one of a rival as my spouse is head of one of the oldest of the colleges at Oxford University, which has encouraged me to think a lot about what makes universities truly and lastingly great.

And then there is Whistler. There are many things about Canada to be admired but authors are allowed to be a bit self-indulgent: as a keen if not particularly skilled skier, and a correspondent on the sport, I did not see why I should not write about a ski-resort if I wanted to. More important, there is something especially and wonderfully Canadian about this tale, which I hope I have brought out.

The USA and Canada are covered but Latin America, I am afraid, is not. The only excuse, aside from the obvious one of a lack of space, is that I am not as familiar with the region as I am with most other parts of the world. I did, however, want very much to include a Brazilian tale and looked at several possibilities, an obvious one being the successful municipal government in the southern city of Curitiba. This is a great example of urban planning – a really well-run city. Another, somewhat more controversial example would have been Protestant churches, which have shot up from tiny beginnings a generation ago to become the fastest-growing Christian organizations in the world.

But the example that I most regret not examining is happiness in São Paulo. It is not that Brazil's largest city is also its happiest but rather that, insofar as such an intangible can be measured, Brazilian people are among the happiest on earth. To some extent a sunny disposition goes with wealth; people in richer countries generally have more to smile about than those in poorer ones. But Brazil is an outlier. Its people are much happier than one might expect from the statistics, and where better to delve deeper into that than the country's economic powerhouse, with all its energy and chaos? Maybe another book ...

China and India both had to be included for obvious reasons. I have made several visits to both countries but, of course, I have only scratched the surface; no outsider from the West can ever feel they will understand countries with more than a billion citizens. In the case of China, however, one choice was easy: the Shanghai municipality. It is impossible not to be astounded, and at one level alarmed, by what has been achieved. The other choice, the Hong Kong Jockey Club, came about because some friends who live there suggested it. I had known Hong Kong ought to feature in the book somehow, but it was not until I researched the story that I realized this was an ideal way not just into gambling (though I enjoyed my day at the races) but also into a remarkable record in governance.

In India I had to write about the hi-tech industries of Bangalore; no one who goes there escapes unchanged by the experience. There are many other examples of hi-tech complexes in India – I could just as well have gone to Pune or Hyderabad – but Bangalore was where the dream first took root. The other choice, Dharavi in Mumbai, was more quirky, or at least it was until *Slumdog Millionaire* introduced Dharavi to millions of cinema-goers around the world. I hate the word 'slum' just as I hate the glamorizing of poverty. So the surprise there is not just that this community works but that it is an important economic powerhouse, generating a billion dollars of GDP each year.

There should, of course, have been other Asian examples, aside from the single Japanese tale – that of public safety in Tokyo. The great Japanese boom that lasted until 1990 brought the world such consumer triumphs as the Walkman and cars that did not break down. The world has certainly learnt from that, just as we have also learnt, less comfortably, about the threat of stagnation from what happened after 1990. (I co-authored a book, published only in Japanese, about the dangers of such stagnation to Japanese society and its influence in the world.) The example here, however, is not economic but social. It concerns how Tokyo, the largest agglomeration of humankind on the planet, is also the safest large city in the world, giving its citizens a greater degree of freedom to go about their daily lives than the people of any other city. Young women can return home on public transport late at night without any concern they might be attacked or hassled. Salarymen the worse for wear after an evening in the bars can do likewise.

I regret not including Singapore, for it is a fascinating experiment and a hugely successful one. Its attributes, however, are well known. There should be success stories from South-East Asia, for example from South Korea, Malaysia and Indonesia; my only defence is that you cannot cover everything.

The Middle East and Africa have each fielded a tale. I first visited Dubai at the height of the boom and decided there and then that this was a story demanding to be told. I next visited when it was rolling over towards the downturn and the question was whether to keep it in for by then it was clear that it would hit the buffers. Should the example be broadened more generally to the Gulf states, including Abu Dhabi, which has moved to rescue its fellow United Arab Emirates member, and also neighbouring Oman, which has been extraordinarily successful in creating a harmonious mix of ancient and modern? In the end I kept Dubai, partly because it is such an extreme example of property development but more because, for all its shortcomings, I believe it will maintain its role as a trading hub in the years ahead and succeed at it. Meanwhile, the lessons are obvious.

Africa was difficult because the continent is so diverse and its problems so challenging. Primary education in Ghana was one possibility, an example of public sector success under difficult circumstances. I would have liked to highlight the vibrancy of commerce in Nigeria, a success story against an even more difficult background. But in the end the obvious choice was surely the right one: mobile telephony. That is a great story in its own right but also illustrates some of the most remarkable features of the continent, including the ability of its people to adapt technologies to suit the special circumstances of Africa and the sheer commercial creativity of many societies there.

Australia provided an outstanding example, sports education, and even if it is an obvious one, I am happy with that. The message that it does this better than any place on earth has already transformed sports training in Britain, among other places, and in any case I think the story really should go beyond sport: governments can achieve in education if they are determined, set up and fund the project, and are clear about their objectives.

Finally, there is one non-geographical example, the International Baccalaureate. This is an education movement that is genuinely multinational: its legal headquarters are in Switzerland, it has an administrative base in Wales, its largest market is the USA and its fastest-growing areas of activity are in Asia. Schools all over the world are turning to the IB as a way not just to give their students a global academic credential, but much more to equip them to be good citizens of the world in their own individual way. I gave a talk about the changing world economy to a group of IB people and came away thrilled by what I learnt. Visiting schools in the UK, the USA and, by chance, Estonia totally confirmed this view. It is wonderful to know that the next generation of people who will be running the show is so good.

That brings me to the final point: the sense of a global community that came through strongly when I was researching and writing this book. Some general themes of *What Works*, together with the more specific takeaway lessons, are set out in the concluding chapter. Here are some thoughts about the global context of this book: how these stories exemplify a world where power is shifting and good ideas come from every quarter.

3. THE POWER OF GOOD IDEAS –
AND THE VARIETY OF PLACES
THEY COME FROM

The world is at one of those inflection points that historians will look back upon with awe. Economic power is rebalancing away from Europe and, to some extent, North America and principally towards Asia. It is the biggest shift of power since the Industrial Revolution, which enabled Europe and then North America to leap ahead of the more populous Asia. In 1820, by far the largest economies in the world were China and India. Fast forward and, within a generation, China seems set to overtake the USA as the largest – it probably overtook Japan to become the second biggest some time in 2009 – while India is likely to move into the number three slot. Other countries, including Brazil and Russia, will not be far behind. Most people in the West are vaguely aware of the rising power of the so-called emerging economies, particularly of China, but have hardly begun to think through the consequences of this.

This shift is not just about economics; it is also about ideas. We are moving from a period when most of the ideas that have driven the world economy have come from the West, to one where many will come from the East – and the rest of the emerging world. For the moment the mixed-economy model of Europe, Japan and, in a slightly different form, the USA remains the one that is being adopted in the rest of the world. On the surface it looks as though a form of Western capitalism is being recreated in China and to some extent in India. In the summer of 2009 the Shanghai Stock Exchange became the second largest in the world after New York, in the sense that the value of the companies traded on it was second only to those traded on Wall Street. But that was in part because Chinese banks had adopted a different set of business practices to those of their US counterparts and it was in part, too, because the Chinese government had followed a totally different fiscal strategy from that of the USA or most European governments.

China and India, together with many other emerging nations, came out of the economic downturn in far better shape than the USA, Europe or Japan. On the face of it, the ideas of the emerging world look rather more effective than those of the West.

The purpose of this book is not to look at the future shape of the world, and the way it is changing, from a macro-economic perspective. That is what I spend much of my day job doing, and it was also the approach of *The World in 2020*. My aim here, in starting from a series of stories, is to illustrate how there are great ideas and innovations in Western societies but also similarly great ideas and innovations in the emerging world.

That surely is the future. Good ideas will increasingly come from anywhere and everywhere. We need to learn from each other. You cannot, of course, lift one way of doing things, transplant it to the other side of the earth and expect it to flourish. You could not create an Edinburgh Festival in China any more than you could make New York as safe as Tokyo. You could not build as good a university as Harvard even in Bangalore, or at least it would take several generations to do so. And you could not transport Hong Kong's lean government to the welfare states of Western Europe, though there are some things we could learn from that. Indeed I hope we can all learn a bit from each of these stories, and try to apply some elements of their success. I've picked out three key lessons (bulleted) in each example and highlighted some further lessons in the conclusion.

We can also learn from the weaknesses. While every single example here is one of something that has been successful, every single story in some way encompasses threats that must be overcome or flaws that must be fixed. I have tried to highlight these for this is what makes the stories real. One of the great puzzles is the way in which clever, thoughtful and decent people can get things wrong.

What interests me most about these examples is partly the extent to which the baton of success can be passed on from one generation to another but it is also the extent to which an entity has the capacity to correct its course when the winds change.

As noted at the beginning of this introduction, the winds have changed sharply during the writing of this book. That makes for a much more interesting world, a much more challenging one, and one where we should dump ideological explanations and responses and simply build on 'what works'. I hope you will enjoy the journey.

The UK
and Ireland

CHAPTER ONE

Edinburgh Festival

The biggest arts festival of all

I. WHAT IS THE STORY?

A shouted warning for the audience to stand back and a burst of fire from a human flame-thrower surges towards the crowd of onlookers on the Mound. A troupe in silver body-paint hands out leaflets for the night's performance. Down the High Street, a jazz band bangs out the sounds of New Orleans. It is clamour, clamour – 'come and see us, the most brilliant act ever' – as every group of talent demands your attention. For it is August in Edinburgh and the prim grey capital of Scotland is once again home to the largest arts show in the world.

As the International Festival guide puts it: 'There is no place on earth like Edinburgh in August.'

Nothing, but nothing, prepares the first-time visitor for the scale of what is on offer. You could in theory set to work every morning at ten, jam-pack the day with visits to shows and go all the way through the wee hours to 4 a.m. – and still see only a tiny fraction of what is available. There are more shows, more world premieres, more tickets, more new talent, more critics, more media moguls, more authors and playwrights – in short more talent on display – than at any other arts festival anywhere. What have Rupert Murdoch, Billy Connolly and J. K. Rowling got in common? They have all, in one way or another, appeared on a stage in Edinburgh in August.[1]

In fact, so, too, has just about everyone involved in the British arts or media scene. Every student theatre troupe in the land wants to put something on there; a dear friend commissioned a new piano composition that had its world premiere there; other friends have done book readings or shows; one of my cousins puts on or acts in a play there most years ... and my own modest contribution was once to go on stage as a panellist for a TV event.

There is a host of other arts festivals around the world but Edinburgh is three times the size of any of them.[2] It is an extraordinary, if improbable achievement – and one that many other cities would love to emulate. How has Edinburgh done it?

The short answer is slowly. This is not one festival but – depending what you include – ten. Each reinforces the others, giving the city an artistic critical mass that makes it impossible to topple.

There is the original arts festival,[3] organized like so many others by the city authorities. There is a jazz and blues festival,[4] Europe's largest, bringing in groups from all over the world. There is the book fair,[5] the largest of its kind on the planet. There is a film festival,[6] the longest continually running one in the world, for Cannes had a break during the Second World War.[7] There is a television festival.[8] In 2003, a video games festival joined the clutch;[9] Scotland is one of the key world centres for creating new video games.[10] There is the Mela,[11] a celebration of life in the Indian sub-continent, run by Edinburgh's Asian community. In 2004 the city added a visual art festival for the first time,[12] though actually modern visual arts had been celebrated since the early years, with local galleries putting on individual shows. In a slightly different category from all the rest, there is the Edinburgh Tattoo,[13] where military musicians – again from all over the world – put on a show on the forecourt of Edinburgh Castle. The Tattoo is actually the second-largest of all the shows in terms of ticket sales, offering more than 200,000 seats through its three-week run, and military visitors come from all over the world to see how it is done.

And the biggest of all? That honour goes to the Fringe. Edinburgh's special feature, the thing that distinguishes it from every other celebration of artistic endeavour, is the Fringe – the open access given by the city to the thousands of events that take place in August. Others have tried to copy it. None has really succeeded.

The story, though, offers a lesson for anyone wanting to run an arts event. Back in that drab aftermath of the Second World War, many cities sought to recapture the life and joy of pre-war Europe. Thus Cannes restarted its film festival – it had opened for just one night, on 1 September 1939, before Europe was plunged into war. In 1946 and 1947, respectively, Avignon[14] and Edinburgh both started arts festivals[15] – the pattern being the classic one where a group of civil and artistic leaders invite companies to bring their acts, organize venues – and usually offer subsidies to get them to come. The original Edinburgh International Arts Festival was exactly that. But in the very first year something happened that changed Edinburgh and the arts world for ever.

Eight groups that had not been invited, six from Scotland and two from England, decided to gatecrash the show. They found their own venues, stumped up their own money and put on a performance.[16] That first Fringe has defined the movement ever since: no performers are invited – there is complete open access; they use unconventional theatres; and they carry all the financial risks themselves. More came the following year and an Edinburgh journalist pointed out that interesting things were happening on the fringe of the main festival – and so coined that expression to describe them.[17]

Since then, the Fringe has gradually acquired a modest infrastructure. The first programme to bring the various independent acts under one loose umbrella, rather than have them compete against each other for spectators,[18] was put together on the initiative of a local printer in 1954. A box office run by Edinburgh students followed in 1955 and the Festival Fringe Society in 1958.[19] One of the key aims of the society was to help would-be performers put on shows, a theme that continues to today. The event became famous across the UK in 1960 after the success of the comedy show *Beyond the Fringe*[20] (ironically part of the main festival, not the Fringe), but the first full-time paid employee was not appointed until 1969.

The Fringe raced on, getting into the *Guinness Book of Records* as the globe's largest arts festival in 1992 and becoming the first arts organization in the world to sell tickets online in real time in 2000. In 2009 an estimated 19,000 performers took part in more than 34,000 performances at more than 2,000 shows in 265 venues. Nearly 1.9 million tickets were sold and the event generated £75 million for the economy. Those figures beat all records by a huge margin. Indeed the Fringe had doubled in size over the previous six years.[21]

Then finally there are the shows that are literally 'Beyond the Fringe'. The Fringe is an enabling organization that aims to help would-be performers. No one needs to use its services to put on a show, though, in practice, it makes life easier to go through the central ticket office and benefit from the publicity associated with the Fringe programme. But lots of performers simply turn up. Most busk in the High Street or on the Mound, the public space by the National Gallery of Scotland, but some simply put on a show in friends' flats. You may not get noticed by the critics, but if you want the experience of performing before a huge and interested audience, Edinburgh provides the ultimate opportunity. Edinburgh in August is the world's stage and anyone, but anyone, can be a player.

But how? How has one medium-sized city managed to achieve this position?[22] To relate the chronology helps explain a little, for the burst of energy that the Fringe brought from day one has been the catalyst driving the growth of the other elements of the festival. Critical mass matters. Once the Fringe was established as the premier showcase for British, later world, theatrical talent, it was natural that Edinburgh in August should attract other festivals too. The market was largely ready-made, for people who are interested in new experimental theatre are probably also interested in more conventional drama, in classical music and jazz, in new books – in all the other experiences that Edinburgh offers. But Edinburgh is not just a retail show for interested individuals; it is a wholesale show for the different artistic trades. For a young performer to get noticed at Edinburgh can be a life-changing experience. Win one of the top awards and nothing will ever be the same again.

So for the (mostly) youthful performers and producers at the Fringe, it is a career tool. 'I am here,' a friend who put on a show there explained, 'to invest in my future.' And for the more mature critics and impresarios, as well as the ordinary punters, it is 'the chance to see it before it happens'.

2. WHAT ARE THE LESSONS?

Edinburgh has long had a lot of things going for it – things that would naturally make it the ideal backdrop for an arts and entertainment festival. It is, physically, the most beautiful city in Britain, with its castle, its gardens, its medieval Old Town and its Georgian squares. It is a capital city and – important in the entertainment world – an English-speaking one. But none of this, of course, would have been enough. There are at least three special features about the Edinburgh Festival that carry a message for other cities seeking to develop their own special face to the world.

Lesson one is the willingness to create and permit a completely open marketplace. This means accepting that what happens cannot be controlled. Edinburgh has tended this marketplace wisely, not by piling in huge amounts of money or building infrastructure, but rather by clearing bureaucratic blockages that might stifle it. For example, one of the keys to the Fringe's success is the use of unconventional performance spaces, often in old buildings designed for another purpose.[23] That means applying sensitive fire and access regulations – to make sure audiences really are safe – rather than insisting that venues fit box-ticking requirements.

It also means accepting that the city will, for one month, be a quite different place from what it is during the rest of the year. Residents and businesses alike in effect lose control of the centre of their city. It is business, of course, but it is also disruption. Were it badly managed, the disruption could damage the core activities that drive the city through the rest of the year. All tourist centres have to cope to some extent with surges of visitors with different values to the locals, but this is extreme stuff. The lesson therefore is not just to permit the creation of a market but also to relish it.

Lesson two is to blend top-down and bottom-up. There is no single mind planning what happens in Edinburgh; there are and always have been lots of minds, which work in different ways. Some of these, such as the director and governing body of the International Festival, have to exert a top-down discipline. The companies performing have to be invited. Funding has to be found, venues secured and the events publicized. To get the right mix, there has to be some artistic direction.

At the Fringe, by contrast, the minds have to focus almost exclusively on logistics. They do not concern themselves about the artistic merit of the performers; all they have to do is make sure that anyone who fills the basic requirements is able to set up a show, for this is entirely a bottom-up exercise. There is, however, one crucial function that the Fringe performs beyond logistics. This is teaching.

Every year it holds a series of seminars to show would-be performers and promoters how to put on a show. These include: how much the different venues will cost; how to manage publicity; the timescale for decisions; the need to go for as long a run as possible to cover costs, and so on. It is in the interests of everyone that people go into the project aware of the costs and how to budget for them. Even performers have to eat.

The trick, which the various organizers of the Edinburgh festivals have managed to pull off, is to achieve balance – to plan but not to over-plan, to lead but also to follow the demands of the market.

That leads to the third lesson: the need to listen. This has been central to Edinburgh's development at three stages.

First, what started as a conventional arts festival, and might have remained so, was swiftly transformed by the demands of the market into something much bigger. Had there been no uninvited guests at the first party, the Fringe might never have taken off.

Second, in the middle years, Edinburgh allowed market forces to develop the Fringe, rather than trying to stifle it. Technically, the Fringe has become extremely innovative, from the first comprehensive programme to the centralized ticket office and, later, to internet booking.

Third, whenever a new festival wanted to tag along, it was welcomed. So films and TV, jazz and books were all grafted onto the official and Fringe core. This tradition continued into 2004 with the formal addition of the art festival – though as I noted earlier, the visual arts had been represented at Edinburgh for many years in an informal way.

By chance, on a visit to the festival in 2007, I met the key person in bringing modern visual arts to Edinburgh – a man called Richard Demarco,[24] who grabbed me by the arm and taught me something else. A tiny, mercurial Italian Scot in his late seventies, he had gone as a 17-year-old to the very first festival – and been so enchanted that he decided to devote his life to bringing art to Edinburgh.

And so over the years a string of European and Scottish artists had their works exhibited in Edinburgh at Richard Demarco's gallery, and in 2007 his archive was put on display at the Scottish National Portrait Gallery in Queen Street. It was an amazing jumble of stuff, bringing together the work of renowned artists such as Joseph Beuys[25] and Richard Demarco's role in the whole festival scene. (He had, for example, co-founded the Traverse Theatre[26] in 1963.)

As we talked, two things became clear – two things at the core of the spirit of Edinburgh. One is that it is vital for the different aspects of art to commingle; theatre should not be separate from the visual arts – it is all part of the whole. And, of course, Edinburgh mixes everything together. The other is that you need failure; people need to be free to fail. Richard Demarco himself always maintains that he set out on his career in the arts because he had failed his exams at school, but the point is much bigger.

What I think Edinburgh does is to create a platform not just where people can feel free to experiment but also one where they do not need to worry if it does not work. There is surely a wider message there: individual failure is an essential part of the wider success of almost all enterprises – and absolutely to a venture as huge and amorphous as the Edinburgh Festival.

- **Create an open marketplace**
- **Blend top-down and bottom-up**
- **Listen – and accept failure as part of wider success**

3. WHAT COULD GO WRONG?

Nothing is for ever but the sheer size and variety of the talent on display in Edinburgh gives it a stability that other arts festivals lack. Because it is market-driven, it cannot be snuffed out by a squeeze on funding; as long as it provides a useful showcase function for the entertainment industries, it will survive. If you were trying to create a new venue for putting talent in the shop window, you would not invent Edinburgh, but it is there, it is huge and it would be hard to displace. Critical mass matters.

But so, too, does efficiency. In 2008 the film festival moved its timing forward to May, thereby getting the city to itself. This decision was largely due to the global film calendar – a case of trying to fit in between Cannes, Venice and Toronto[27] – but the sheer congestion of Edinburgh in August was apparently a factor too. That year the Fringe booking system broke down and ticket numbers were down year-on-year, though they recovered spectacularly in 2009.

Thus the main threat is not that all the new shows will suddenly up sticks and decamp to New York, London – or Hollywood, rather it is that the festival will become an inefficient showcase, making it hard for the talent-spotters to find what they want and for the best shows to gain their attention.

It may become too big for its own good. This is not principally a matter of logistics – though the city needs to think more innovatively about the way in which it manages the weight of visitors – but of marrying the needs of the ordinary public, who largely fund the whole show, with the needs of the industries that use it to show their wares. If it becomes inefficient for the professionals and they find other ways of locating the new performers, then the city loses a crucial element of its importance.

At a popular level that might hardly be noticed; the more punters who come, the more the market will create stuff to entertain them. The retail trade would continue unchecked, at least for a while. But if Edinburgh were ever to lose its edge – if, for example, the new comedians started to test their acts elsewhere – then after a while the public would begin to notice.

There is an element of danger about Edinburgh in August; not physical danger, of course, for there is remarkably little crime given the number of people. No, it is artistic danger. Alongside the possibility, even probability, of seeing the new stars before they are famous, there is the certainty of seeing some poor hopefuls tank, embarrass themselves and their audience, and disappear from the entertainment world for ever. From the point of view of the visitor, the cost is a wasted afternoon or evening of leisure time. From the point of view of the critic, the cost is higher: it is not seeing something of greater merit elsewhere. From the point of view of the performer, it may simply become better to bypass Edinburgh and find other ways of making your talent known.

There has been a little evidence of this in recent years. The danger sign is key critics not turning up or only going for a couple of days. This is not yet a serious problem but you can see some cracks in the façade. The number of tickets sold is wonderful but some say that the essential edge – the artistic danger – may not be quite as sharp as it used to be. The Fringe is the key here. If ever the word gets round that it is on the skids then, well, the festival could implode.

First, Edinburgh would cease to be as important as a trade fair, or rather a set of trade fairs. The professionals would no longer attend.

Instead, they would find some other place where cutting-edge performers would test their acts on audiences and the critics could gauge their talents. Next, the public would become a different, less experimental audience, seeking entertainment that was more conventional, more 'commercial', more downmarket. Then after a while numbers both of performances and attendees would start to fall and the trouble would become obvious to the world.

Now I think this danger is quite small because every year the artistic focus shifts as demand for different types of artistic experience waxes and wanes. In recent years there has probably been an excess of stand-up comedians, as Richard Demarco complained, though that reflected a demand from the somewhat cynical early 2000s. But there were also a number of religious-themed events – something that reflects society's changing values and would not have happened ten years earlier. There was much about Christianity, as you might expect from the home of the Church of Scotland, mostly questioning it but also celebrating its musical traditions. There was everything from early Christian music in pretty early Christian churches to the Soweto Gospel Choir. There were also a Yiddish song project, Buddhist tutorials and a small Islam festival, which featured Arab calligraphy, talks and music at the Edinburgh Central Mosque.

Edinburgh has a great plus in its organization in that there is not and never has been a single mind running the show. So there is little danger of the city taking a decision that would undermine the festival phenomenon. But this also means that were, for whatever reason, the movement to lose its edge, it would be hard for the city to do much to recover it. Edinburgh sings to Mao's dictum 'Let one thousand flowers bloom', rather than his policy of Cultural Revolution. There is no mind to mess things up, but equally there is no mind to sort things out.

As well as being the biggest set of arts festivals in the world, Edinburgh is also the most commercial in two senses. One is that it receives less of a subsidy proportionate to its size than any festival anywhere;[28] arguably it subsidizes the city as a whole, for the additional revenue it brings in is far greater than the modest municipal contribution it receives. The other is that because it is completely open access, it gives an early signal of what the market for artistic or creative endeavour is seeking, hence the growth of religious events noted above. It has prospered because it both fills a market need and has a sense of mission to be the greatest show anywhere.

The chances are it will carry on doing so. However, tastes change in the worlds of arts and entertainment as much as in other areas of human endeavour.

So far, Edinburgh seems to have caught the fickle shifts of fashion and retained its lead. Long may it continue to do so. Meanwhile, anyone in the world who is interested in the arts should have at least one shot at braving the cacophony on the High Street of Edinburgh one August. Go to ten shows in a day and stagger back to the hotel battered and ready for some more tomorrow. Better still, put on one: back some students or even commission some music and give it a world premiere.

At some stage the ever-greater size of the festival will become a more serious obstacle. Maybe the re-timing of the film festival carries a warning here – it cannot go on growing for ever and the switch from its present very big bang to some sort of steady state will be tricky. But for years to come it will remain, quite simply, the greatest show on earth.

CHAPTER TWO

The City
of
London

The world's international financial centre

I. WHAT IS THE STORY?

It is almost too obvious a tale – the way in which the financial services industry in London has outpaced other cities so that by the early
years of this century, the UK capital had a credible claim to be the
financial centre of the world. It is a story on which I have reported all
my adult life, from the growth of the Eurodollar and Eurobond
markets in the 1960s, to the Big Bang reforms in the 1980s, to the
spurt in growth this century. With my wife Frances Cairncross, I
wrote a book about the City of London as a financial centre – indeed
it was because we so enjoyed writing a book together that we had the
confidence to embark on another type of partnership.

I have a further connection with the City. Both my grandfathers
worked there all their lives, one as a textile merchant and the other as
a timber merchant. When I got a job in the City as a financial jour-

nalist, the first office I worked from, the side of Bracken House overlooking Friday Street, was on the site where my paternal grandfather's office had been before wartime bombs swept it away. So this is very familiar ground.

However, as often happens with something familiar, you tend not to look properly. It is only when you open your eyes and try to pin down what makes it so special that you realize the depth and complexity of your subject. And so it is with the City. Let us call it that because although London's financial operations are now located in three parts of the capital – the square mile of the old Roman City of London, the new Canary Wharf tower blocks[1] and an increasing proportion of the St James's area in the West End – the City is where it all began and it is a City ethos built up over many years that still drives the London financial services industry.

The key point is that in most areas of international financial business, London is the largest centre[2] in the world. New York is slightly bigger overall on most measures – not all – thanks to its huge domestic business. Much the same applies to Tokyo. But if you take cross-border business, London is the clear leader from New York, and Tokyo is hardly in the running at all. So London has a fair claim to be called the financial capital of the world.

The reasons for this are partly historical, going back to the days of empire and the pre-1914 role of London as supplier of investment capital to the world. But that role was to be severely undermined by the loss of wealth from two world wars, while Britain's proud status as a manufacturing nation gradually declined. The resulting weakness of the pound meant Britain could not return to its previous position.[3]

In the 1960s, however, the City began its revival when it discovered it did not need to use sterling but could turn to other currencies instead. That insight, coupled with applying the telephone trading system of the foreign exchange market to dealing in deposits, lead to the creation of the various Eurodollar markets. Banks borrowed other currencies, mainly dollars, and issued bonds and made loans in these rather than in sterling.

This allowed the City to regain its status as a world banking centre, with foreign institutions flocking in to trade in these new markets: by the end of the 1960s, there were more foreign banks in London than in any other city in the world.[4] Gradually the merchant role of the capital diminished. Instead of being a place where goods and raw materials were actually traded, the job of my grandfathers, finance ruled.

There was no plan – no single mind that declared the balance of activity should shift in this way. What happened was that the banking techniques built up to finance trade and investment became more profitable than the actual trading itself.

The Euro markets were discovered almost by accident, with a couple of City bankers spotting the opportunity for London to do business that had previously been carried out in New York. In 1963 the USA introduced a tax on foreign bonds issued in New York – a spectacular own-goal.[5] And when it did so, the Bank of England helped choreograph the City's response. But it did not plan it; what it did was to welcome foreign banks that wanted to set up in London, even providing them with staff to help them do so.

What the City was very good at – still is – is exploiting opportunities as they arise. Indeed its whole ethos is not to plan but to respond with astonishing vigour to market signals. One effect has been to secure London's position in international banking; another, to allow foreign banks to have the largest share in London's business.

A second example of this opportunistic approach – and its consequences – was the Big Bang of the 1980s. While London had become the largest single centre for international banking, its securities trading – issuing and dealing in bonds and shares – remained a parochial business. There was a set of interwoven restrictive practices that kept foreign companies from taking part in British business. For one thing they could not in practice become members of the London Stock Exchange, and for another, London operated on a different trading system from the rest of the world, splitting all trading in domestic securities into two separate types of company. There were brokers, who could only act on behalf of customers buying and selling shares and could not deal on their own account. And there were jobbers, who were only allowed to deal with brokers. Commissions were fixed. The Bank of England issued government securities, or gilts, only through a handful of specialist banks called discount houses. And so on.

Meanwhile, other parts of the City were busy trading in international shares and bonds, where these restrictions did not apply. On one day, 27 October 1986, all the barriers were blown away – hence the expression Big Bang.[6] London shifted to the global system of share trading.

What then happened was that foreign financial institutions took over the British-owned ones. Nearly all the larger brokers and jobbers sold out, and after a few years most of the City's famous merchant banks disappeared too.

In essence, this was a deal: Britain traded national ownership of its investment banking business[7] for dominance of international securities trading. It was not planned this way; most people expected that British-owned businesses would succeed in keeping a decent proportion of trading, and there were in the early days several large British groups. But they all disappeared, selling out to foreign competitors or simply shutting up shop. London retained even less control over investment banking than it had over commercial banking. It created the marketplace and cared little as to who might play on it.

The most recent example of the City's pragmatism has been the way in which it has jumped into the gap and gained ground on New York post the terrorist attacks of 11 September 2001 and after the collapse of the energy group Enron[8] in a whirlwind of financial scandal. Since 2001 the USA has introduced a number of restrictions, some designed to improve security, some to improve financial regulation. Among these are simple measures such as visa restrictions, making it harder to employ non-Americans in New York. Others are more complex – the interplay of the Sarbanes-Oxley[9] corporate legislation, which puts onerous restrictions on companies listing their shares in the USA, and various other financial regulations.

There was no specific plan for London to use all this as an opportunity to increase its share of financial business, but that was the outcome. In 2006, for the first time, more money was raised for businesses in London than New York. US businesses found it easier to expand in London; it was not hard to hire non-national staff and they found the regulation more pragmatic. Meanwhile, international companies preferred to list their shares in London because that avoided Sarbanes-Oxley. And international investors, particularly those from the Middle East and Russia, preferred to deal through the UK rather than the USA, partly for political reasons, partly for time-zone reasons, and partly because of the social and other attractions that London offered.

The result: London becoming once again, as it had been 100 years earlier, the centre of the earth for finance. The difference is that this time it is foreigners as much as Britons, and foreign money rather than British money, that have driven it to this position.[10] This has led some to suggest it has been a Faustian bargain. The benefits may be obvious – not just the wealth and employment the industry generates but the intangible advantages of being the most important single place choreographing the process we call globalization. The costs – the loss of national control of a key industry and the heavy reliance on a single industry – must raise concerns.

The downside of the Faustian bargain became particularly evident after the collapse of confidence in international financial markets in the autumn of 2008. London was as hard hit as anywhere, though it is worth noting that the principal problems arose in the USA rather than the UK and that within the UK it was the two banks headquartered in Edinburgh, not London, that were hardest hit.

The damage to the global financial services industry was severe and it will take the best part of a decade to reconstruct the industry. As far as the UK is concerned the globalization of financial services has enabled the country to gain international influence in exchange for the loss of national power. Until the autumn of 2008 London's financial services industry had been one of the great beneficiaries of this phenomenon as well as a driver of it. I am pretty confident that in the medium term it will retain that role, as it has done in the past when faced with equally severe challenges. But, as we have seen, the interaction between globalization and finance does mean that while there are lessons in the City's success story, there can be dark twists to it too.

2. WHAT ARE THE LESSONS?

The lessons come at three levels. The simplest, and the one most closely studied in places as diverse as Dublin and Dubai, is how to create an international financial services industry. The second is how people interact to create a lasting marketplace that is flexible to new demands yet carries on a set of core values that are passed like a baton to the next generation. And finally there is the broader impact of the financial services industry and in particular how, in the case of London, it is associated with other aspects of the economic success story in the south-east of England.

As far as the first is concerned, consider the parallel with the motor industry. If a country wants to start a motor sector from scratch, it either encourages some of its existing industrial companies to set one up or it goes and gets in foreign companies to do it instead. South Korea took the first path; Slovakia the second. You just need expertise, which you can buy, and reasonably cheap labour. But with finance things are more complicated. Why should international financial organizations come to a new place to set up a business? How do you develop the pool of talent? It is much easier to build a motor industry or indeed lose one to foreign competition, than it is to build and retain financial services. A car factory is a car factory; a financial centre is a complex web of different skill-based businesses that takes years to develop. That is one reason why London has fought off challenges from other European centres, such as Frankfurt and Paris.

So the base of skills in London is deeply embedded. But the City has done something more: it has become a magnet for skills too. Indeed had London financial institutions just managed on the available pool of British workers, the City could never have succeeded in the way it has. It has imported talent at the highest level from all over the world. How? Well, of course, the answer is partly about money:[11] an international financial post in London pays, as a rough average, double the rate for the equivalent role in Paris or Frankfurt. At the top skill levels the disparity is even greater. In some specializations, though not all, the London pay package is larger than the New York one.

But it is also culture – the open attitude to foreign talent. This goes back centuries: most of the top merchant banks of the nineteenth and twentieth centuries – the Rothschilds, Schroders, Kleinworts and Warburgs – were founded by people from the Continent. Go to the huge Reebok health club at Canary Wharf and listen to the cacophony of foreign languages and accents.

The City is also open to Britons of modest background and education – there is no 'credentialism'. Even now, many high-earners in the dealing rooms and insurance markets have not been to university. There is a long tradition of that open attitude. For example, both my grandfathers had modest starts in life: one was the son of a Highland Scottish shepherd, the other came from a poor family in the East End of London.

The first question, then, for any budding financial centre is how to attract the people. Getting financial capital is easy: you give tax breaks to companies. Getting human capital is much more complicated.

People are the key to building a financial centre. They are also the key to its survival down the years. Somehow each new generation has to take on the ethos built up by the previous generation – or at least the positive aspects of it – and modify it to fit new conditions. There are fascinating similarities between people in the City now and those a generation ago. Most obviously money is a powerful motivator, but it is not just that. Money is a way of keeping the score – it says how good you are – and successful people are hugely competitive. But there are also social limits to competition in this business, for people have to play in teams; loners do not do well. Sustained success is achieved partly by competing, but also by co-operating.

A further element for lasting success is effective regulation. Even ahead of the current crisis London has had its regulatory failures: in banking the collapse of Bank of Credit and Commerce International;[12] in pensions the stealing from workers by Robert Maxwell;[13] and in insurance the near-collapse of Lloyd's of London.[14] We now know that the changes to the system put in by the Labour government of 1997 at best failed to insulate London from inherent weaknesses in the international financial system and at worst contributed to the failure. On the other hand the model adopted by the British authorities for the rescue of the banking system worked comparatively well and became a model for bank rescues in other countries.

But to see the City through the prisms of regulation and rescue seems to me to be a narrow and distorted way of looking at the place. In any case banking is only one part of the financial services industry, albeit an important one, and over the years London's regulatory advantage over New York has encouraged most major US banks and securities houses to base their international business there. As for Tokyo, its obstructive system is one of the reasons why it has failed to become a truly international centre, as many had expected back in the 1980s.

Regulation is only a means to an end. That end is to have efficient, open and transparent markets. And arguably London is able to get away with lighter regulation because it has managed, compared with other centres, to sustain a reputation for fundamental straight-dealing through many incarnations of regulatory environment.

I do not think anyone fully understands how this spirit endures down the generations. There must be some element of peer pressure to do the right thing. There must also be a continuing climate of openness – of looking to the world rather than just to the UK or to Europe. But I think the strongest glue holding the City together over time is simply the profound embedded appreciation of the power of the market. Do not over-intellectualize. Respond instead to whatever the market signals that people want and then you will make money. And by making money you will have served a social as well as an economic purpose.

This may be a bit idealized – a vision of City aspirations that is, for many workers in the financial services industry, a long way from their own experience. There are plenty of greedy people in London, quite a few crooks who will manipulate markets to their own advantage. There has been quite a lot of insider dealing and, as we are now well aware, quite a lot of excess. To many people this is distasteful, and even enthusiasts for the City would have to acknowledge that these excesses undermine both its reputation and ultimately its performance.

But there is no denying that it has brought home the bacon for the economy of the capital and the south-east of England. Inner London is the richest place in Europe in terms of GDP per head.[15] The biggest single impetus transforming the UK from having a per capita income towards the bottom of the European league table in the early 1980s to one close to the top by the early 2000s has been the strength of its financial services industry. That dominance brings problems, of which more in a moment, but it has brought prosperity to millions.

There is a list of features about London that goes beyond finance: more visitors through its airports than any other city in the world; more international telephone calls; the largest non-national professional community on the planet; more book titles published than anywhere else. According to United Nations data[16] the UK exports more cultural products and services than any other country including the USA.

There are, of course, many other elements of the economy, especially education, communications and culture. But the City has been the engine driving it all along.

- **Become a magnet for skills**
- **Develop an open attitude to talent**
- **Appreciate the power of the market**

3. WHAT COULD GO WRONG?

In 2008 the engine faltered. The world had a classic financial market crash, leading to a serious global economic recession, one that may eventually turn out to be deeper than any since the Second World

War. Writing at the end of 2009, it was still not possible to judge the extent to which London-based institutions contributed to the collapse. The blame game had some way to run. Pointing out that, as far as UK institutions were concerned, the most serious problems occurred in banks that were headquartered elsewhere, particularly in Edinburgh and the north of England, cut little ice. The financial breakdown originated in the USA rather than the UK or continental Europe but financial institutions everywhere found themselves under the cosh. It is true, too, that there have always been crashes and there always will be crashes in the future. But inevitably and understandably the reputation of the City was seriously damaged, just as it was by previous disasters, including the dot-com bust and the subsequent collapse in share prices. And while all financial centres that were involved in international business suffered, the London economy and financial services in particular took a huge blow.

Markets recover; confidence returns; growth resumes. It is too early to make any firm judgements but to me the damage of 2008/9 both to the world economy and specifically to the City feels very like the damage during the 1970s. The world then was racked by runaway inflation and experienced what was its most serious post-war recession to date. The key difference, aside from the fact that inflation is under control, is the world economy is vastly more global than it was forty years earlier.

That leads to what seems to be an even bigger issue than the fallout from the 2008/9 recession. It is what happens to globalization. A number of things trouble me here. One is rising inequality. As a rule, globalization of the world economy decreases inequalities between countries but increases inequalities within them. Perhaps the most important consequence of the present burst of globalization is the rise of China and India from developing to some sort of developed status. Rising inequality is most evident in these countries as some people get left behind, but it is also a feature of the US economy and of the London one. This creates strains and injustices that must be tackled.

It may be that in trying to cope with these strains, a British government makes the same mistake as US administrations have done, bringing in legislation, taxation or regulation that has the effect of shifting business elsewhere. There will in any case be some rebalancing of international finance, with Asian centres taking on a larger role. As China moves towards becoming the world's largest economy, is it almost inevitable a Chinese city will become the principal financial centre of the region. The main issue would seem to be whether it is Hong Kong or Shanghai. That will depend as much on the willingness of the authorities to permit such a development as the acumen with which both cities are run. Tokyo is the prime example of a domestic financial centre that has not developed significant international business because the Japanese authorities have maintained a regulatory environment that has deterred international participation.

Beyond this, however, we have to accept that as financial power shifts east so, too, will the value system of international finance. Global capitalism will no longer march principally to the beat of the West. For Europeans and North Americans this will be disturbing – far more disturbing than late twentieth-century concerns as to whether the 'Anglo' or the 'continental' or the Japanese versions of capitalism were the most effective. We are not used to a world where financial power is located in China and India rather than Europe and North America. Despite the size of the Japanese economy, its financial model has had little influence on the rest of the planet. And, for the moment, the financial services industry of China remains primitive by global standards. But it will become both larger and more influential as China moves closer to becoming the world's largest economy. My own view is to welcome that, but, of course, this process will create strains.

That leads to a wider concern – of something happening to the world economy that undermines the fundamental role of international trade and finance. The shift from an ever-more global economy to one where international trade and investment fall back a bit, for example, could easily trigger protectionism – restrictions on the movement of capital and maybe goods and services. That happened in the 1930s.[17] Were it to happen again, London, as the most dependent city on international business, would suffer most. However, what happens to the City, or indeed to the UK economy, is less important than what happens to the world.

Put bluntly, were anything to go wrong with globalization – and it has had a pretty severe blow – that would herald a most dangerous period not just for the world economy but for humankind. At some stage in the first half of the twenty-first century, the world will probably cease to become more global. International trade and investment will stop growing faster than world output. We may go back to protectionism and a collapse of world trade, as happened in the 1930s; though maybe we will move to more of a plateau rather than falling backwards. But it is not hard to hear the voices against globalization, calling for protection from cheap imports from China and India, or resenting the shift of power away from Europe and towards Asia. Were the general economic downturn also to be associated with widespread conflict, such as happened in 1914, that would be even worse.

This hardly bears thinking about. My point is simply that no one should assume the present burst of global prosperity, which involves more of the world's population than ever before, will continue for ever. It will not. With luck, thoughtful political leadership and a sensitive attitude within the financial services industry, the threats to world prosperity will be averted. But there will be nail-biting years ahead. This future will be shaped in part by a handful of politicians in the various world capitals, but also, maybe to a rather greater extent, by the myriad anonymous players in the world's business and financial community.

Arguably, at the beginning of the twenty-first century, the City of London has become the focal point for this community. It is a gigantic responsibility to carry. In the years running up to the First World War it was widely believed that war was impossible because the world economy was so interdependent. It was unthinkable that countries that depended on each other for their prosperity and had invested so substantially in each other could throw that progress away. Countries were by definition national but finance was international. Yet the financial markets failed to discipline the European politicians into co-operation. The world was allowed the slither into the First World

War. The markets failed to educate the politicians on the economic disaster (let alone the human catastrophe) that nationalistic policies might provoke. Now we face similar dangers, at least potentially. Yet the markets have themselves misbehaved, or more specifically some of the protagonists in those markets, including some in London, have failed. Their moral authority is under challenge, and understandably so.

Maybe it is too much to ask when the future is so uncertain, but I still think the question is worth putting: who on balance over the years are likely to be better custodians of global prosperity, politicians or financial markets? I think, comparing their records over the past couple of centuries and notwithstanding the disaster of 2008/9, it is no contest. That is why I respect the City. It is why I believe it has much to teach the world. It is why, too, I believe that global prosperity will be rekindled and why world financial markets have a crucial role in that process.

CHAPTER THREE

1995   2009

The Celtic Tiger
From boom to bust … to recovery

I. WHAT IS THE STORY?

During the 1990s something amazing happened in Ireland. At the beginning of the decade it was about the poorest country in the European Union. By the Millennium it was among the richest. In between it had become by far the fastest growing economy not just in Europe but in the entire developed world.[1] The most obvious parallel was with the explosive growth of the Asian 'tiger' economies, such as Singapore and Hong Kong, and in 1994 a friend, David McWilliams, the Irish economist and TV show host, came up with the phrase that caught it all: the Celtic tiger.

My own perspective on this is acutely personal. I grew up there.

In the spring of 1951 my father was in Dublin for a business trip. He walked down Grafton Street and, on a whim, went into a phone box to call my mother. 'I am looking at the happy, smiling faces here in Dublin,' he said, 'and I think we should come and live here.'

We were living in the Isle of Man at the time. My mother was eager to live in a larger place and immediately agreed. We would, my father warned her, be very poor. She pointed out that we were very poor already. I was seven at the time – and so that was how I came to be brought up in County Wicklow just south of Dublin.

But it was not just us who were poor. The whole country was poor and it continued to be right through to the 1990s. Of course, the poverty was relative: people were well fed, rather better fed than they were in Britain, which still had rationing at the beginning of the 1950s. The Dublin of the 1950s and 1960s had a cheerful if shabby charm: the place was indeed full of happy smiling faces. But while, of course, there were pockets of wealth – I remember the father of a school friend who had a huge American car with a wiper on the back window – for most people, including my parents, it was a struggle to get by. The life was pretty simple too. We eventually got a car but even well into the 1950s, the milk arrived in a horse-drawn cart with a huge churn on it and they measured the milk into your own jug. Right through the middle 1950s there was a recession.

By the 1960s things were picking up a bit, but not by enough to employ the flood of young people coming onto the job market.[2] The young left for jobs in America or more often Britain; some three-quarters of my economics class at Trinity College Dublin[3] left the country on graduation. We were the lucky ones for economists then were in short supply. For the mass of emigrants who did not have a university degree, the more likely occupation was on the building sites of Britain.

Despite the highest birth rate in Europe,[4] Ireland's population slowly shrank. There were lots of children, lots of older people, but few young adults. The population of the twenty-six counties, the Republic of Ireland, was down to 2.8 million by the middle 1960s.[5]

And now? Well, it is no secret that the Irish economy has been among the hardest hit by the global recession, of which more later. But despite its current difficulties the centre of Dublin has become a shining modern European city. Superficially it is just a smartened-up version of its old self: Grafton Street is still the main shopping area and you can still drink at Davy Byrnes, the 'nice quiet bar' in James Joyce's *Ulysses*, round the corner in Duke Street.[6] But now it is a seafood dining haven, whereas then it was just somewhere we used to go for a drink after lectures. Trinity still occupies its thirty-five prime acres at the very centre of the city. You still walk through the front gate from the bustle of a capital city to the calm Georgian front square. But the streets around it are smart and stylish instead of, well, pretty drab. And despite recession they are filled with a multitude of different languages as well as different accents, for what has been the fastest-growing economy of the European Union has also been the fastest-growing job market.[7] During the boom years the young of Europe came not just to spend money; they came to earn it.

Just south of the centre of Dublin, in Ballsbridge, the contrast between the old and the new is even sharper. A genteel suburb of late nineteenth-century villas has become the new hot location for offices, hotels, bars and apartments. Dublin is the fourth-most expensive city in Europe in which to rent, behind only London's West End, Moscow and Paris, and is in the global top ten for office rents.[8] Further south, stretching round Dublin Bay, are the rich suburbs, but alongside the older and grander houses are vast tracts of new suburbia. The expanding population of the Dublin area, at 1.6 million in the 2006 census,[9] looks set to reach two million by 2021, making it the fastest-growing conurbation in Europe.

Ireland became a magnet for Europe's ambitious youth. When the European Union was enlarged to include a new wave of entrants from Eastern Europe in 2004, only three member states fully opened their labour markets to this new workforce: Sweden, the UK and Ireland. In absolute numbers the largest wave of migrants went to Britain; unsurprisingly, since it too had a strong job market. But proportionately Ireland took more than anywhere else.[10] The Dublin streets are full of young people again, and this time it is not only the Irish themselves but throngs of French, Germans, Scandinavians – and now Poles, Czechs and Hungarians too. Even in the 1960s Dublin had a different, almost continental feel to it, but now that feeling is immediately evident even to the weekend visitor.

I find this thrilling. Ahead of the recession Dubliners complained that people no longer seem to have time to talk to each other, though their felicity with language remains as extraordinary as ever. They fretted about the new immigrants, though they seemed to me to be pretty well behaved – a lot better than we were as students. They say that Dublin has changed and, of course, they are right. But a city that immigrants have flocked to is bound to be culturally different to one from which emigrants leave. People are voting with their feet for the new Dublin, the new Ireland. Success may bring problems but it is a sight better than failure, and Ireland has had too much of that.

We will come to how much ground has been lost during the recession in a moment. First, we focus on how the transformation happened. How in the space of less than ten years did the poorest member of the European Union become almost the richest? The story intrigues much of the rest of Europe – obviously those two other Celtic nations of Scotland and Wales but also the new EU members to the east: the Baltic states, Poland, the Czech Republic, Slovakia and so on. Anyone who knows anything about the Irish boom is bombarded with questions: what can we learn and how can we do it too?

The short answer is that Ireland was almost uniquely placed to benefit from the burst of globalization that took place through the 1990s, following the end of the Cold War. Its success was built on openness to the world market. But it had been held back by political errors, which saddled Ireland with high taxation and other restrictions. Once Ireland got its policies right, it was like a coiled spring, ready to uncurl. So it was a classic case of sensitivity to the needs of the market but also radical (and quite brave) decisions by a group of politicians with a mission. They realized that Ireland did not have to be an economic failure and that it was intolerable it should continue to be one.

The market element to the story runs like this. By the late 1980s there were at least six forces helping to give Ireland's economy a tailwind. They were:

- The European Single Market, which from 1987 onwards encouraged foreign investors, particularly American ones, to choose Ireland as a base from which to manufacture for Europe.[11]
- The associated massive increase in global capital flows, which Ireland was able to tap into.
- Favourable demographics, for in the 1980s half of Ireland's population were under the age of twenty-five;[12] that many were unemployed further increased the potential labour supply.
- The strong investment in education (at all levels) going back many years, but with a change of emphasis in the 1980s to encourage more maths, science and business studies.[13]
- EU structural and regional funds,[14] which Ireland spent well on infrastructure, especially roads – even if most Dubliners would say these initiatives did not move nearly fast enough.
- Political stability, which has ensured that ever since 1957 the country has encouraged outsiders to invest in Ireland.

So the potential was there. It just needed the right policies. Here, Ireland had been unfortunate. Following its political independence from the UK, it had adhered to a policy of economic independence that ran right through to the 1960s. One key element to this was protectionism.

To give just one example, in the 1950s and 1960s nearly all the cars in Ireland were assembled there. Kits were imported in CKD (completely knocked down) form. The cars were made first on the original production lines in the UK, France, Germany or wherever, then taken to bits and packed into crates to be reassembled, painted and trimmed in Ireland. The rare imported vehicles suffered a large duty to protect the local industry. But there was no rational reason for the industry to exist at all. The quality was worse even than the same cars assembled in the UK – quite an achievement – and they cost more. Eventually, but not until the end of the 1970s, the industry was swept away.

From the 1970s onwards, after entry to the European Economic Community in 1973, the principal flaw in Irish economic policy was financial ill-discipline. Public spending rose, budget deficits soared, then tax rates were increased to try to curb the deficits ... and the result was stagnation. There was a short-lived property boom at the end of the 1970s but that was followed by a slump in the early 1980s. By 1987, Ireland's unemployment had risen to 17.5 per cent and its GDP per head was only two-thirds that of Britain's, producing a vicious circle wherein public funds were pre-empted to pay social welfare and interest on the debt. Emigration eased the pain but many educated young people left.[15] The following year *The Economist* magazine dubbed its survey of Ireland 'The Poorest of the Rich'.

Then came the miracle. Just nine years later the magazine returned with another survey, and the title said it all: 'Europe's Shining Light'.

So what changed?

It started with politics. Ireland, like the UK in 1979, had hit an economic wall. The country's political leadership knew it could not carry on with high-tax and high-spending policies. There was a real threat it would have to go to the International Monetary Fund for a loan to bail it out, as the UK had done in 1976. But by the middle 1980s change was in the air. In 1985 a pro-business, low-tax party called the Progressive Democrats[16] had been formed and that helped create the momentum for change. It was started by Desmond O'Malley and Mary Harney to try to break the mould of the two major parties, Fianna Fáil and Fine Gael. Along with Fine Gael they also provided a constructive approach to the ongoing conflict in Northern Ireland. They won seats in the Dáil (the Irish parliament) in 1987, the same election that put in a Fianna Fáil government into power under Charles Haughey, the hugely controversial veteran rascal of a politician, who fought the election vowing not to cut public spending and then did exactly the opposite when he got in. Arguably he made the great boom possible, but my own hero of that period of Irish politics was the leader of Fine Gael, Alan Dukes, who lost the election but agreed to support the new government provided it followed Fine Gael's economic policies. That was bad for the party – he lost the leadership soon afterwards – but great for Ireland.[17]

Thus the policy of cutting VAT, income tax and, perhaps most important, corporation tax has been sustained and expanded by all subsequent governments, whatever their political make-up. The mission and the market came together and the Celtic tiger was born.

2. WHAT ARE THE LESSONS?

As you might imagine, this is a story that has been picked over thousands of times. Every country with a sluggish economy wanted to know how to fix it, and the Irish model seemed the best one to bet on.

The problem is that this is a subtle tale. For it to be helpful as a model, you have to get beyond saying it was the result of low taxes and good education. You also have to acknowledge the mistakes that were made and finally to see how the country has set about correcting those mistakes. The way it has coped with its excesses is almost as useful to others as the success story itself.

We start with success. There have been several elements to this and the trick is to judge which of these were crucial and which merely nice to have.

The easy part, and one emulated by the new EU member states, is to be 'business friendly'. That means low taxation. Ireland became a magnet for inward foreign investment thanks in fair measure to its low corporation taxes, 12.5 per cent in 2009, less than half the average EU rate. For the new EU members it has been a flat-tax system, a single low rate on both individuals and companies.

While any country can cut its taxes at a stroke, the other general element of Ireland's success, the availability of educated young people, takes time. Ireland reformed its education system back in the 1960s, improving secondary schooling and pumping money into its universities. The depression provoked longer stays in the education system producing a steep rise in the education levels of the Irish workforce which, accompanied by low wage expectation on its part, presented good value to potential employers. For many years another large part of the resulting human capital had left the country. Skilled people emigrated. But when growth did take off, that very emigration became a benefit, for people returned, thereby boosting the local labour pool but also bringing back the practical skills they had learnt working abroad.

Beyond these two core elements there is a well-known litany. Students of the Celtic tiger point to EU subsidies being spent rather more effectively. They cite deregulation of the service industries, the development of a new financial centre with associated tax benefits, and so on. There is also the advantage of size: it is much easier to turn round the economy of a country of three or four million people than one of fifty million plus. But while all this is true enough, I think to focus on the mechanics of the story is to miss its cultural and romantic element. That is much harder to replicate; indeed it cannot be done.

Ireland is one of the most powerful 'brands' in the world, with people from completely different cultures yearning for something Irish. Some thirty-five million people in the USA claim Irish ancestry.[18] St Patrick's Day is celebrated around the globe. There are Irish pubs all over the world, which bear little resemblance to the bars we went to in Dublin. (We did not even call them pubs. Pubs are an English tradition, not an Irish one. In Ireland it is a bar.) Many of the most successful rock groups are Irish, with U2 top of the league. One of the prime reasons why US companies chose Ireland as their base for the European market was that they liked the place. The tax and other incentives prodded them into doing what they rather wanted to do anyway.

But if other countries cannot be Irish, they can learn from Ireland's experience. They can reconnect with their own citizens who have emigrated. They can promote their own cultures and identities. They can cherish, promote and benefit from their own unique qualities in an ever more homogenized world.

They can also learn how to cope with success. Many Dubliners would greet that thought with a hollow laugh, and there are certainly some negative lessons too. Dublin suffers hugely from traffic congestion, partly because of under-investment in roads and in public transport but also because the planning response to such pressure has been weak and – on some occasions, I am afraid – corrupt. Infrastructure has scrambled along behind the growth, never quite catching up. Much of the new private housing is uninspiring, while some of the new public housing is associated with social deprivation. Dublin also has a serious drugs problem.[19] But in other areas of great importance – most particularly the human relations between the 'new' Irish and the existing population – I do think Ireland has got it pretty much right.

You have to appreciate that no other developed country anywhere in the world has seen as rapid a rise in immigration proportionate to the population. This is not just the biggest migration that has taken place in the world over the past decade or so; it is one of the largest that has *ever* taken place over such a short time. And it has happened to a country that had no experience of inward migration in living memory. Of course, it has not been easy and if you read the Dublin papers there are plenty of examples of friction. But somehow the country has risen to the challenge.

For economic success is not just about getting richer. It is also about creating a society where people want to live – a place where they can be happy. Ireland's achievement has been wider than prosperity. And that has something to do with that quality my father recognized in Grafton Street all those years ago.

- **Be 'business friendly'**
- **Promote your own culture**
- **Learn to cope with success**

3. WHAT COULD GO WRONG?

In one sense that is no longer the right question. The Irish economy has gone wrong. As I write in 2009 it is experiencing just about the most serious downturn of any developed economy, and is forecast to contract by more than 10 per cent between 2009 and 2011. It is too early to do more than sketch the reasons why the country should be so severely affected but it is clear that it allowed its property boom to get out of control and permitted wages and salaries to rise too quickly.

The reasons for these failures will be picked over by economists almost as closely as the reasons for the prior success but my own view is that given the rate of the climb some bump was inevitable. The property boom[20] of the Dublin region had got out of hand and there is little the Irish authorities could have done about it. The boom was fuelled by the low interest rates of the Eurozone and Ireland could not increase rates while it remained a member.

Ireland's decision to adopt the euro has brought it the benefit of being the only English-speaking country in the zone. That helped attract foreign investment. But it meant that Irish business people could borrow at below the rate of inflation, which they did with great abandon. While property values continued to go upwards, these loans were good; when values faltered following the credit crunch, many of those became bad debts.

With 20/20 hindsight the crisis could have been managed better. Maybe Ireland could have placed direct curbs on its banks, restricting their lending, particularly to property. It could and should have had more restrictive fiscal policies and might accordingly have been able to put itself in a better position to withstand the global recession. But what is done is done. What I find much more interesting is the way in which the Irish authorities, and society as a whole, has responded. Wages have been cut, often with workers offering pay cuts in exchange for greater job preservation. Public spending has been cut, more sharply than in any other EU member state. So Ireland is adapting to tough times.

Eventually growth will resume in Ireland as elsewhere. When it does Ireland will become a more 'normal' economy in the sense that it will grow at a rate of 3 or 4 per cent, not the 7 or 8 per cent of the boom years. Much of the growth spurt was catch-up, getting to where Ireland should have been. By the middle of the first decade of the twenty-first century it was just about there, so it was always going to have to adapt to slower growth. That will inevitably be tough both financially and socially.

The sudden burst of wealth that has hit Dublin from the early 1990s onwards has led to all the excesses you would expect. Stylish sure, but also flash, and that flashy element is much resented – and understandably so – by the hard-working people who have only partly shared in the dream.

The central point here is that, of course, all booms create excesses, and it is only when there has to be a shift to a more stable state that you can separate the froth from the substance. I have tried to argue here that there is solid substance to the Celtic tiger story, in particular in the education and quality of the Irish workforce and in the carefully crafted tax system of the country. It has faced a tough test and it will continue to struggle until secure growth is resumed. But when that happens, it will be an Ireland that is utterly different to the Ireland of even the early 1990s – an Ireland that looks outward, that is truly multicultural, that is increasingly influenced by the new Irish. For Ireland has been both an economic experiment and a social one.

The first has turned out to be a success story, albeit a flawed one. I am confident that in economic terms Ireland will resume its place as a beacon for the rest of the developed world.

The outcome of the great social experiment is less clear. It has invited huge numbers of other people to its shores – people who will become Irish but Irish with different attitudes and expectations. Over the next couple of decades, the new immigrants will create a new Ireland that will feel quite different to the familiar stereotype.

So there are risks but ultimately I see this as a human success story. It is about a group of political and economic leaders who got together with a mission not to carry on failing, and who then transformed the opportunities for millions of people – the old Irish and the new Irish – as a result. Walk down Grafton Street now and the place is still full of the 'happy, smiling faces' that led to my being brought up in Ireland. But they are different faces in the sense that they have come from all over the world. I think it is great.

Continental
Europe

CHAPTER FOUR

Traffic Management in Copenhagen

I. WHAT IS THE STORY?

Cities are for people. Walk out in Copenhagen on a summer evening and the streets are full of … people. They are sitting in the cafés in the squares, dangling their legs over the quays of the old port, chatting, drinking, reading. At the Tivoli Gardens, the oldest funfair in the world, they are riding the roller-coasters. In summer the city is a festival of fun, like many other successful European centres. But Copenhagen has also managed, despite its northerly latitude – the same as Glasgow in Scotland – to become a nine-month summer city, one where people extend the café society on the squares and streets to all but the very darkest of winter days and nights.[1]

How has it done it? Well, it could not tame the weather but it could succeed in taming the motor car.

All the cities of the developed world face traffic problems and some have coped better than others. But Copenhagen is special because it gradually, cautiously, and with the general support of its residents, transformed the medieval core back into being a place where people do not drive or take buses; they walk. Some 80 per cent of the journeys in the centre are on foot,[2] with another 14 per cent by bicycle.

This transformation has brought a string of benefits. One is economic. Walking is the most efficient way of using crowded city centre space: if there are no cars or buses, thousands of people can go up and down a narrow street. The result is that the shops and bars are passed by more people – and pedestrians also spend more money. When a survey was conducted into how people travelled to the centre of Copenhagen, as opposed to the way in which they moved around once they had arrived, it was found that those who walked, or came by public transport or bikes, spent much more than those who had driven in.

Another benefit is social.[3] As cars were discouraged, the heart of the city was used by a much wider band of ages – more children and older people. And with the streets evolving into centres of recreation, places to be enjoyed in themselves rather than being seen simply as points on a route to destinations that people actually needed to get to, so they have come to feel safer.

How has all this been achieved? It took a vision. That was supplied by a Danish architect and professor of urban design called Jan Gehl, who has become the global leader of a movement to improve the quality of life in city centres. But it has also been driven by the long-term, market-friendly, practical backing of the city authorities in Copenhagen since 1962, when the main shopping street, Strøget, was pedestrianized. Successive municipal leaders have followed a cautious, step-by-step process, making the series of incremental changes to the streets and buildings that have, over a generation, transformed the city.[4]

As streets were changed from cars to people, Copenhagen found that all sorts of activities sprang up. Cafés and restaurants opened; small, specialist shops started selling antiques and handicrafts; the streets themselves became filled with café seating. Sometimes this happened quickly, as with Strøget. In other places, for example some of the large city squares, it has taken a while for people to learn how best to use the newly available space.

Gradually, the pedestrianized area has been extended: it was 15,000 square metres in 1962, 95,000 by 1995.[5] This has not been the rather token exercise in traffic-free high streets and shopping centres seen in some other European towns and cities; bit by bit, the car has been taken out of the equation so that the two-kilometre-long Strøget now serves as the central artery for a whole network of pedestrianized blocks, with more than 100,000 square metres set aside for walkers.

As this has happened, not only has the number of people shopping increased so, too, the number of people carrying out some kind of stationary activity, such as having a cup of coffee at a pavement café, watching buskers, sitting down on a bench or simply standing chatting. This has all been measured. So we know that on a typical summer day in 1968 there would at any one time be an average of 1,750 people involved in one of these stationary activities; by 1986 this had risen to more than 4,500 and by 1995 to nearly 6,000.[6] As a result, the streets in the centre of the city are being used in a different way. They are no longer just a way of getting from one place to another; they are in themselves a destination.

But does this really indicate a rise in the quality of city life?[7] In their book *Public Spaces, Public Life* (Danish Architectural Press, 1996), Jan Gehl and Lars Gemzøe, a senior consultant at the firm of Gehl Architects, make the distinction between two types of activity: necessary and optional. The first are things people have to do and most walking belongs to that. The second are things people want to do – various forms of recreation – and are mostly stationary. People will only make the choice to linger in city streets if those streets are pleasant and safe places. So the extent to which the city centre has people doing some sort of stationary activity is a measure of its health.

In an interview, Lars Gemzøe pointed to the seamless manner in which the city's way of life has been transformed – to the extent of being an invisible revolution.[8] 'The character of Copenhagen has changed very much,' he explained. 'People sometimes talk about how nothing has changed for a long time in Copenhagen, because there have been no new buildings for a long period. But everyone was think-ing about that so much as a symbol of change that they forgot that we have, in fact, changed urban culture completely. Before, we did not have the space for outdoor activity or indeed the culture for it.'

Just shutting off streets from cars, however, does not in itself guar-antee that the urban environment will be safer or more pleasant. There are plenty of examples of pedestrianization creating urban wastelands, deserted after dark, with graffiti-scrawled walls and aban-doned shops. Getting rid of cars has sometimes meant getting rid of business activity. Copenhagen has taken a number of steps to avoid this fate.

First, there has been a lot of attention to the detail of the planning so that traffic is not simply pushed from one street to another. Devel-oping the project very slowly, over more than forty years, has meant that each new phase can build on the lessons of the previous ones and, where necessary, avoid evident mistakes.

Second, the street furniture and paving have been improved. More seating is provided, both formal (park benches, for example) and informal (raised kerbs, steps, edges of fountains etc.). Paving seems to matter enormously: squares paved in granite attract activity whereas those covered in asphalt do not.

Third, Copenhagen has looked at the street façades and encour-aged owners and tenants to make these people-friendly. For example, bright shop fronts attract window-shoppers in the evening, whereas shuttered fronts are threatening. Streets with doorways and steps are more interesting to walk along than those with solid glass or concrete walls.

Finally, the city has encouraged the use of bicycles as a way of getting about, including dedicated cycle-ways and a special rental scheme, which has enhanced its ability to function while it goes about cutting car use. By 1995, as a result, more people were cycling to work or school, 34 per cent, than driving, 31 per cent – the rest going by train or bus. Even on wet days, 60 per cent of those cyclists still used their bikes. More recently the proportion of 'two-wheel' commuters has risen to 36 per cent (with car journeys decreasing proportionately) and, through improvements to the bike network, the municipal authorities plan to increase this figure again to 40 per cent by 2012.[9]

No city is perfect. Cyclists are not perfect, and can behave just as selfishly as other citizens. Copenhagen has its social and economic problems. The key point is that by thinking carefully about the purpose of a city centre as a cultural and social magnet, as well as a business one, it has managed to cope more effectively with pressure from traffic than any other city on the planet.

2. WHAT ARE THE LESSONS?

The first conclusion is that it is possible, over time, to make radical improvements in the quality of life of a city by looking at the space between buildings rather than the buildings themselves. Unsurprisingly, what has happened in Copenhagen is studied by urban planners the world over. Gehl Architects has been commissioned by many other organizations, including Transport for London and the Department of Transportation in New York, to see what part of that experience can be applied elsewhere.[10]

But all cities are different. They have different histories, a different balance of activities and differences in basic layout. Copenhagen itself has a number of unusual features, some of which have made things easier, some harder. For example, it has a medieval core,[11] with a street pattern originally based on pedestrian traffic – plus perhaps some handcarts. It is largely a single-level city in the sense that there is no underground railway system, no underground shopping malls, no pedestrian footbridges. It has very few privately owned shopping arcades attracting people away from the streets and squares. It is also flat, making bicycles a much more attractive prospect than in hilly cities.

In a sense Copenhagen has been forced to use its street-level public spaces better – but it has also taken the opportunity to do so.

For lessons, though, it is best to start with the medieval core – even though few non-European cities have a similar central zone laid out hundreds of years ago. The most important lesson here is that where it is practicable to turn that core back into a place where people walk there are huge advantages in doing so. For any journey of less than about one kilometre, a little over half-a-mile, walking is the most efficient method of transport. It uses by far the least road space per person and, with the partial exception of using a bike, it is also probably the fastest way of getting about. For any journey taking up to ten minutes, most people are happiest as pedestrians.

But if they are to walk, while sharing the space with other traffic, the process has to be made pleasant. This requires great attention to detail. For example, there has to be enough space so people do not feel crowded and can move at a steady pace. When they cross a road, the lights have to be designed to give them priority, not other traffic. They must not be forced down steps into underground passages or up steps onto pedestrian bridges. So it is not enough to get rid of cars. Street furniture has to be improved, trees planted, pavements made attractive. Lots of design details, each small in themselves, have to mesh together.

Some of these changes can be made easily, but others imply radical rebuilding. For example, the slab-sided tall buildings that are the standard office block of the developed world can whip up vortex effects, increasing the winds at street level. That means it is much less pleasant for anybody walking and makes it impossible to create places where people will linger, such as outdoor cafés. But you cannot tear down every office block.

Copenhagen starts with the advantage of being largely on a single level and its old core is largely made up of four- and five-storey buildings. But it suffers from slab blocks outside the centre and not much can be done about that, except not to repeat those mistakes in the future. There is, however, the lesson that whenever new buildings are constructed, the designers and the planning authorities should consider their impact on the space in between.

That leads to a more general point about coping with weather. There are many ways in which cities in cold climates have sought to adapt, one being to offer people an alternative, as far as possible, to having to go out into the open. In Toronto there is a huge shopping-centre complex underground; in Minneapolis the central business area is linked by walkways one storey up. Copenhagen lacks such facilities. Instead, it has sought to turn the city into a place where people will use outdoor public space in winter as well as summer.

Basically this has been achieved through small details: outdoor cafés supply blankets for their guests and there are space heaters under large umbrellas. And the city is looking at other ideas: big entertainment screens that emit light on dark evenings; heated benches; skating rinks and so on. But the important change – and this applies to cities in all cold locations – is not to fight the winter but to celebrate it.

Perhaps the biggest lesson of all from Copenhagen is that city centres work best as places where a mixture of functions can flourish. They have long been centres of commerce as well as leisure and entertainment; but they also work better if they are residential centres too, particularly with young student populations.

The thing to avoid is letting any one function dominate or being too rigid when new projects are on the drawing board. The parts of Copenhagen that work least well are the planned blocks and streets of the 1960s; since then, the market has been allowed to signal what people want, not what planners think looks good on paper. To illustrate the point, far from being one of those pedestrianized areas that turn into urban wastelands after dark, Copenhagen's centre is now home to around 7,000 residents – a development welcomed by local people who report that the atmosphere is both warmer and safer thanks to the thousands of city homes emitting light out onto the streets.[12]

The authorities have worked with the grain of demand to decide on the best use for the different parts of an ancient city. This has worked remarkably well.

- **Make the process pleasant**
- **Consider your impact**
- **Allow a mixture of functions to flourish**

3. WHAT COULD GO WRONG?

Well, in one sense nothing can go wrong – or rather, wrong specifically as a result of the urban policies followed by the Copenhagen authorities. Thanks to the incremental approach they have adopted, if something does not work then it can be reversed without serious damage.

There are certainly things that might go wrong with the Danish economy and with Copenhagen's contribution to it: the city might become overpriced; the competitiveness of Denmark vis-à-vis other European countries might slide backwards. But those are general issues. The specific problem that might result from Copenhagen's policies is that too much economic development is pushed to the periphery of the city, so the main business activities are located outside the centre, while the core becomes little more than a museum.

But the landscape seems to be changing for urban planning in the post-industrial developed world. The model of a downtown central business district, where all the offices are located, surrounded by a suburban sprawl where people live, already looks outdated. We are still at the very early stages of the communications revolution but we can glimpse some of the implications, the decline of the regular commute and the rise of teleworking from home being one of the most apparent.

The more substantial charge is that what works in Copenhagen is specific to that city. For example, it is easier to re-establish the old medieval core as a place where people walk if you have a medieval core to start with. It could also be said that it is simple to encourage people to cycle more if the highest point of the city is just a few metres above sea level – or that the egalitarian Scandinavian society is conducive to the street lifestyle established by the city. Or more generally, it could be pointed out that Copenhagen is a dinky little city by world standards in a very rich country, and the real urban issues are those faced by the mega-cities such as São Paulo, Shanghai, Mumbai or Lagos.

Those are reasonable arguments. But the conclusion flowing from them is not that Copenhagen has little to teach other cities. Rather it is that attention to urban detail can make any place function better for its citizens – with the important qualification that each device used to that end has to be specific to the city in question. You need heated benches in Copenhagen if you want more people to sit down in winter; you do not need them in Mumbai.

But sometimes the transfer of principles really does work. Take Melbourne,[13] where Gehl Architects was involved as a consultant in importing the concept of mixed-use development to a city that had come to be described as a 'doughnut' – a sprawling suburban ring to which everyone would return at the end of the working day, leaving an empty, hollowed-out downtown centre in the evening. To begin with, Swanston Street, the main thoroughfare, was partially closed to traffic and then a whole range of improvements cascaded down to turn Melbourne into something like a twenty-four-hour city: a huge increase in residential housing; an expanded pedestrian network; wider pavements; and an explosion in shops (sometimes punched at street level into the city's office towers). As a result, according to the online magazine Worldchanging.com, the downtown residential population mushroomed by 830 per cent, pedestrian footfall rose by 98 per cent in the evenings and 250 new outdoor cafés opened. 'You cannot just pick up one model and transport it to another city,' said Roy Adams, director of Melbourne's urban design department. But you can, he added, 'pick up the principle that we're going to make the city more liveable'.

Lars Gemzøe in an interview[14] again:

> Jan [Gehl] and I wrote a book called *New City Spaces*, which looks at nine cities with visionary public-space policies. For example, Barcelona tried 'urban acupuncture', where you put a good spot here and there and the whole body becomes better, but it actually did not do much for traffic in the city. You have Lyons with its 'human face', Strasbourg with its streetcar tramlines and so on. The office has been working with Melbourne. In 1994, Jan did a survey of public space in Melbourne and discovered that the city was like a doughnut – the centre was empty of activity. He made recommendations, and in 2004

we made a new study on how they have improved, and they have performed fantastically. They had a 200 to 300 per cent increase in the number of people using downtown public spaces to hang out. Melbourne is a fantastic example because they have seen a huge change, but in a much, much shorter time than Copenhagen.

That is a tremendously powerful point. Melbourne is based on a grid, rather like so many North American cities that have suffered from the doughnut effect. If the principle works there, as it has done, any city in the world can make itself a better place in which to live. That is Copenhagen's core message to the world.

CHAPTER FIVE

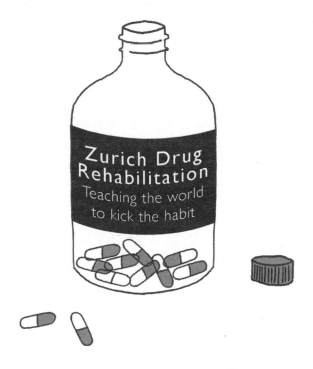

I. WHAT IS THE STORY?

The burghers of Zurich have arguably both the highest standard of living and the highest quality of life in the world.[1] As anyone who visits will quickly appreciate, Zurich is prosperous, comfortable and calm – even, well, just a little dull. It seems like a city without problems.

It has not always been so. In the late 1980s and early 1990s this orderly bourgeois city had the worst drug problem in Europe.

The story goes back to the 1970s. Zurich, like so many other rich cities in the developed world, saw a gradual increase in drug use, particularly among the young. To start with, they would gather in small groups by the river and no one took too much notice. Then gradually the numbers increased. Instead of there being a dozen, there might on a summer evening be a couple of hundred. Residents and shopkeepers complained. The police would break up the groups and move them on, but then they would regroup somewhere else nearby.

Fed up with chasing these people around, Zurich held a liberal social experiment. It allowed drug users to buy and inject drugs in one place without any police intervention. The place they chose was Platzspitz, a pretty park in the centre of the city between the principal railway station and the main river. It was contained by water on two sides and the station on the other and therefore seemed an ideal location.

It was a disaster. The park became a magnet for drug users from all over Europe. More than 2,000 of them would congregate every day. Their discarded syringes gave it the new name of 'Needle Park'. The citizens, who had initially supported the project, were aghast. Far from keeping the drug problem limited to one location, the social problems associated with drugs increased even faster than the number of users. There was misery, crime and prostitution. Central Zurich became horrid. Eventually the city decided that this could not continue and in February 1992 the police used rubber bullets and tear gas to disperse the drug users. The park was shut down. In the months afterwards, workers had to remove the top six feet of soil to get rid of all the syringes.

This made the problem less visible but the drug users regrouped, first in local streets and then in the Letten railway station nearby. They were allowed to stay there because the citizens felt it was better than having them on the streets. But so many people were arrested that some 60 per cent of the inmates in the jails were drug users. Switzerland was spending more per head on law and order than even the USA. Drug abuse and the associated crime continued. Nothing worked.

Then came a change of approach. The Swiss government had already developed a harm-reduction programme for drug addicts, with needle exchanges and treatment centres, back in 1991. So when in 1995 the crackdown came in Zurich and the station was closed, there was a programme in place to help the addicts. Treatment centres provided injection rooms. Patients could choose their own doctor and treatment was free. There was also a big methadone project, for methadone, as elsewhere, has generally been the favoured alternative to heroin.

This initiative was called the Four Pillar programme – the pillars being prevention, treatment, harm reduction and enforcement – and it has gone on to become the model for many cities around the world. But at first there was a lot of resistance from local authorities and its first major application did not come until 1994 when Zurich began putting it into practice. In the same year the Swiss government started trials in heroin prescription, a further controversial move. But when the results of these were evaluated, it became clear that for the most strongly addicted people, it was more effective to give them heroin rather than a substitute. Addicts' health improved, their illegal use of drugs decreased and people on the programme committed fewer crimes. So the programme was approved for general use and other regions of Switzerland introduced heroin prescription too. This scheme, while controversial, seems to have been a key advance.

Further lessons? A number of people were involved in turning things round but perhaps the most important was Professor Ambros Uchtenhagen, president of the Addiction and Public Health Research Foundation in Zurich. He points out that the Swiss managed the shutdown of the Letten railway station much better than they had that of Needle Park three years earlier. Ahead of closure they arranged for people to have access to sheltered accommodation and to enrol on a drug-substitution programme. So when they did shut it down, very few drug users were there anyway.

There have been many studies on the effectiveness of the initiative but let us just cite two. One, by Dr André Seidenberg, another of the key doctors behind the programme, was featured in the journal *General Practitioner*, published in Zurich, in 1999. In it he noted the 'hard' measures of success: a halving of the death rate from overdoses, for example, or the 80 per cent fall in HIV infection rates. But perhaps even more impressive were the results of one specific element of the programme: the prescription of heroin for heroin users, rather than a substitute. This produced excellent results even in patients where drug taking had become most embedded. You could see this in the 'soft' measures of improvement: people who had been unable to function normally for an average of ten years were able to rejoin mainstream society by receiving their drugs under medical supervision; after treatment, two-thirds found jobs; they started to pay off their debts; they gave up crime, with offences falling to a quarter of the previous level; prostitution more or less stopped; and the taking of cocaine and other hard drugs fell right away.

Dr Seidenberg's central message was this: 'There is no better measure or treatment for reducing the criminality and cocaine consumption of heroin addicts than the medical prescription of heroin.'[2]

That was the view of one of the people behind the scheme. But it has been backed by outside independent studies, of which one of the most recent was published in the medical journal *The Lancet* in June 2006.[3] This looked at the statistical evidence: how many people were on the programmes and what had happened to the incidences of drug use. This was really useful because by now there were many years of hard data about drug taking in Zurich. At the peak in 1990, around one person in every 1,400 was taking up heroin; by 2002, the number had fallen to about a fifth of this figure. That peak was similar to the level reached in New South Wales in Australia, but the fall has been much faster.[4] Not many people on the programme actually kick the addiction, about 4 per cent a year, but it seems the scheme has the effect of cutting the number of people taking up the drug in the first place.

What seems to have happened is that by making the taking of heroin a medical issue rather than a legal one, it has become less fashionable among the young. The report explained that heroin had become 'a loser drug'. If you can get something on prescription, it stops being glamorous. So while the programme may not have been particularly successful at getting people off heroin completely, it has been very effective in stopping the young from taking up the habit in the first place.

But that is heroin – what about other drugs? Here the story is less encouraging. It seems, unfortunately, that the use of some drugs –

including cannabis, cocaine, ecstasy and amphetamines – is rising.[5] There is also a problem with binge drinking. There is no open drug scene in Zurich, or indeed elsewhere in Switzerland, but the problem remains.[6]

It might surprise many people but Switzerland is actually a large exporter of cannabis: it can be cultivated legally and exported as 'hemp'. Farms have sprung up all over the country and Switzerland has become Europe's largest hemp producer. A lot is used locally too. The Federal Commission for Drugs Issues, an independent panel that advises the government, estimates that half a million people out of Switzerland's population of seven million smoke cannabis at least once a month.[7] In fact, it has become so widespread that at the end of 2008, the Swiss held a referendum on whether it should be made legal. The vote was against but the issue will hardly go away.[8]

So the programme pioneered in Zurich is not perfect. It is just the best that has yet been developed. And as such it carries practical lessons for cities and societies seeking to improve the health and welfare of their people – trying to stop them harming themselves, trying to help them escape the scourge of drugs and lead happier and more fulfilled lives.

2. WHAT ARE THE LESSONS?

At one level it is all very simple. Switzerland developed a model and applied it to the city with the most serious drug problem in Europe. So other places can pick up this model, adapt it to local conditions and roll out similar programmes. Many have done so. Particular elements of the Swiss approach now widely used elsewhere are injection rooms in pharmacies and needle-exchange programmes. The twin ideas of harm reduction and turning drug use into a medical issue rather than a law-and-order one have been widely imitated.

It has been applied, for example, in Britain. At the first stage three clinics were opened, one in south London, one in Darlington in north-west England and one in Brighton on the south coast. It has, according to Professor John Strang, the head of the National Addiction Centre at the King's College in London, who is leading the study, been a huge success. In 2007 he reported that instead of buying street heroin every day, about 100 of the 150 volunteers were buying it only four or five times a month – while the rest of them had completely stopped 'scoring' the drug on the streets.

Professor Strang said: 'This is genuinely exciting news. These are people with a juggernaut-sized heroin problem and I really did not know whether we could turn it around. We have succeeded with people who looked as if their problem was unturnable, and we have done it in six months.'[9]

So the medical approach works. But there is another element to the programme that is arguably just as important: alongside the medical approach, there was in Switzerland a fierce legal crackdown. Just before Letten was closed, the Swiss passed legislation giving police the power to search, arrest and detain anyone suspected of living without permission in Switzerland. All illegal foreign addicts and dealers were to be deported. These laws were dubbed 'anti-foreigner' but they had the authority of a referendum behind them. Two new prisons were built for foreigners suspected of committing an offence, and they were held in jail for up to a year without trial while waiting to be deported. As for Swiss drug users, if they were not from Zurich itself, they were sent to their home cantons for treatment. The tough legal approach was widely criticized – indeed by the advocates of the harm-reduction approach. The Association of Drug Specialists warned that the closure of Letten would force addicts to regroup elsewhere or go underground. Its president said the price of drugs would rise and the quality would fall as the scene was driven underground. As a result, the health of addicts would deteriorate still further. Fortunately, thanks to the treatment centres that were in place, those fears proved unfounded.[10]

So the Swiss approach has been a mixture of tender and tough. The Zurich experiment, focusing as it did on harm reduction and treating drugs as a medical rather than a criminal matter, was extremely liberal. But it has been more effective in Switzerland than elsewhere because it was backed by extremely illiberal legislation. The authority to hold foreigners without trial for up to a year is at the outer limits of the legal powers of Western democratic governments. Swiss powers to deport foreigners with relatively little right of appeal are much tougher than those of EU states. Even the power to force addicts to return to their home cantons for treatment is not something that other democracies would find easy to sanction.

The message therefore is a 'both/and', not an 'either/or'. You must have proper anti-harm treatment but you also need tough anti-crime legislation. However, those tough laws did not focus on the crime of drug taking because that in itself is not considered a crime. Rather they focused on the dealers, and particularly the foreign dealers.

Many people will find this a difficult combination to accept. Indeed the tough elements were much criticized by many of the proponents of the emphasis on treatment rather than punishment – as the soft ones were criticized by people who put punishment first. The distinctions in the treatment of foreigners accused of drug dealing – the holding them without trial and the willingness to deport them – would be difficult for most European countries to adopt as, on the face of it at least, they breach their human rights. Switzerland has neither signed nor ratified the relevant protocol in the European Convention on Human Rights on expulsion of foreigners. In practice, it is inevitable that some people will be treated harshly and unfairly. But many will recognize there is a common-sense element here: a country is responsible for its own citizens but not for people who come to it and break its laws.

There is, finally, another tantalizing possibility. It is that you curb drug use by acting on the demand side rather than the supply. If you could cut demand, the whole drugs industry, and all the social evils associated with it, would collapse. The clever idea behind the tough/tender Swiss approach is that it has made heroin in particular less fashionable. If it has really been turned into a drug for losers, then that leads to another question: could one make other harmful activities – excessive drinking, say – something for losers too? Even if there can be no simple answer to that, a radical decline in drug use is a prize worth chasing.

> • **Mix tender and tough**
> • **Act on the demand side rather than the supply side**
> • **Seek balance between extremes**

3 . WHAT COULD GO WRONG?

One difficulty will be obvious from the above: Switzerland has a serious cannabis problem. While the treatment of heroin addiction has been very effective, there has been less success in the treatment of softer drugs. But the bigger question mark over the Swiss experiment is the extent to which its success was down to the special circumstances of the Swiss drug problem at the beginning of the 1990s and therefore how much of this model can be replicated elsewhere.

Those circumstances included a sense of desperation and public shame. The Zurich authorities were forced to confront their failure but were also given the legal tools, backed by a national referendum, to take the tough steps as well as the soft ones. Now other places can do bits of the policies it pioneered. The treatment centres are relatively simple to transplant and prescription and administration of heroin, rather than substitutes, is easy in the sense that it merely requires legal consent.

But if the soft side is relatively easy to scale, the tough side is much harder. There is a political problem in that the places where there is a willingness to regard drug taking as a medical condition rather than a criminal one are not those where there is support for, say, holding foreigners without trial for a year. Conversely, perhaps an even bigger problem is that the places where there is support for the tough measures are unlikely to have the funds, facilities or political impetus for the medical approach. The USA, where 55 per cent of the people in federal prisons are serving time for drugs, is the obvious example of the latter.[11]

There are also a number of 'third rail' issues – the ones that people are afraid to touch in case they are electrocuted. Switzerland does not have historic connections with areas with a long history of the

production and transfer of hard drugs. It has a huge immigrant population, more than 20 per cent of the total, but relatively few are from
Latin America, West Africa or the Caribbean.[12] So Switzerland does
not feel the same need as other Western democracies to tiptoe round
the racial associations of the drug trade, or indeed crime generally.
Some 70 per cent of the inmates of Swiss jails are foreign-born.[13]

It is hard, then, to transplant the Swiss experience wholesale.
Harder still is the chase for the greatest prize of all: having a real
impact on drug demand. But that goes beyond the realms of both
medical intervention and law enforcement and into marketing,
psychology, brand advertising and so on. No one has yet succeeded
there. Advertising can project the notion that drug taking is harmful
but it has yet to succeed in convincing young people that it really is
an illness. There are some elements, though, in what Zurich has
achieved that point in this direction. It is not glamorous to have to
make a daily appointment at a drug clinic to get one's fix.

All our experience of drug taking through the ages is that it does
not head forever in one direction. It goes in cycles. One form of drug
abuse, or more broadly one set of social problems, recedes while
others take its place. But well-designed policies can have an impact.
We know what does not work; we know that the hands-off approach
of Zurich in the 1980s did not work; it is pretty obvious that the
turning of drug taking into a criminal offence, as in the USA, does
not work either. The way forward must be some balance between the
two extremes, and this experiment is as good an example of that as
any in the world.

CHAPTER SIX

The Mittelstand
Germany's industrial powerhouse

I. WHAT IS THE STORY?

Germany is the world's most successful goods exporter. In 2008 it sold more manufactured goods to other countries than the USA, more than China, more than Japan – all countries with far larger populations.[1] It did so despite not being particularly strong in the new electronics industries and it has managed to overcome the problem that most of its European neighbours are slow-growing markets.[2]

So what is its secret? Part of the answer is that there are many great German corporations – the household names such as BMW, Siemens or Volkswagen. But another part of the answer is that it is home to thousands of medium-sized companies – ones that most people have never heard of, but that are wonderfully successful in their own specialist fields. They each employ perhaps a few hundred people (though some have staff counts running into the thousands) and are usually family-owned[3] and managed, so they do not have huge resources behind them. Yet they dominate the markets in which they operate, often being number one or two in the world. They are the German 'Mittelstand'.

Notions about their size and their dominance of the German economy vary. On one count they employ more than two-thirds of all employees in private business, according to the Institut für Mittelstandsforschung in Bonn, the research body that studies and promotes their activities.[4] They contribute half the value-added of the entire country and produce directly a third of all exports. All other countries, of course, have small and medium-sized businesses, but no other nation has anything on this scale. Perhaps most surprising of all, this sector has survived the devastation of defeat in two world wars, the hyper-inflation of the 1920s and the challenges of lower-cost companies in Eastern Europe and Asia. Germany is an expensive place to make things – on some counts the most expensive in the world.[5] Yet while there have obviously been individual corporate casualties, as a sector these small and medium-sized companies have survived and prospered.

Why and how? Mittelstand businesses have a number of common characteristics. One is that family plays a core role. In some instances the same family has carried on for generations, both owning and managing the firm. In others the family ownership has become diluted, with other shareholders being brought in. In still others the family owns the firm but has it run by professional managers. The point in common is that families are able to take a very long view of a company's future – far longer than the shareholders of publicly quoted businesses.

A second characteristic is that most of the firms are in manufacturing rather than services and they usually have highly specialized, intermediate products that are part of the manufacturing process, rather than being finished goods. So the products are invisible to the consumer. The companies focus on a narrow market niche, aiming to dominate that niche worldwide. Typically a firm might have 70 to 90 per cent of the world market for that product.

That leads to a third characteristic. They tend not to have grand strategic visions but instead work in great detail with their customers to meet market demands. They are helped by the good technical training in Germany, so are able to draw on an innovative and educated workforce. The main competitive advantage this seems to give the firms is that they offer better customer service – something that enables them to justify their higher cost base.

Finally, many of these companies are located in small towns, where they are the dominant employer, rather than in large conurbations. This binds the workers into the company because they have fewer options for alternative employment. You could argue that it is dangerous for any town to become too dependent on one company, but the effect has been to align the interests of staff with those of the business, which probably makes management easier and fosters innovation by workers.

These characteristics were highlighted by the author and consultant Hermann Simon, who in the early 1990s identified more than 450 'Hidden Champions' – companies that had global leadership despite their small size. His book, published in 1996 with that title, still offers the best description and analysis of the sector.[6]

My own introduction to the Mittelstand came rather earlier, as from the 1950s onwards my father had the Irish agency for a number of German companies. He had a little one-man business as a textile agent, selling material on commission to Irish shops and clothing manufacturers. The most important of his agencies was a textile producer in Augsburg called Christian Dierig – you could almost say commission from the firm paid for my education. As it happens, this has proved a very good example of the longevity of German companies.

The company, named after its founder, dates back to 1805, and since then there have been six generations of the same name. The family still controls the company and it is still in textiles. That said, it is atypical in several ways. It was founded in the very early years of the Industrial Revolution, long before the notion of Mittelstand companies was conceived. At one stage it was one of the largest companies in Germany: just before the Second World War it employed nearly 19,000 people, whereas now it has some 200. But it survived wars, it survived the partition of Germany, it survived the decline of the European textile industry. And while its product mix has changed radically and it now makes quite a lot of its money from property development, it is still in the business in which it set out more than two centuries ago.

Boasting somewhat less longevity but a prime example of how the Mittelstand can touch our daily lives while remaining invisible is Webasto. Indeed many of us literally touch one of its products when we get into our car. You might think that if you bought a BMW then most of the car, aside from obvious components such as the electrics, would have been made by BMW. Not true. That goes for the vast majority of European-made and US-made cars and many others around the world. If a BMW has a sunroof that will have been made by Webasto – until quite recently it had more than half the world market for sunroofs, though as China has ramped up its car production that proportion has come back to about one-third. (Webasto started work on a factory near Shanghai in the middle of 2009, so expect it to garner a larger share of that market too. Mittelstand companies retain their German roots but think global for their future.)

Webasto has been making car sunroofs since 1932, when it invented the first folding roof for saloon cars. The company itself goes back even further, to 1901, when it started making things out of sheet metal. It moved to its present headquarters, in Stockdorf near Munich, in 1908 and has been a family-run business ever since. In 1935 it started making heaters for cars with water-cooled engines, and after the war branched out into products such as heating units for buses, electric steel sunroofs and parking heaters (so you can get into a warm vehicle on a cold morning). Now it has two broad product ranges. One category comprises the various car-roof products, from a simple tilt-and-slide to the complex glass roofs for MPVs. The other product line is made up of heaters and air-conditioning units, like parking heaters and heaters for boats and ventilation for lorries. It has some 7,000 employees, mostly in Germany but also in the USA and Asia. Its turnover in 2007 was $2.4 billion, so it is a sizeable operation.[7]

An equally sizeable company that most people have never heard of is Körber AG. But if you smoke cigarettes, what you have in your hand almost certainly involves the work of Körber, because more than 90 per cent of the machines in the world that make cigarettes have been built by the company.

Körber only goes back to 1947, a stripling compared with the other two companies. Its founder, Kurt A. Körber was born in Berlin in 1909, but when the war broke out he was an engineer at J. C. Müller, a cigarette-machine manufacturer in Dresden. He survived the bombing of the city in 1945 and after the war managed to get from Russian-controlled Dresden to Hamburg, in the British sector, where there were three cigarette factories. He helped them re-establish production and then got the licence from J. C. Müller to set up a cigarette-machine factory under the name of Hauni. That was the basis of the present business, which now dominates the world market.

But it kept on diversifying, adding business lines in which it could build a similar degree of brand leadership. So it went into paper processing in 1970 and then, as demand for cigarette machines declined, added an electronic manufacturing unit that produced a machine for extracting oxygen from the air. In the 1990s it developed a system for cutting small pieces of paper (such as cheque books) and has 90 per cent of the world market for that. But cigarette machines are still its largest division.

Kurt Körber died in 1992 and since then the business has been owned by a non-profit foundation that he set up, so it remains a 'family' business in this sense. And like many other Mittelstand family firms, it is run by professional managers, who report to the foundation. So in terms of ownership it is as secure as any commercial company can be.

2. WHAT ARE THE LESSONS?

Germany did not make some sudden collective decision that it would dominate the world market for certain types of manufactured products or that it would create a collection of medium-sized companies to help it do so. The development of the Mittelstand was not the result of any policy but rather derived from an attitude that technical education and commercial competence were essential for economic prosperity. That emphasis on technology and education goes back at least to the emergence of Germany as a modern state in the second half of the nineteenth century, under, most notably, the chancellorship of Otto von Bismarck. But one of the companies highlighted here precedes that, for Christian Dierig can trace its roots to the early days of the Industrial Revolution in Germany.

Attitude, it would seem, matters more than policy. Germany has created some huge companies, as have all developed nations, for that is part and parcel of the process of economic development. Nor has the country sought to restrict the size of its companies so they remain medium-sized; that would be absurd. For some reason, though, no other nation has managed to sustain such a body of excellence, and the special characteristics that have permitted the Mittelstand's companies to thrive despite huge military, political and social upheavals carry messages for the rest of the world.

There are, I suggest, a number of these messages.

The first is that dominance matters. To be successful over a long period, a business has to be a leader in its particular market segment. In fast-growing economic conditions, many indifferent companies can thrive as they simply get carried upwards by the tide of growth. The German economy has had its periods of rapid expansion, including the Wirtschaftswunder, or economic miracle, in the years after the Second World War.[8] But it has also gone through the fire and, particularly after the unification of East and West Germany in 1990, struggled with slow growth and high unemployment.[9] For medium-sized companies to survive such times they must have deep strength – and one of the sources of strength is dominating the market they serve.

That also means serving niches, the second message. If you are only medium-sized and want to dominate your market, you are bound to pick a few narrow areas of excellence. You cannot compete on price so you have to be better, in your chosen field, than anyone else. You have the advantage that you can know all the possible customers in the world, and they will make you aware of any potential competition. If your customers want some new product or service, you are in the best position to supply it.

This leads to a third message – that although most of the Mittelstand is in manufacturing rather than services, much of the added value lies in adding service to the product. Most of these companies are selling to other companies, not to the end user, so there is less need for conventional marketing skills. Instead the quality of service they give, in terms of back-up, sticking to delivery times, fixing problems and so on, makes it worthwhile to pay the additional cost of German wages. How does Germany remain the world's largest exporter, while having about the highest wage costs anywhere? One of the answers is that back-up is superlative. That is very deep-rooted. I recall as a child that my father found his German suppliers were much better than his British ones at attention to detail, from little things such as responding to customer queries to the rather larger one of paying his commission on time!

The next message is that, to survive, these companies have learnt to become nimble. All the three firms highlighted above – Christian Dierig, Webasto and Körber – have diversified. The firms of the Mittelstand are led into some things by their customers but also spot parallel niches where their skills, mostly in engineering, enable them to achieve similar advantage. So they seem to have a bottom-up approach to innovation: they take something they are doing and work forward from that, using the embedded skills of their workforce. They do not do 'blue sky' innovation.

They have also recently become a driving force for educational reform. The highly selective German school system, particularly in the small towns where most of the Mittelstand firms are located, no longer delivers the right mix of qualifications. For example, companies need technical skills but also foreign languages as they are selling to the world. The message here is that companies need to become involved in the education of their workforce and cannot just rely on the schools to deliver the skills they need.

And finally they operate with great discipline and control. If they expand abroad, they usually keep complete control of their overseas operation. They do not in general go in for joint ventures or takeovers. If they do buy another company, it is swiftly integrated into their core business. They do not pay huge executive bonuses and they usually grow their management from within. They are in a curious way quite modest about their achievements – local companies that happen to sell their products all over the world, but still local in their ethos.

All this is very impressive and perhaps most of all because the model has come through some very difficult times. And now, in 2009, it is entering yet another of those times. It is to those issues that the next section turns.

- **Attitude matters more than policy**
- **Dominance matters**
- **Encourage a bottom-up approach to innovation**

3. WHAT COULD GO WRONG?

The conventional wisdom is that the Mittelstand is now in trouble for a number of reasons, the most general one being that these family firms are finding it hard to manage the succession. There are many strands to this.

One often cited is that the post-war generation of owners have been loath to hand over control to the next generation, believing it has become self-indulgent and undisciplined. Another is that the young do not want the responsibility of running the firm and in any case have plenty of other career options that were not available to their parents. A variant of this is that, with Germany's low birth rates, there are not many people in the next generation who would want to go into the family business anyway – maybe none at all. So there is a human management issue.[10]

There is also a financial issue. Mittelstand companies are not quoted on stock exchanges and so do not have access to equity capital, and as a result they tend to rely on the banks and retained profits to finance expansion. But all banks in Germany are under pressure, and while that is true of other countries too, similar-sized companies elsewhere can go to alternative sources for outside funding. A model that works when banks are well capitalized and solid is unusually fragile when the banks themselves are weak.

There is a further concern. It is that Germany has low business start-up rates, and worse, falling ones. They were much lower in the 2005–8 period than they were ten years earlier.[11] Quite why this should be is a bit of a mystery. A more widespread lack of dynamism in the German economy? Globalization shifting competitive advantage away from smaller companies and towards larger ones? Changes in taxation and regulation that discourage start-ups?

Whatever the explanation, this must be a concern for the future, for if the stock of new companies is not renewed, the model that has served the country well for upwards of 200 years will die.

I suppose what it really comes down to is whether enough German people want to create businesses. It cannot just be about money, though obviously that is a powerful driver for most entrepreneurs. It has to be about service – the idea that by setting up a business that serves the needs of the country and the world, you are doing something worthwhile, perhaps even making a noble contribution to humankind. Or has the social and political climate that led to the creation of the Mittelstand somehow changed? Has this mixture of drive and service gone?

There can be no answer to this other than to see what happens. My instinct is very much that this extraordinary phenomenon will persist and flourish. We know it is adaptable to the challenge of globalization, for it has proved that you do not maintain a position as the world's largest exporter if you cannot cope with global competition. We know the Mittelstand can adapt to the very high cost structure of modern Germany. Indeed it seems to come stronger out of every economic downturn.

Writing in 2009, it is clear the challenge ahead is huge, but I would not want to bet against the Mittelstand. The spirit that has survived two catastrophic world wars will not give up easily, and I much admire it for that. Indeed I would be really astounded if, in another 50 or 100 years' time, people around the world were not still looking to Mittelstand companies to see how to make things that other people want to buy. More than that, they will surely also continue to look to these companies as a way of building harmonious links between employers and workers, between the producers and the community that they serve. The companies themselves will rise and fall but as a group they will continue both to be commercially successful and to carry on bringing these wider social benefits to the German people.

CHAPTER SEVEN

I. WHAT IS THE STORY?

Forty years ago most people in the developed world cooked their own meals – but bought their furniture fully assembled. Now we eat out or buy ready-prepared meals – but increasingly have to screw together our own furniture. The flatpack has been one of Ikea's most important innovations, one that has changed the way in which millions of people kit their homes.

Like many great innovations, this one was discovered by accident. In 1956, when Ikea was a small furniture mail-order business in rural Sweden, Gillis Lundgren, a young local draughtsman employed by the company, was trying to fit a table into a car. It would not go. So he took the legs off.[1]

Ikea's founder, Ingvar Kamprad, immediately appointed him as a designer. He realized that shipping furniture in flatpacks had a host of advantages over shipping it made up. It took out the labour cost of assembly, of course, but it also cut transport charges because less bulky items were being moved. Flatpacks used up less warehouse space, so there was a saving there, and there was less chance of damage when delivering the furniture. All you had to do was adapt the design so that an ordinary person could put the thing together. Gradually, product by product, Ikea set about doing so.

The flatpack revolution fitted in closely with social changes in Europe – and particularly Sweden – in the 1950s. Working hours for men were falling, giving them more leisure time and hence more time in their homes. But taxes and labour costs were climbing fast, making it more economical for people to use their own, untaxed labour rather than the taxed services of another worker.[2] And at that time young people were starting to live together and have children at a much younger age than their parents, so they wanted to be able to furnish their homes as cheaply and stylishly as possible.[3]

Ikea was on the right side of a tidal wave of social change and received the commercial rewards for that. Its success in helping young families to live in affordable comfort is such that an estimated 10 per cent of babies in Europe are conceived on an Ikea bed.[4]

Soon that may apply to other continents, for though four-fifths of its sales are still in Europe, Ikea has become the largest furniture retailer in the world. In 2008 its sales were $28 billion; it had 253 stores; and it employed 128,000 people in 39 countries. It printed 198 million copies of its catalogue and 565 million people visited its stores.[5]

Ikea was founded by Ingvar Kamprad in 1943 when he was 17. He used his initials for the first two letters and those of his family farm and local village for the final two.[6] He started the business as a mail order one, selling any goods that he could find cheaply: pens, wallets, picture frames, watches etc. He added furniture in 1947, launched his first catalogue in 1951 and opened his first showroom in 1953. The company began to design its own furniture in 1955, leading to that fateful invention of the flatpack, but the first store did not open until 1958.[7] Its management is still Swedish, its designs are mostly Swedish and the company is still controlled by its founder and his family.[8]

So Ikea is at one level simply a tremendously successful business. It is one that has come to dominate its field in Europe and is branching out with increasing penetration in the rest of the world. Like all successful businesses, its management has an instinct for what people want – in this case, clean, modern design and very low prices – and has developed special ways of delivering this. The flatpack was a key innovation because it held down prices by eliminating the cost of assembly and cutting the cost of shipping. But there have been many others. Some of these involve using new materials: particleboard with a lacquer finish for cheap but stylish furniture; plastics for chairs; and applying the board-on-frame way of making doors to cabinets and other furniture. Further innovations are about clever design: making easy assembly part of the initial design of the product, or developing the idea of the modular kitchen, where people can put in an entire kitchen or just add bits to one in the same style.

Ikea was very early, too, in outsourcing supply to low-cost countries.[9] Initially it pioneered production in Eastern Europe and more recently in China. In 2008 over 20 per cent of its purchases were from China and a further 12 per cent from Poland. The relationship with Poland goes back to the start of the 1960s, a time when the word 'outsourcing' had not been invented and when buying from Communist Eastern Europe was almost unknown in the West.

The company remains, however, indubitably Swedish. Its logo is blue and yellow, the colours of the Swedish flag. As any of the hundreds of millions of shoppers know, the stores have a proselytizing air about them. Traditional Swedish dishes such as gravadlax and meatballs with lingonberry relish are on sale in the restaurants. The designers are largely Swedish and continue to produce the classic mixture of clean, unfussy, stylish, informal and accessible product lines.

The Swedish element extends into concern about less developed countries and a stress on environmental and social responsibility. In 1998, for example, the company set up a project to rehabilitate rainforests that had been devastated by logging and fires on the island of Borneo. In 2000 it launched a programme with Unicef in rural India to try to reduce child labour (the 'Ikea Social Initiative' has since committed around $200 million to the charity's projects) and in 2001 came an initiative to move goods wherever possible by rail rather than road. The same year it started sending students on a course on sustainable forest management, and since 2002 it has worked in tandem with the World Wildlife Fund to combat illegal logging and maintain biological diversity.[10]

As citizens of big-government Sweden accept, there is a certain bossiness about Ikea's treatment of its customers. You can buy some but not all of the goods online; you can look at everything on the website but to purchase the items where there is a cross through the shopping-trolley icon, you have to go to a store. There is a delivery service but people are encouraged (not least by its cost) to pick up the purchases themselves. Inside the outlets, you are directed to meander right round the store along a yellow road, so that you see the entire range rather than being able to zero in on the thing you want. Meanwhile, Ikea's complex if egalitarian sourcing arrangements – it has suppliers in fifty-four countries – can sometimes lead to items being out of stock, which is a particular problem for shoppers buying multi-component products such as Ikea's kitchens. But the prices are so astoundingly low that people are prepared to accept all this. They vote with their wallets.

There is a cultural criticism too, though. The Nordic way that seems attractively egalitarian to some comes over as offhand, inattentive service to others. The USA, where retail expectations are different to those in Western Europe, has been the firm's toughest market. The drive to hold down costs means that service is inevitably thin – with minimal advice for shoppers in their buying decisions – while at the same time the success in holding down costs means the outlets are often crowded. But at the most basic level, by combining a powerful Swedish culture with commercial zeal, Ikea has done something more than just commerce: it has transformed the way Europeans live.

2. WHAT ARE THE LESSONS?

The first and most obvious is that price matters: Ikea is simply the lowest-cost producer in the world of a particular line of output and has ridden to global success on the back of that. But the underlying lessons are much more subtle – and much harder to replicate. Ikea is different to almost all other retailers; this is not a specialized European version of Wal-Mart. Price matters certainly, but so, too, do three other features of the company's proposition: style, culture and education. All carry important lessons.

The first of these messages is that cheapness, efficiency and self-assembly are not any barrier to producing something that is functionally stylish. The result, at its best, is a supreme elegance of design.

There are lots of examples of this. Some are concepts, of which the flatpack is only the most famous; the invention of a modular design for a kitchen brings up a considerable vanguard. Others are products, such as the Skopa chair, made out of plastic, or the Dagis children's stackable chair. The idea that a chair should be made from plastic is now commonplace but it was not before 1974; the idea that children's chairs should be stackable, just like grown-ups', is common sense but no one had thought of it until 1995 – or if they had, they had never made it available to a global audience.

None of this would be possible were it not for the cultural base from which Ikea grew: Swedish, or perhaps more general Nordic, egalitarianism. There is a certain irony that Ingvar Kamprad should be ranked by *Forbes* magazine in 2008 as the seventh-richest person in the world and live in Lausanne, in low-tax Switzerland, rather than high-tax Sweden. Some may also think it ironic that he should drive an old Volvo and fly economy class – using the minor symbols of equality – while locating himself in a tax haven. Arguably, too, the fact that he was in his youth a Nazi sympathizer (something he says now that he much regrets) chimes oddly with his subsequent elagitarian zeal.[11]

Nevertheless, the idea that people should assemble their own furniture is essentially egalitarian: you do things for yourself rather than pay someone to do them for you. And, of course, the Nordic influence runs much deeper. Ikea designs for families – there is a huge emphasis on what works for children – and for couples who share tasks, including the bringing up of their children. An Ikea kitchen is not designed to impress the neighbours; it is designed to be a calm, cool, clear environment where a family, probably a young family without a huge amount of money, can live a stylish, classless life.

This is very Swedish, as anyone who visits the country will immediately recognize. But while the Swedish element is captured in colours of the company logo and the food in the stores' restaurants, these are just outward symbols of a deeper desire to imbue in shoppers the ideals of the Nordic way of life. Ikea is not selling furniture; it is selling a lifestyle. To judge by the company's growth, there are elements of this way of life that other Europeans in particular find very attractive.

This cultural element also explains why Ikea has made only slow progress in the USA. The first US store opened in 1985 and there are now thirty-six, accounting for 10 per cent of the company's global sales and ranking the country second behind Germany as Ikea's biggest market. However, this is also the largest market in the world and the push into the USA has been arduous. Why? The straightforward answer is that American tastes are different to European ones and it has taken a while for Ikea to come to grips with that. But behind this explanation lies the cultural story. It is not just that Nordic egalitarianism plays better in Europe than it does in the USA or that Americans have less leisure time to bolt things together than Europeans do; the overriding cultural force behind Ikea means it has found it harder to adapt to the US way of life than it has to other – ostensibly even more different – societies such as Saudi Arabia or China.

That leads to the third element of the Ikea proposition: education. The company's mission is not just to educate customers; it is also to educate suppliers. Ikea learnt very early on that if it wanted to cut costs, it had to pioneer sourcing from lower-cost regions; Sweden was too expensive a place to make things. In the early days, this meant looking to Eastern Europe and in particular the then Communist Poland, which had a reservoir of craft skills in the 1960s but could not boast companies with the ability to make the sophisticated products that Ikea designers wanted. So it had to teach them.

That led to a mission to teach Eastern European suppliers not just how to produce to quality and to time but how to meet Western European environmental and ethical standards.[12] From that base, Ikea has sought to go on and teach Nordic ethics to suppliers in China and other low-cost countries.

So the company is an academy. It is, to be sure, an academy driven in some measure by self-interest, for it knows its customers would rebel if, for example, they found that suppliers employed child labour. So it has worked hard to ensure this does not happen. Its aim here is to show suppliers on the other side of the world not just that child labour is wrong, but inefficient.

Pull these three special elements of the Ikea proposition together and what lessons emerge?

First, it cannot be replicated as such because its success is too deeply derived from its embedded Swedish cultural attitudes. But parts of its mission can be adapted by any wise business. One is the idea that design should start from function and efficiency. Train great young designers in this way of thinking and great innovative products will emerge. Another is that one should look at the way a society is evolving to understand what the next generation of consumers will want; Ikea was lucky to be based in a country that, in many ways, has been a European social leader. Still another is that not-very-rich people can and should have access to great style. Style does not need money.

And there perhaps is the most important lesson of all: money matters but other things matter more. It is possible, in an advanced economy, for the vast majority of the population to be able to afford to lead decent, fulfilled lives. The material goods needed for that can be delivered by thoughtful, well-organized, ethical companies.

The trick, looking forward, will be to convert what Ikea does for furniture not just to other products but the services we need for a better quality of life. For example, in line with the company's proposition of customers meeting an organization halfway to buy something they value at a low price, the concept of do-it-yourself wills and probate arrangements is already taking shape in some countries. Alternatively, the Ikea way could be applied not just to what we put in our properties but the properties themselves – in other words, good-quality but low-cost or social housing. Here the company has put down its own marker with its BoKlok ('stylish living') homes – light, functional, timber-framed constructions that follow the flat-pack model in that they arrive on site in pre-assembled units. Already installed across Scandinavia, the BoKlok has now landed in England, aimed squarely at people earning in the range of £15,000 (around $25,000) to £30,000 a year.

If Ikea can educate suppliers on the other side of the earth, could not the ideas and attitudes it has developed influence providers of products and services across the planet? And could it not help educate children around the world as well?

- **Don't sell a product, sell a lifestyle**
- **Educate customers, educate suppliers**
- **Money matters but other things matter more**

3. WHAT COULD GO WRONG?

Ikea is very focused. It was founded by one person with a sense of mission and it does one job supremely well. But all our experience of such focused enterprises is that quite suddenly the winning streak can end. There are two main ways in which this can happen.

One is that when the founder dies, the succession is mismanaged. Maybe the children squabble; maybe the professional management that has performed fine under the founder's tutelage fails to find the right blend of skills and makes strategic errors. For whatever reason, the business is gradually overtaken by newer, more innovative competitors.

The other is that a grand social or economic change overtakes the company so that what it is doing, or the way it is doing it, is no longer required by the community.

Ikea is vulnerable to both risks. Ingvar Kamprad was born in 1926. Eventually it is assumed that one of his three sons,[13] all of whom work at the company, will be named as successor. No one can know whether the growth will continue when that happens. There is huge momentum in the business and solid managerial depth, and the Ikea board itself is not led by a family member. However, ultimate ownership still rests with the Kamprads through a Dutch trust and, because of this family control, it has not established the public reporting and control structures of a typical quoted company – structures that would give more confidence about the future management direction. In that sense, Ikea is more vulnerable than, for example, Wal-Mart. The experience of other private businesses in similar positions is not encouraging.

Retailing, any form of retailing, is a curious industry – one in which a single intuitive and talented individual can carry an entire business. It is also one in which a business can rapidly lose its way and where size alone is little protection.

The other risk is that young people no longer want the Swedish style of goods or indeed the accoutrements of the Nordic lifestyle. Partly this is just a matter of changing fashions; one has only to look at the rejection by many societies of the architecture of 1960s modernism to see that what appears smart and stylish can become shabby and sad. But it is also a question of the changing ways in which people live. It may be that the youth of tomorrow will want to buy service with product and will not be so prepared to bolt things together themselves.

That Ikea has found expansion in the USA tough carries a warning. If the rest of the developed world is to become more like the USA then it may be difficult, working out of a Swedish base, to continue to dominate it. Will, for example, the newly rich of China and India take their style notes from Europe or from America? Why should a young couple in Shanghai want European style as opposed to USA?

Japan, where Ikea now has five stores, has tended to look to the USA for its design guidance. As Europe inevitably becomes less important in the global economy, it may be harder for its companies to give a lead to the world.

The key with both these risks, of course, is the ability to adapt. Ikea has been extraordinarily nimble in the past and there is no reason why it should not be equally so in the future. If it can adapt then the force of message it gives to the world will be all the greater. Meanwhile, it carries on improving the lifestyles of Europe's young people in that most practical of ways: making their homes more comfortable and stylish places to be.

North America

CHAPTER EIGHT

New York Philanthropy
The most generous people on Earth

1. WHAT IS THE STORY?

Americans are the most generous people on earth. People in the USA give away more of their income than do those of any other nation.[1] With that wealth the country creates wonderful institutions, filling in the gaps in human relations that pure market transactions pass by. And they have been doing it for 400 years, long before the USA became an independent country.

You could start the story with what on most measures is the greatest place of learning on earth. It came into being in 1636 but was to bear the name of its first benefactor, a British clergyman called John Harvard who had emigrated to America in 1637. He died the year after he landed, leaving his books and half his estate in Cambridge, Massachusetts, to the new university. Or you could cite James Smithson, another Briton though he was born in France. He never visited the USA, but after his death in 1829 his funds were bequeathed for the creation of the Smithsonian Institution in Washington DC.[2] Or consider the experience of Andrew Carnegie, the Scottish-born American steel baron, who became the second-richest man in the world and then gave away 90 per cent of his wealth, believing that: 'The man who dies rich dies disgraced.'[3]

In those three cases, their names live on in the institutions for which they were benefactors, for philanthropy can buy a form of immortality. It does so particularly in the USA, because while those donors were born outside America, there was and remains something about the ethos of the USA that enables and encourages such philanthropy to flourish. The desire to use personal wealth to make for a better world exists everywhere, but somehow that spirit seems to be harnessed more effectively in the USA than anywhere else.

That is partly a function of the country's genius for organization. Its foundations are stunningly effective at fund-raising. The joke goes, why do Harvard alumni never get lost? Because the university's development office will always find them. Note the term 'development office', which has become a sort of euphemism for fund-raising, because some people, particularly outside the USA, find this aspect of American society distasteful. That seems a shame; there are genuine concerns about the power of philanthropic organizations, of which more later, but to carp at them for being effective at fund-raising is surely a pretty sad response.

The spirit of philanthropy is alive and well all over the USA. What is surely its most notable current example, the Bill & Melinda Gates Foundation,[4] is run from Seattle, while those three historical examples noted above have their roots in Cambridge, Washington DC and, among many places, Pittsburgh, home of the Carnegie-Mellon University. New York, though, is really the centre of the movement and so the best place to catch what is so special about it – and the Big Apple has Carnegie Hall.

There is, though, a puzzle in the scale and spread of this giving.

A vast array of information is available on the subject. The Center on Philanthropy at Indiana University publishes a survey, *Giving*

USA, which calculates that Americans donate more than 2 per cent of GDP to charities.[5] (The figure for Italy is 0.1 per cent.[6]) It also does a survey for the Bank of America on what high net worth individuals give away each year, and logs all donations of more than $1 million in the Million Dollar List. There are many books on the topic giving further details and perspectives. But despite all this work, there is a huge gap in our understanding. It does not answer the question: why?

We can observe that Americans give away much more, absolutely, of course, but also relatively, than the citizens of other nations.[7] And we can see some of the inducements for them to do so, including favourable tax treatment and the enhancement of social status; while Americans cannot be inherently more generous than Italians, they can be seen to be using their wealth to do good works.

So you could perhaps explain the lower commitment to charity in continental Europe by noting the higher personal tax rates there.[8] Maybe the more people have to give to the government, the less they are willing to support charities. If the state is going to take away so much of their money, this argument goes, then there should be no onus on them to hand out even more of it. However, there are plenty of low-tax regimes where the level of giving is also relatively low, and vice-versa.

You could point to how philanthropy conveys status in the USA, in contrast to much of continental Europe. But that does not explain why Americans seem to be different, especially given that new immigrants to the country quickly pick up the giving habit. Indeed they pass on a much higher proportion of their income than established residents in that they send huge amounts of money home. That is not exactly philanthropy, for most of the money is for their families, but the effect is an informal aid programme analogous to the formal aid programmes of other countries. And it is certainly giving.

In any case the practice of giving is different in the USA from elsewhere. People who move there from Britain and Europe find it is expected of them to support charitable causes to an extent that would be unthinkable at home. It is not a question of being generous or not generous; it is just what people in the USA do.

This gives a different tone to American society. Part of that difference is religion. More than 35 per cent of charitable donations in the USA are to religious foundations, according to *Giving USA* and Johns Hopkins University (which itself owes its existence to the American businessman and Quaker of the same name who in 1873 endowed the university, and a number of medical institutions, with a legacy of $7 million – at the time, the largest philanthropic bequest in US history). In Britain and Europe the proportion is less than a quarter of that.[9]

Another distinguishing feature, however, is a sense of global drive. Many charities outside the USA, for example Oxfam in Britain and Médecins sans Frontières in France, were founded for the very purpose of helping people in poorer countries. But there is a qualitative difference between them – their structure, their growth and their focus – and the foundations of the great American benefactors such as Bill Gates and the financier George Soros.[10] An organization whose funds are derived from a single individual who is still alive and so able to provide direction is different to one founded a generation or more earlier, however well funded, however competently run and however true to the intentions of its founder.

Greater fortunes have been made over the past quarter of a century in the USA than anywhere else, so it is natural the ideas of the people who have created them should dominate global philanthropy. These people know how to get things done. Most of us naturally find that combination of enthusiasm and effectiveness extremely impressive. These foundations do good in the world.

That, however, is a known story. Anyone with a few billions has a model to follow: all you have to do is make the money in the first place. What is less widely appreciated is the special quality that philanthropy can bring to its own society, the society in which that wealth is created, and this is where I suggest New York carries its special message. To see the reasons why, I visited two bodies there – one large and famous, the other small and unknown – to see what they have achieved.

The large one is MoMA, the Museum of Modern Art. It sits on a prime site in Midtown just off Fifth Avenue, has recently renovated is

buildings and nearly doubled its exhibition space, and is unquestion-
ably one of the great museums of the world. Though it now lags
behind the Tate Modern in London in terms of visitor numbers (2.6
million against 5.2 million in 2008) it has been and arguably still is the
most influential museum of modern art there is. What interested me,
though, was not its influence on art and design but rather its relationship with the city: what it gave to New York citizens and what those
citizens gave to it. I went to Glenn Lowry, its director, whom I had
met in Oxford and London, to learn about this.

Dr Lowry saw American philanthropy as something of a miracle:
the extent to which people were 'astoundingly generous for no apparent reason'. There are, of course, tax benefits but he found that donors
would give money far beyond the point at which they could have any
such advantage. Besides, there were lots of people with just as much
money who did not donate to charity at all. The reason why people
did donate? The sense in New York that if you were in any way privileged you were part of the tradition of collective civic responsibility to
support culture: 'to make things happen'. There was also a powerful
sense, too, that the private sector can do it better. There were the large
donors, such as the Rockefellers, who have been hugely important in
supporting MoMA, and other people told me that the museum was
lucky to have a particularly strong and supportive bunch of trustees.[11]
But Glenn Lowry pointed out that most American giving did not
come in massive donations – 'heroic philanthropy' – but rather in
smaller amounts from millions of people of relatively modest means.

It is a ten-minute cab ride from glitzy Midtown to the modest
offices of Visiting Neighbors, on Broadway in the lower part of
Greenwich Village.[12] I had heard about them from a friend who lives
in the Village and whose wife is a volunteer. Its director is Cynthia
Maurer, who explained to me how they operated. Their principal aim
was very simple: it was to enable older people to carry on being able
to live in their own homes. In addition, they sought to promote
volunteering and to try to improve attitudes towards ageing in
general. Their main programme was also very simple: they paired an
older person with a volunteer who would visit them for two hours

once a fortnight. The volunteer would not do any professional service though if the client needed some kind of additional help then Visiting Neighbors could find it. So it was not a nursing service; nor would volunteers do housework or anything like that. The job was to go and visit, as a good neighbour would, and have a cup of tea and a chat and apply some common sense.

Dr Maurer explained to me that they had discovered 'what works' – I liked that phrase for obvious reasons. First of all a volunteer needed to be a social person: they needed to like other people. There needed to be a support system for volunteers, so they could get help on the problems they came across. They needed to be matched correctly – the right person had to visit the right person. And you had to be honest about what becoming a volunteer would entail. They also found that the commitment of two hours a fortnight worked because it was a reasonable amount of time for someone to give. If you asked for more, people would find it too much and drop out.

So here were two charities less than three miles apart doing utterly different things but both in their way hugely successful. MoMA has extended its buildings; Visiting Neighbors has extended its range and now reaches up towards Midtown. Both are based on philanthropy and respect the freedom that this gives. As Glenn Lowry stresses, MoMA benefits from the input of its supporters and they give it freedoms that a European museum dependent on public sector funding perhaps would not have. As for Visiting Neighbors, it did get some funding from the city but Dr Maurer points out that it is better not to be fully funded because you have more freedom that way.

But the overriding impression that I got was something more. It was that both work because the people who help them get something intangible out of doing so. In the case of MoMA they are supporting one of the world's great museums and that must be deeply satisfying. And in the case of Visiting Neighbors? Well, in Dr Maurer's phrase people find that 'volunteering feeds some part of their soul'.[13]

2. WHAT ARE THE LESSONS?

There are two broad ways of looking at philanthropy. One is to examine how effective it is at achieving its goals. Is it better, for example, at helping to fight malaria in Africa than other forms of action, such as official aid deployed through the World Health Organization? The other is to look at what philanthropy does to the identity and cohesion of a community.

On the first, the key point to appreciate is that the sums distributed through philanthropy are very small beside the transfers made by governments. In the USA, all charitable spending on social welfare is less than one-tenth of the state's expenditure on welfare; in the UK the ratio is about thirty to one and in other countries the proportion is even lower.[14] So philanthropy is no substitute for government action. The only area where the numbers might be comparable would be between immigrants' remittances and official aid. Obviously this varies vastly from country to country and the figures are at best hazy. But in the case of the USA, the numbers are of a similar order of magnitude, and in a city full of immigrants such as New York, its people finance a lot of development in poorer countries. However, the money immigrants send home would hardly fit in the normal definition of philanthropy, though perhaps it should.

As for effectiveness, it is really very subjective. As a general principle, if money is given freely, rather than taken in tax and redistributed, the relationship between giver and recipient is more direct and more personal. It would be nice to think that as a result there is less waste – that the funds are better allocated and supervised; that the recipients themselves choose to use the money they receive more wisely because they know it is given by real people rather than distributed by some amorphous government agency. That is nice to think but hard to prove conclusively. In any case, advocates of the virtues of 'the gift relationship' (to borrow the title of the book on blood donors by Richard Titmuss, the British social researcher)[15] have to admit that philanthropy is not democratic. Why should rich people use their money to determine social priorities? The answer is that they are rich and they can spend their money in any way they like.

Nevertheless, it seems a reasonable expectation that philanthropists can achieve things that government officials cannot. They can move more quickly. They can inject greater drive. And on the balance of probability, the funds are more wisely spent as a result.

If the benefits of philanthropy to society at large are hard to assess, there is no such difficulty in identifying the benefits to the local community. They are there for all to see, and more so in New York than any other place on earth.

For just as the Big Apple has created many of the world's great fortunes, so it gains hugely from the way in which those fortunes have been deployed. It is a city built on philanthropy.

I have taken two examples of that but there are a host of others. There is the New York Public Library, which unlike most other great libraries of the world was largely financed by private donations, from among other people Andrew Carnegie, the multimillionaire fur trader John Jacob Astor, Samuel Tilden, a governor of New York, and James Lenox, the millionaire bibliophile.[16] There is the Frick Collection, the Manhattan art museum founded by the industrialist Henry Clay Frick, not widely liked in his lifetime but immortalized since.[17] There is the Guggenheim. There is the New York Botanical Garden, founded in 1891 on part of the grounds of the Belmont Estate in the Bronx, with money raised from wealthy New York families. There are many more such institutions, mostly set up with private wealth, and it is those that make New York such a special place.

In the case of MoMA, the achievement has been to make New York the world centre of modern art. In the case of Visiting Neighbors the achievement has been to make the lives of thousands of people more fulfilling. We can learn from both.

- **Move quickly**
- **Inject drive**
- **Spend wisely**

3. WHAT COULD GO WRONG?

Philanthropy faces a host of challenges worldwide. The most obvious is that it is vulnerable to the swings in personal wealth. In a boom there are more resources to share around; in a slump people are more cautious. That is the preoccupation of the moment but on a long view it hardly matters. (MoMA, incidentally, was founded in November 1929, just after the Wall Street crash.) While there will inevitably be peaks and troughs in the flow of funds, the durability of philanthropic foundations is remarkable. Indeed they are much more durable than the industries and companies that brought about their creation. For example, the American steel companies and railroads that led the late nineteenth-century US boom are a shadow of their former selves, yet the Carnegie foundations continue all over the world, the Frick Collection remains a jewel in New York's crown and the New York Public Library is one of the great libraries of the world.

So the economic cycles of the twenty-first century will see fluctuations in the flow of funds into philanthropic activity, just as previous cycles have done. But once a charitable organization has been firmly established, it is likely to endure. Naturally there are the threats of fraud and incompetence, as there are in all walks of life, and it is true that American philanthropy has been gravely damaged by the financial market downturn of 2009 and by the frauds associated with that.[18] But on a long view it is robust in bad economic times as well as good.

Another concern is perhaps more troubling – that philanthropy can become perverse in its objectives when the donors have strong ideological motives. One example is the extent to which terrorism in Northern Ireland and the UK during the 1970s, 1980s and 1990s was in part at least financed by US donations. The stated purpose was the relief of poverty, but in practice much of the money funded the purchase of arms, and even when this was revealed, the flow of funds continued – much to the frustration of the authorities on both sides of the Atlantic and both sides of the border within Ireland. The flow did, however, dry up after 9/11 when the consequences of terrorism were brought home to the American people.

There is also the argument that sometimes the heart can rule the head in philanthropy so that givers end up achieving the opposite of what they had intended. In *The Bottom Billion*, his 2007 book about the world's failing nations, Paul Collier, a former director of research at the World Bank, notes that many civil wars in the developing world are financed by gifts from the developed one as what was meant as aid gets diverted into military spending.[19]

How will the next generation of Americans develop their philanthropic instincts? On this point I heard a heartening story. I was at a lawyers' conference in lush Connecticut amid the white-washed houses and paddocks with children's ponies. The firm represented wealthy American families, often with assets around the world, and one of its most popular services, the one that made clients' eyes light up, was helping to teach the next generation how to do philanthropy well. So the children would be given a certain amount of the family's charitable trust to deploy. They would come up with projects to support and make a presentation at the family charitable meeting. They would then monitor progress, reporting to the family every quarter on how well the charity was performing.

'Gosh,' I said. 'That's wonderful. What age do you start the children at this? About 15?'

'No,' the lawyer replied. 'We suggest they start at about 8.'

So philanthropy will continue. It will continue until the demise of our species, for it is deeply embedded in our behaviour as human beings. At various times it will achieve a particular prominence and identity in one place. For the moment, the first years of the twenty-first century, that place is New York. Indeed it has been the prime centre for philanthropy for more than a century.

There will be aspects of the way the people of this great city choose to deploy their wealth that will cause concern to others. There will be failures and sometimes even perverse effects. But what New York does – what New Yorkers do – is surely a beacon for the world.

A final word. When I visited the city in the summer of 2009 several people told me to go and see the High Line. What was that? It is the city's newest public space, a narrow park built on the tracks of a disused freight railway running right up the west side of Manhattan from the Meatpacking District towards Midtown. It will eventually run for one-and-a-half miles. It is an inspired piece of urban design, packed with young stylish people enjoying themselves and thereby giving a lift to what had been a pretty dingy part of the city. And the connection with philanthropy? Two young New Yorkers spotted the possibility of creating a park, organized an action group, collected seed money and set the whole process into action.[20] Eventually the city came on side and helped fund the project but nothing would have happened had ordinary New Yorkers not exercised their sense of civic duty and performed another miracle of American philanthropy.

CHAPTER NINE

Main Street America
Core values for the world

I. WHAT IS THE STORY?

Why bother with the Disney version when the real deal is so much better? 'Main Street USA' stands at the entrance of the various Disneylands around the world. It is an idealized take on the main street of some small American town of a century ago – a mixture of shops, taverns, public buildings and homes. Why? Perhaps because the genius of Walt Disney was to understand what Americans saw as the core of their civilization's special gifts to the world: the values of community, of order, of people having their own place in a society, of getting along together, of being free to live out their dreams. Other countries have their central meeting point: the marketplace of the northern European trading cities, the Roman forum, the Italian plaza, the English high street. But they are not the same. They are either public places provided by the municipal or religious authorities, or they are purely commercial developments, taken over, in the case of Britain, by chain stores. They are not the mix of public and private, personal and communal that is Main Street USA.

Or rather was. For so many of the activities that used to be on Main Street have gone to the shopping malls on the outskirts and the anonymous office blocks, while the people have decamped to their suburban homes sometimes many miles away. So what is worth celebrating is not the place but the spirit – the spirit of the hundreds of medium-sized towns and cities across the fifty states.

Say 'Main Street values' and to Americans that conjures up the notion of conservative small-town values, fine in their way but maybe a bit narrow-minded. These are the places in the fly-over states, so dismissed by the sophisticates of the great cities. Yet these medium-sized cities are in their way just as innovative and dynamic as their larger counterparts, and on balance far more so than the equivalent places in Europe and Asia. So think of Main Street today not as the Main Street of Disneyland, nor as some sort of contrast to Wall Street, but rather as shorthand for the virtues of all those communities across the nation.[1]

A place and a story. The place is Billings, the largest city in Montana.[2] I have chosen it because it happens to be the place I have visited every few years since 1964, seeing it grow from the 60,000 population then to the 100,000 or so today.[3] The reason for going there was simply that like so many Britons of part-Scottish descent, I have cousins in the USA. Some had settled there and I wanted to meet them.

The story starts on the road from Red Lodge, a small town in the Rockies on the way to Yellowstone National Park an hour's drive from Billings. Archie Cochrane, owner of the Ford dealership in Billings, was driving back and stopped to pick up a dishevelled man called Joe who was stumbling beside the road. He was in a pretty bad way and during the drive explained his problem. He could not get a job because he had this drinking problem and he had a wife and family to support. Archie told him to turn up at the garage on Monday morning and he would give him a job. He added: 'But one drink and you're done.'

Joe worked for Archie for the next twenty-five years. On the Monday when he came in to sign the job contract Archie discovered something else. Joe signed with an X. However, it transpired that he had a particular ability, perhaps associated with being unable to read or write, that was tremendously useful for a car dealership: he could take one look at the ignition key of a car and remember which vehicle it matched. The garage had a huge wooden board with hooks for the keys and he would know every one. So he ran the yard.

Cars would come in needing to be washed and serviced and then taken back to their owners, and Joe did it all. He had another quality, which was that he was the only person who could cope with Archie's elderly father. John Cochrane was not an easy man, especially in old age. But Joe would in effect act as his carer, driving him to his club or into town and generally making sure he was looked after. That made the whole family's life much easier for many years to come.

Archie died some years later and the business was sold, though it still lives on under his name, but I know the story from his daughters because he was married to my cousin. The point about the tale is partly that in a well-functioning society everyone who can make a contribution gets an opportunity to do so. It is partly that there should be second chances for people who fall through the net. It is partly, too, that people with some form of disability, such as not being able to read or write, may have remarkable skills; what matters are not a person's credentials but his or her ability to do a job.

Archie ended up as a Republican senator in the state legislature and I recall him being outspoken about the values of the liberal media – at that stage I was working for the *Guardian* newspaper in London – but also about the need for the Billings authorities to make sure people had the training to make them employable. It was the duty of the city to help its people, he said, and it was the duty of the people to help themselves.

This is not, of course, just a Billings thing; the very core of any society that is functioning well is this ability to strike a balance between rights and responsibilities. That seems to me to be the special contribution of medium-sized cities in the USA. Why?

There are a number of reasons. For a start, they differ from cities in most of the rest of the world in that they spring up more quickly and often decline more quickly too. Americans move. If a new business springs up, people flock there for the jobs. If the factory or the mine shuts, the workers and their families move on. The combination of a more adventurous people, a tradition of migration, fewer planning controls, plenty of land and a thinner social security net makes US towns much more fluid entities than European ones.[4] They adapt better because that is the nature of their people.

You can see this clearly in the case of Billings. It started as a railway town in the 1880s, the major staging post of the Northern Pacific Railroad, and its early prosperity was as a communications hub. It was one of the Montana boom towns of the early part of the twentieth century, but unlike so many of the others it did not shoot up and fizzle out.[5] Back in the early 1900s the copper mining town of Butte, three hours to the west, was larger than Billings is now. But that was a single-industry town, built on mining wealth, and when the mines retreated, it shrank back. It is now less than one-third the size of Billings.[6]

Billings, by contrast, kept on growing and today is a successful service industry centre, the largest town for something like 300 miles in any direction. It has strong medical facilities, two university campuses, one private and one public, and a financial services business. It is still a key communications hub but the airport has replaced the train station. The big decision there was to extend the runway of what had been a small airport, something that Archie pressed hard to get done. Having good communications has helped make it a tourist centre in its own right, as well as being one of the jumping-off places for Yellowstone.

As in many cities, there is the usual cluster of social problems: assaults, crime, drugs, alcoholism and so on. There has been a big effort at gun control, interesting in a state where guns are part of the heritage. Still, Billings ranks towards the top of the 'quality of life' league for cities in the USA, so it must be doing something right. But the thing I most like is its ordinariness. Some years back we were in town for the annual rodeo. Unlike most rodeos, which are mainly shows for the visitors, this was one for locals – much more an opportunity for farmers to show their animals and their produce than for entertainers to thrill the crowds. So the standard task of roping a steer was not the skilled ten-second job that the professionals manage. Indeed most of the contestants, who seemed to be the children of the farmers, failed completely and the steer scuttled off. But that was just fine, for this was not for show; it was real people having a fun afternoon.

There is the nub of it. What is special about Main Street USA is that it is not special. The best medium-sized towns and cities in the USA are not picture-postcard preservations of the country's past, and neither are they glitzy, celebrity-ridden showcases. They are places where people can get on with their jobs and look after their families – places where people look after each other and enjoy themselves but most of all seek to give back to the community more than they take out. The Disneyland version of Main Street was never a reality; the real version is alive and well in thousands of places across the land.

2 . WHAT ARE THE LESSONS?

You cannot transpose Mid-American towns onto the rest of the world, nor would you want to. They are what they are. What you can do, though, is recognize the host of qualities here that can help guide other societies to live more happily with themselves. You do not need to buy the dream to see the virtues or what the world can learn.

For a start they are communities that people choose to join and choose to leave. The ties that bind their citizens are wholly ones of consent. They are encouraged to see themselves as competing with other towns, seeking to attract the talented and hard-working people who will be good citizens and help the community function better. If they succeed, great; if they fail, well, the people just drift away.

This has all sorts of consequences. It means power in US towns is bottom-up, not top-down. It is bottom-up not just because of the democratic process – the election of a mayor and town council – but also the economic dynamics. If the leaders do not perform well, the population falls and the town's revenues slip away. If the town is seen as being well run, it attracts people and grows as a result. This makes for tremendously practical politics: local people become involved as it is in their interests to do so, rather than stepping back and blaming national politicians instead.

It also strengthens non-political activities – church, school, sports club. Take the last of these: in a society where people tend to come and go, it has the option of becoming a magnet for that community. If it has better facilities or better coaching, or simply a more welcoming attitude, it can actually attract people to the town. So there is a reward for the people who participate in these groups if their activity is seen as a successful enterprise.

In essence, then, the very fact that US towns are so fluid and competitive creates virtuous circles that go far beyond the narrow economics of it all.

Foreigners who move to the USA are frequently amazed by the welcome they receive. They are invited into people's homes, asked to join clubs and faith organizations. But with that welcome comes the expectation they will participate themselves. It is inclusive but it can also be intrusive. You do not have to live in the place, but if you do, you are expected to join in. This is the glue that helps hold these societies together.

That leads to a bigger point. All societies have to strike a balance between the communal and the individual and there will always be tension between the two. But the special thing about medium-sized American towns is that, to a much greater extent than towns in Europe and Japan, they are not single communities but lots of interlocking ones. No one needs to be, or could be, a member of all of them.

True, almost every adult has a vote and so has a voice, however diluted, on the municipal authority. But that is about the only thing everyone can do. In other aspects of life, people have to make their choices. They choose their church or faith community. They choose which clubs to join and which charities to support. They choose which sports to follow. No one forces you to play golf or shoot quail, but if you do, you become a member of that part of the community.

In other words, people can define their individuality by choosing the communal activities with which they particularly identify. And if your own special interest is not catered for, well, you start one up. This has a number of consequences. It means, for example, that you are not excluded unless you actually decide to be; you are allowed to be a loner but you are not forced to be one. It also means the society has multiple decision points: if the municipal authorities will not fund something, maybe the private sector will step in; if the Rotary Club decides not to sponsor a student going abroad to study, maybe one of the faith groups will create a scholarship instead.

That creates inherently optimistic societies. If there is a problem, people will get together to fix it. Had Billings not extended the airport to take the jets it might have declined as rail traffic fell away. Naturally, if something is too big for the community to tackle on its own, it will look to the state or even federal authorities for help, but in the first instance communities look to themselves.

Or at least communities that are working well do. Any enthusiast for Main Street USA has to acknowledge two worrying aspects of American civic organization. One is that 'pork', government-funded projects, is a huge element in the system too.[7] That is not going to change fast and tends to promote a dependency culture whereby communities look to government agencies to solve problems rather than rely on their own initiative. The other problem is that there seems to have been a general trend in the past generation or so for civic engagement to decline, as famously charted by the political scientist Robert Putnam in his essay (and subsequent 2000 book) *Bowling Alone*.[8]

More of that in a moment. Meanwhile, consider this question: how might the admirable elements of Main Street USA be recreated elsewhere?

Of course, you cannot just tell people to form more clubs or get on better with their neighbours; the impetus has to come from within those communities. However, many of the innovations of American society do get picked up elsewhere, most dramatically the online social network services such as Facebook. So maybe the best hope for spreading Main Street USA characteristics is through the new communications technologies. Now people sitting in different places tapping out messages to each other are not creating much of a community, so technology by itself can be more a barrier than a benefit. But there could be some municipal involvement in the sense that towns seeking to strengthen their internal links could use the new technologies to learn about the hopes and needs of their residents. The more that people can be involved in the running of the show, and the less that is subcontracted to professional politicians, the greater their sense of identity and control.

One of the fascinating aspects of US towns – at least to this British onlooker – is the extent to which tax and spending decisions are taken by the citizens themselves. Can the town afford a pay rise for its workers? How should the money for a new school be raised? Americans are connected to their locality in a way their counterparts in British and most European towns are not. You cannot change the way long-established places are run but you could bring in something of the involvement that, when it is working at its best, epitomizes Main Street USA.

- **Be fluid, be competitive**
- **Strike a balance between the communal and the individual**
- **Encourage involvement that conveys a sense of identity and control**

3. WHAT COULD GO WRONG?

Main Street USA faces many pressures but American towns are not going to 'go wrong' in the sense there will be widespread social breakdown. The main social threats to American society come surely in the big cities, not the medium-sized ones.

Inevitably many smaller towns and cities in the USA will shrink as the economic conditions that led to their creation and growth change. This is a big issue in parts of the Mid-West and West, for as agricultural employment declines, the towns that service the farms decline too.[9] But as argued above, the rise and fall of towns is the key to the vigour of American society: contrast Billings and Butte.

The fundamental challenges are not so much those associated with individual towns or regions; they are more about the whole model of Main Street USA. Do the young want to stay or do the opportunities seem too limited? How does a city of 100,000 or 50,000 match the services of one of, say, three million? Do people still want to live in towns where everybody pretty much knows who is doing what, or would they prefer the privacy (and with it the loneliness) of a mega-city? Even if they do stay, will they still participate in the civic life, or will they 'bowl alone'? Boil it down and the question is whether these places still deliver the lifestyle that Americans want.

A general rule when trying to get a handle on giant questions such as these is to look not at what people say but what they do. Here there are several troublesome trends. The centres that are growing most quickly, such as the retirement towns in Florida or the immigrant communities of California, tend to be all of a kind. They are specialized places created by, and catering for, people at a particular stage of life. There is nothing wrong with this if that is what people want. It just is not the ethos of Main Street USA, where all generations and incomes are mixed up together. And then there is the further challenge of gated communities, where there is none of this mixing at all.[10]

Against those trends, though, stand communications technology and changing work patterns. Anyone who works on screen has a fair ability to locate wherever they want, and as work patterns fragment so more people will have that freedom. So if Billings really is the third-best place in the country to raise a family, as some surveys in the USA suggest,[11] then more people will have the freedom to choose it. In any case, these medium-sized cities will continue to evolve and attracting more teleworkers will be one way in which they do so.

Main Street USA cannot go backwards to the dreamland of 100 years ago; towns and cities now have to figure out what attracts people to them. They have to be safe, of course, and they have to be able to create job opportunities. But they must also have something else – something that distinguishes them, makes them a magnet. Billings is lucky to have its position as a regional hub but it works hard to maintain that role. Others are less lucky and will have to try even harder. But the ethos of Main Street USA is alive and well and will be secure, I suggest, for generations to come.

CHAPTER TEN

Harvard
The world's top university

I. WHAT IS THE STORY?

The USA has the best universities in the world and the best of the best is its oldest place of higher education, Harvard University, founded in 1636.

Make a sweeping statement like that and you annoy people. Their responses usually start with 'What about …?' or 'Yes, but …' So as far as the first response is concerned, let us acknowledge straight away that there are other great universities in the world that in some areas do a better job than Harvard. Within the USA, the nearby Massachusetts Institute of Technology is pre-eminent in its field, Chicago is terrific at economics among other disciplines and Johns Hopkins excels at medicine. Stanford, Princeton and Yale also have world-leading faculties; indeed on some counts Yale ranks level with Harvard. Outside the USA, both Cambridge and Oxford are not only the equal of any institution on the planet for research but arguably do the best job of teaching undergraduates. Put it all together, though, and on just about every world index of universities, Harvard comes out tops.

As for the 'Yes, but ...' response, it has indeed become easy for Harvard to maintain its position. It is the world's richest university, with an annual income of $3.5 billion[1] and, after the market crash of 2008–9, an endowment of some $26 billion.[2] Success brings money, particularly from alumni, and money enables you to reinforce your success. If instead of measuring absolute excellence, you looked at value for money, then there would be many universities in the USA and elsewhere that would naturally score higher. But it would be wrong to dismiss Harvard's success just as an extreme example of the 'winner takes all' phenomenon in higher education worldwide. This university is at the top because it works hard to stay there.

Besides, Harvard is important not just in itself but as a beacon for American universities in general, for US higher education is the best on the planet on almost any measure. If you take as a starting point the famed (though much criticized) world rankings from Shanghai's Jiao Tong University,[3] the only other institutions in the world that can mount a serious challenge are Cambridge and Oxford in the UK – the only non-US universities in Jiao Tong's top ten.

How did the USA come to dominate higher education in this way? We regard this almost as a natural state of things now, an inevitable function of the wealth of the American economy, but the education world did not look like this at all back in the second half of the nineteenth century, when the UK led in the humanities and in some areas of pure science, while Germany was the master in the technical application of science, and France excelled in medicine. American universities were not really in the game.[4]

One person, more than any other, changed this. He was Charles William Eliot, president of Harvard from 1869 to 1909, who turned it into a modern institution centred on research.[5] In his twenties he had travelled widely in Europe, noting the connections between the new technical universities and industries, and when he became president of Harvard, aged only 35, he sought to apply best European academic practice – and then develop it further. So he brought in an entrance exam, organized the different disciplines into separate faculties and set about hiring the best staff. He also realized that the USA could and should adopt a different funding model to Europe. Whereas European universities relied to a fair extent on government money, he sought to persuade the private sector to supply the funds, and as a well-connected Bostonian he was ably equipped to do so.[6] During his forty years in charge, it became the richest private university in the world.

It also became a model for other centres of higher education in the USA. By the end of his tenure, the country had a number of universities that could match the best of Europe.

I think it would be fair to say that the USA had not established intellectual leadership at this point, for that really came after the Second World War. But what might be called the Harvard revolution did set the USA on a path, so that when the continental and UK university systems were undermined by the disruption of two world wars, America could surge ahead.

After the Second World War, Harvard moved forward, widening its student base both socially and ethnically by encouraging applications from outside the elite feeder schools.[7] It merged with what had been its 'female annex', Radcliffe College, and it massively increased its postgraduate numbers.[8] These are developments common to higher education elsewhere in the USA and indeed in the rest of the world. The point is simply that Harvard has made a particular success of this transformation, and especially in the quest for attracting the best students irrespective of their background and then helping them achieve their full potential. You have to note, too, that Barack and Michelle Obama were fellow students at Harvard Law School.

That points to another source of strength: the breadth of its different schools and the way in which they are structured. Breadth first: while Harvard has not always been a first mover in spreading the university model to new schools, it has invariably been a quick responder.

The pioneer law school in the USA was at the College of William and Mary, in Williamsburg, Virginia, and founded in 1779 during the American Revolution. But it has had a bumpy ride, shutting down during the Civil War and having to be revived. For this reason, Harvard Law School, founded in 1817, is the oldest in continuous existence in the USA and ranks with Yale at the top of US law schools.

Much the same has happened in business studies, though Harvard does not dominate here to quite the extent it does in law. The first business school set up in the USA was the Wharton School at the University of Pennsylvania in 1881, with Chicago following in 1898. Harvard Business School was not founded until 1908. But while Wharton ranks top in the world, an illustration of the first-mover advantage that business schools so often cite when studying other industries, Harvard is just behind it,[9] while Harvard Business School Press is the premier business publishing enterprise. (I should disclose an interest here, having been published by it and finding it excellent!)

Take another example, the John F. Kennedy School of Government, whose origins go back to 1936 when it was founded as the Graduate School of Public Administration. Viewed internationally it is generally reckoned to be the premier school of public administration in the world, though on one US ranking it is pipped to first place by the Maxwell School at Syracuse University in New York.[10]

It was a former dean of the John F. Kennedy School, Joseph Nye[11] (whose big idea of 'soft power' has had a profound influence on perceptions of America's role in the world), who explained one special quality of Harvard schools to me: they do not rely on handouts from the university and have to raise the funds themselves to keep going. Indeed most schools are net contributors to the university and this sense of responsibility for their own future reinforces the drive that defines them.

There is a positive feedback loop. The schools have to maintain their reputation for intellectual excellence to maintain the flow of revenues from students and outside funding bodies. Meanwhile that flow of funds enables them to hire the best faculty members, which is, of course, essential to their intellectual standards.

There is a further point, which I had not understood. When a department wants to hire a new professor from outside or give tenure to someone already there, it has to have its choice approved by what is called the Ad Hoc Committee[12] – a body with outside representatives that scrutinizes the appointment with the aim of ensuring that this is the best person in the world to do the particular job. At least that is the theory. I do not doubt there are imperfections in practice and there have also been suggestions that ad hoc committees inhibit academic freedom. But the core idea – that you try to hire the very best – must surely be the right place to start.

Inevitably there have been controversies, arguments, protests and resignations – all the normal turmoil of academic life that seems to occur everywhere on the planet. There are tenured professors whose best work is in the past but who cannot be moved. There are schools that are fine but could be better. And two recent resignations also highlight the tensions within the university.

Harvard lost its charismatic but difficult president, Lawrence Summers,[13] in 2006 following a loss of confidence vote by the faculty. He had, by and large, the support of the student body and of the Harvard Corporation, the ultimate board that controls the university, but fell out with a faculty over criticism of one of the professors and amid suggestions of sexism.

The year before it also lost Jack Meyer, the legendary head of Harvard Management Company, the company that handles its endowment. He had helped bring the university pot from $4.7 billion in 1990, when he arrived, to $25.9 billion when he left.[14] Obviously there was new money from donors included but it has been calculated that the high returns achieved by Harvard meant that over those fifteen years it gained more in capital growth than the entire endowment of the next-richest university, Yale. When he left to found his own management company, he took twenty of the staff with him.

There will always be tension between the academic staff of a university on the one hand and the overriding management body and the fund management arm on the other, and actually there probably should be some tension for each has different objectives. There are, however, other concerns. For example, undergraduate students complain sometimes about the quality of teaching, and I think it is a legitimate criticism that Harvard is not as outstanding here as it is at the postgraduate and research levels. Some undergraduates say they are taught by postgrads rather than the famous professors at whose feet they thought they were going to sit. And while Harvard has its admirable application policy and, thanks to its endowment, can afford to subsidize bright students from modest backgrounds, family connections and donations probably skew the admissions in a way that would not happen at Oxford or Cambridge.

It is easy to carp, for no organization can be perfect. It is vital to remember, too, that there are many other wonderful universities in the USA, doing work that is just as good and sometimes better. But while size is not everything, the sheer scale of Harvard, in particular the facilities, the breadth of the faculty and the quality of its postgraduate students, gives it a critical mass that nowhere else can quite match. The USA benefits hugely from this because Harvard is a beacon of excellence for the university system as a whole. It is the one to beat. And insofar as it is also a beacon to the world, other countries benefit too. That surely deserves celebrating.

2. WHAT ARE THE LESSONS?

There are three powerful lessons, but I fear the first two are hard to replicate.

The first is that age matters; first movers do seem to gain an advantage. One of the troubling features of higher education everywhere is that it seems to take a very long time to build excellence. Japan could become the dominant producer of consumer electronics in a generation and the USA became the dominant producer of computer software in little more than a decade. But if Harvard (or Oxford and Cambridge) is any guide, building great universities seems to take centuries. So what hope is there for China or India or Dubai to catch up?[15]

It is not quite as dire as that, as other great but more recent universities in the USA and elsewhere bear testimony. But they are still old by the standards of, say, commercial or industrial corporations. Just about every one of the top 100 universities in the world on the Shanghai index was founded more than a century ago. To build a new university from scratch is a daunting and lengthy exercise. To some extent it may be possible to take an existing institution and develop it further, but it is impossible to get away from the point that it seems to take the best part of a century to establish a great university.

There is, however, a second part to this message, which is to ponder why some very old universities have failed to maintain their reputation. Why is the University of Bologna, founded in 1088, no longer one of the world's great higher-education institutions? Why did Latin America,[16] in contrast to North America, fail to develop great institutions? Why are the many old continental European universities, of which there are on a quick tally no less than forty-four, not doing better?[17] Age, of itself, is clearly not enough, particularly if age breeds complacency. One of the most remarkable aspects of Harvard is that complacency is rare and, if it does sprout, it seems to be swiftly squashed.

The second big lesson is diamonds polish diamonds, or to put it less elegantly, there is a positive feedback loop in the quality of students and the university. Harvard gets great students both at undergraduate and particularly postgraduate levels. Great students attract other great students, great research gets done and the reputations of the professors soar, which in turn attracts more good students. There is a way of breaking through this, which is to hire the best professors and give them the money to pursue their research, which will quickly start to attract the students. But to do so you have to be credible in the first place – to have a good enough brand name as well as the cash. So while there is indeed a possible course for other universities to follow, they have to be able to get to the starting gate.

Perhaps the most useful part of this lesson is that a well-known university with a weak department can turn that department round by scouring the world for the best professors and then trying to create a package that will attract them. In the academic world, talent is mobile. This, of course, cuts both ways; universities need to know how to retain talent as well as how to attract it.

That leads to the third big lesson. Complacency is a catastrophe. You might imagine that Harvard would feel pretty secure, with its huge reputation and enormous endowment. It does not. Moreover, it has structures to make sure that it does not. There is the outside scrutiny of appointments, noted above, with young junior professors knowing that the odds of gaining a higher position are against them, for there are always several good candidates for each tenured post. In that respect it is a competitive place: you have to produce good research and you are expected to go on doing it.

Managing academic staff can be pretty difficult. Some top academics are team players, particularly in the sciences, because they have to be. But many are not; like journalists, they are not herd animals. Their reputation is based on their individual achievement, rather than the achievement of the university as a whole, and they take their reputation very seriously. The Harvard lot can cut up rough, as Lawrence Summers discovered, but it has managed to sustain a culture that remains competitive and genuinely strives for excellence.

There are other lessons from Harvard – for example, that clusters matter. Thus Harvard has been lucky to have the Massachusetts Institute of Technology, just across the Charles River, as a friendly rival, while there are other universities, including Wellesley and Brandeis, just up the road. Put these together and the Boston area stands out as one of the great intellectual hotspots of the world. This brings a practical benefit in hiring, for dual-academic families have many options for employment; if Harvard wants to attract a star, the star's partner can usually find a similarly suitable post. It also gives a cultural vigour to the entire region.

But I think, standing back, that the biggest lessons of all are that excellence is driven by the spirit of competitiveness instead of complacency and that the relentless pursuit of excellence brings benefits not just to the institution but the entire community and beyond. The world needs great universities and – for the moment, and in all probability for many years to come – Harvard is top of the pile.

- **Age matters – use it to your advantage**
  - **Diamonds polish diamonds**
  - **Complacency is catastrophic**

3. WHAT COULD GO WRONG?

There are lots of things that will go wrong at Harvard, plus one spectacular thing that has already gone wrong as a result of the financial meltdown of 2009. But on a long view it is surely hard to see it being toppled from its place at the top of the global league of higher education for at least another generation.

The damage to the university's endowment wrought by the market crash, with a $37 billion pile falling by something like $11 billion, has made it along with other less wealthy US educational establishments think hard about the way they organize their finances. The blow to Harvard's endowment could hardly have come at a worse time for it made the classic mistake of assuming the boom years would continue for ever and set about a building programme of monumental proportions. Part of that had to be delayed as the money dried up. The university is also having to make other cutbacks.

In the hothouse of Cambridge, Massachusetts, Harvard's difficulties are viewed with a mixture of schadenfreude and fear: schadenfreude, for the university, like any elite institution has its enemies; fear because a lot of decent people involved in some way or other are getting hurt. Viewed from a distance it seems that the university has made one of the errors typical of large enterprises when they allow themselves to be dazzled by their own success. The adjustment is painful but ultimately the experience should make it stronger. It certainly makes it less likely that complacency might creep in, at least on the financial side of the equation.

All this is obvious and in any case the university's finances will recover. There seem to me to be two other broad threats to Harvard and indeed the entire US higher-education establishment that are more fundamental.

The first threat, widely accepted in the USA, is that the whole system has simply become too expensive. It is too expensive even for an economy that is booming, let alone one that periodically hits hard times. At the top-flight schools, such as Harvard, only about 10 per cent of the students are able to pay, in that direct expression, 'the full freight'; the rest are helped, in some way or other, by the university. Undergraduate fees at Harvard in 2009 were approximately $48,000 including tuition and accommodation, and while top schools can and do subsidize their students, particularly at postgraduate level, the system as a whole leaves students with massive debts. On average, new graduates leave university in the USA with around $20,000 of debt.[18]

So there is not only a burden on parents to stump us as much as they can but also on the students themselves. And this burden is carried by middle-class families simply so that the next generation can maintain their position in the US job structure. There will always be a handful of high-school graduates who achieve great things in life, just as there are university dropouts who make fortunes. But for most young Americans, to get a decent job you certainly need a good undergraduate degree and, increasingly, a postgraduate one too.

So the US university system has become almost a tax on maintaining middle-class status – something that young people have to pay one way or another just to get as good a job as their parents. For the very low-income families there is financial help available; for the rich there is the family money; but for the mass in the middle this is a huge problem.

There is a further twist here. Even if a few elite universities manage to maintain and develop their endowments so that they can offset more of the cost of the service they provide, the rest cannot hope to do so. There is a real danger that the massively endowed institutions will increasingly outpace the rest.

The other threat is whether US higher education is too American. To any US citizen, that might seem absurd; how can any US institution be 'too American'? In the case of Harvard, that concern might seem particularly misplaced as it has 4,000 foreign students and many non-national faculty members.[19] But from a British perspective, Harvard is profoundly American in that it sees the world entirely through US eyes. To illustrate, take just the contrast between Harvard and Oxford or Cambridge: Harvard has never had a non-American president, or even one whose main career has been outside the USA; the present vice-chancellor of Oxford, although English by birth, worked in the United States for thirty years before he assumed the role, and his predecessor was a non-national.[20] The current vice-chancellor at Cambridge spent most of her career at Yale.[21]

The heads of all the major departments in Harvard are American, though there are some star professors who are not. That is much less the case in the UK. In addition, and for obvious reasons, virtually all the endowment of Harvard is subscribed by Americans, or by people who have made their careers in the USA. I would not try to claim that this skews Harvard's research, hiring policy or choice of students. But it does, I suggest, reinforce a fundamental belief that the US way of doing things is the best way.

Well, in many respects it is. But as the weight of the USA in the world economy declines and the ideas of the emerging economies, most notably China and India, become more important, being 'too American' will become more of a handicap.

It will be a handicap at two levels. One is that the superstructure of US higher education – the pressure to publish in particular journals, the importance of peer review and so on – will be superseded by other ways of organizing and managing educational excellence. The other is that America's ideas about how some aspect of society should be organized – for example, financial services and business management – will be replaced by other ideas. Will the US model of financial services, which led to the catastrophe of the sub-prime crisis, be the global model? This seems less likely following that disaster than it did before. Will the US model of corporate management remain the global ideal? That seems less likely following the bankruptcy of General Motors.

So Harvard, along with other top US universities, will have to become less American and more global. They would claim they are doing so and point to the apparent diversity of the faculty and student bodies. But that is apparent rather than real. The faculty and the students may have different ethnic and social backgrounds but the broad lines along which they think are, I suggest, pretty much the same.

So the challenge to Harvard will come not from other universities that follow the present conventional higher education model but from educational institutions elsewhere in the world that develop a different model. We cannot yet see what that might be or where those ideas will come from. All we can see is that the Western liberal ethos, with its many virtues but its annoying indulgences and arrogance, will not dominate higher education for ever. In another generation Harvard will still be top dog in its particular pack. Other packs of rather different hounds will be snapping away somewhere on the other side of the globe, but that is great too. Ideas are global. Many will come from India and China, and that will force the universities of the West to reinvent how they run themselves yet again. But that will be fine. The world needs great educational institutions, and the more of them there are in every corner of the globe, the better for the future of humankind.

CHAPTER ELEVEN

Whistler
North America's top ski-resort

I. WHAT IS THE STORY?

A Canadian ski-resort? What's so special about that? It might seem almost perverse to include an activity as frivolous as skiing in this collection of essays, especially as there are plenty of keen skiers who feel this particular resort is overrated. My own introduction to the place came when I was the skiing correspondent for the travel pages of *The Independent*, and I have had several good weeks there. But a lot of people feel it is over-hyped – clever commercially but nothing more than that. And as for the skiing itself, while the critics would accept it is reasonable, they would also say it cannot compare with top resorts in the Rockies, still less the Alps.

But there is the story. Whistler's path to becoming North America's largest ski centre is a triumph over, if not quite adversity, certainly pretty unpromising basic circumstances. Moreover, it has achieved success by going beyond the normal rules of commerce and creating something that is special and very Canadian.

First, what's wrong with Whistler, or more specifically Whistler Blackcomb, as there are two main mountains served by the same resort? For a start it is low, with the town only 2,200 feet above sea level and the highest point only 7,500 feet up. It is in the coastal mountains of Canada, two hours' drive up from Vancouver, so while it does get a huge dump of snow most years, it is wet stuff. It is not the wonderful dry powder of the resorts in the Rockies. Its sun record is poor; indeed the original name of Whistler was London Mountain, apparently so-called because it always seemed to be covered in fog.[1] Access was dangerous until the only road up from the coast was upgraded for the 2010 Winter Olympics.

In the resort's early years, two companies were in competition, running a mountain apiece, until one of the firms bought the other in 1997. Only in 2008 was a there a lift between the two mountains. Until then you had to go down to the resort and come back up again on the other side. And the resort has had its share of accidents, and not just the normal skiing ones. In 1995 one of its lifts crashed, killing two people and injuring more – a tragedy that inevitably cast a cloud over the whole complex.

Put all these disadvantages together and by rights it should not be particularly successful. But it is, immensely so.[2] Why? Well, it is competent and well run, though that in itself would not make it worth selecting; there are lots of good businesses around the world. More to the point, there is one particular quality I will come to in a moment – one that is exclusively and especially Canadian and, if it could be bottled and exported, would enable Canada to sweep the world. But first the rest of the story.

This begins in the early 1960s when a group of Vancouver businessmen hit on the idea of creating a ski-resort to host the 1968 Winter Olympics. It was an extraordinarily ambitious notion, for at that time there was not even a road into the valley; the only way in was by rail, built mainly for logging but giving access to a cluster of settlements that became summer resorts for fishing and hiking.[3] Whistler would have to wait for the 2010 Winter Olympics[4] but it did open in 1966 as a ski-resort, initially just on one mountain, Whistler itself, and then in 1980 on its neighbour. There was by all accounts a pretty hostile relationship between the two companies running the shows, but it was the owner of Blackcomb that came out on top and since then the whole resort has passed into the hands of a leisure development company.[5]

This group, Intrawest, has been steadily investing in the place, in particular adding to and upgrading the lift system so that it is now the largest in North America. It has also extended the main village out over what had been a dump.

More than this, the company has managed to create a very harmonious resort. It is big, so it would not claim to be exclusive, but everything is on a manageable scale and is designed sensitively to fit in with its surroundings. The Whistler complex looks as though it has been there for ages, yet most of what you see is brand new.

That gives the clue to Whistler's success. It hits all the spots. Naturally it fulfils the core purpose of the place, to provide good skiing: there is a range of slopes for different levels of skier, including the eight-mile run down from the top of the Blackcomb glacier. (The steely nerved can start from the vertical drop of the 'blow hole' at the top; the more cautious can do the long traverse across the glacier instead.) The something-for-everyone theme means that at one extreme you can do heli-skiing; at the other you can, well, not ski at all and still have a good time. The ski school is excellent, the people in the equipment shops helpful and knowledgeable. You can even eat well at a reasonable price both up in the mountain restaurants and back down in the village, something not always possible in resorts in the USA.

The cleverest idea of all, though, is having mountain hosts. These are usually retirees, tanned and smiling volunteers who greet people at the top and direct them to the best snow. They also run daily ski tours. You show up at the meeting point at a certain time and shoot round the mountain in the tracks of a septuagenarian. This is an entirely free service for the visitor and the hosts are not paid either.

Instead they agree to serve a certain number of days up the mountain in exchange for a free annual lift pass. Free skiing for a year is not to be sneezed at, and the hosts themselves are a great advertisement for the delights of retirement.

At any rate it has worked. Whistler often gets ranked the top resort in North America and sometimes even the world, with people praising the whole experience as much as the skiing itself. Of course, this is partly the result of good commercial management but I think it is something more, something especially Canadian. It is the manners, decency and charm that Canada at its best manages to generate and deploy.

It sounds corny to talk of Canadians being especially hospitable or of finding everyone at Whistler especially welcoming, but it is true. That is the quality the country should try to bottle and sell: the easy charm of a society that is comfortable with itself. From the concierge at the hotel to the students running the Little Red Chair (the oldest and slowest of the lifts), there is that mixture of self-confidence and pride in the place, but most of all a genuine desire to make visitors feel welcome and want to come back. As a result, the visitors themselves behave better and everyone has a good time. It is American hospitality but without the self-conscious jockeying for status (or in the case of resort and restaurant staff, the chasing for tips) you can get in the USA. Just about everyone who goes there notices it: the charm born of the genuine desire to welcome the stranger.

At one level Whistler is just another successful leisure operation. Like any business it has had its ups and downs. Like many others the parent company suffered during the 2008/9 economic downturn.[6] The resort itself has had bad years, for even a place with a good snow record sometimes has seasons when there is little snow.

But, as noted above, there is something more than just commerce here. Maybe it is the harsh winters that encourage hospitality – a survival instinct born of the elements being against you. Or maybe it is a case of the country wanting to define itself in some way that distances itself from its brash neighbour to the south, and charm seems to be one solution. If Whistler were just a business – professionally welcoming because that was good commercial practice – you would feel it. You would know this was a machine designed to make things nice so visitors would be attracted back – and designed also to extract as much from them as possible while they were there. Whistler is not like that.

There are myriad examples of just how charming Canada can be. There are the mountain hosts mentioned above. My own experience includes a boot fitter who spent half a morning working through the various options with me, with the result that I have subsequently skied with comfortable feet. There was the owner of a ski school who threw open his house to visitors with only the most tenuous links to the school. There are the invariably cheerful lift operators, who come from all over the world but seem to be chosen for their charm. The hotels invariably generate good reports.

The most remarkable thing, at least to the European visitor, is that the skiers are all much nicer to each other as a result. It is almost as though they absorb the Canadian ethos by some process of osmosis. Everyone who goes skiing wants to have a good time but everyone in Whistler seems to want to make sure that everyone else has a good time too.

You see that best in the lift queues – yes, even Whistler does have some queues. Instead of the scrum of European resorts, everyone queues neatly, with lines merging alternately with almost military precision. Skiers in all North American resorts have much better manners than those in Europe but Whistler is outstanding. The only other place where I have seen such disciplined queues are those to get over the Lion's Gate suspension bridge from Vancouver up to the resort. Cars let each other in alternately with similar courtesy and precision. The result in Vancouver is that an old and inadequate, if very lovely, bridge gets used to the full and everyone gets home faster and calmer. The result in Whistler is that everyone gets up the mountain faster and maybe calmer too.

2 . WHAT ARE THE LESSONS?

Whistler Blackcomb is a business and there are common features to all well-run businesses. But a resort differs from a conventional business in that the owner does not have close control over the entire operation. It owns the land area and the lift system but it does not control the hotels, the shops, the restaurants, the sports suppliers and so on. Some of the credit for managing the parts it does control and helping to nudge the rest of the service suppliers into good performance must go to the owner, Intrawest, so there will be straightforward commercial lessons, particularly for the leisure industries. But the Whistler experience is more useful to other places for its social lessons: what it can teach not so much about commerce but about a society. Municipalities have as much to learn as other businesses. I can see at least five main lessons.

The first is that you have to do the detail well. One of the most remarkable things about Whistler is its order and that starts with the layout of the resort itself. Since traffic is not allowed in the centre, you can walk about freely, rather as you can in the car-free Alpine resorts such as Zermatt and Wengen. That creates a festive atmosphere throughout the centre. Cars are not banned as such – merely pushed to the sides of the main streets, with access to the backs of buildings, and then tucked underground. There is also a harmony to the architecture: a variety of different styles that look as though they are all 'meant' but without the Disneyland spoof 'old world' character.

The second lesson is that you invest in infrastructure. The complex delivers because the lift system has had a lot of resources put into it. This has been done progressively over the years, initially upgrading to clear the bottlenecks in the system and most recently raising the system to top-of-the-range Alpine standards. The last big gap in the operation, the lack of a connection between the two mountains, was plugged by the Peak 2 Peak gondola in 2008, with a two-mile unsupported span, the longest in the world. There has been some controversy over this final link, of which more later, and the whole system is expensive to run; but it does deliver what visitors want. Obviously the infrastructure investments that other towns make will be different. It may be that a port city needs a better harbour, or a mega-city requires a better underground railway system or better connections to its airports. And there are examples of cities building the wrong infrastructure – Montreal's investment for the 1976 Olympics, for example.

Canada built a new airport, Mirabel, which was planned to be the largest in land area in the world. From 1975 to 1997 Canada forced all international flights to land there. But it was wildly unpopular with airlines and passengers alike, being situated twenty-five miles from Montreal. All passenger flights have now reverted to the old and vastly more convenient airport, at Dorval, only twelve miles from town, and Mirabel is used mainly for cargo flights. The main Olympic stadium has also given huge trouble, being costly to maintain, and since 2004 when the Montreal Expos moved to Washington DC and became the Washington Nationals, it has not had a main tenant. (Mind you, since the Nationals have not delivered a brilliant performance, from a sporting point of view at least maybe Montreal's loss is none too grave.)

But notwithstanding Canada's own goal with the Montreal Olympics, the general rule that investment in infrastructure is usually money well spent surely stands.

This leads to the third point, which is that human beings like iconic structures – and places need them. Whistler now has something that identifies it, and while the gondola does not stand comparison with the Eiffel Tower in Paris, say, or the Sydney Opera, it is certainly more than just another ski lift. It has helped turn what was already a big ski-resort into something more.

Lesson four is that a whole community has to identify with a venture. In the case of Whistler, as in any community, there are some tensions. Homeowners would, in an ideal world, have the place to themselves; people who live there throughout the year may sometimes resent weekenders and holidaymakers. There have been strains over Peak 2 Peak, with some residents feeling that it makes the mountains *too* accessible for visitors, and there is the broader tension between development and the environment. However, Whistler seems to have managed to mediate between these different interests with understanding and sensitivity. It would be wrong to say the community is united because it is not. But there is a common purpose that most people buy into – to make the place something special.

Finally, there is the whole issue of decency. That, of course, is something you find everywhere in the world, often in surprising places, so Canada has no monopoly here. It does, however, produce large quantities of the stuff and this has been measured by the United Nations Human Development Index, on which Canada is one of the highest-placed countries.[7] Vancouver figures similarly highly in separate surveys of the best places to live[8] and, for what it is worth, Whistler is ranked among the best places to ski. It sounds almost improper to talk about skiing in the same breath as human development or living conditions, and I do not mean to. My point is simply that because the people at the front line of Whistler – in the bars, on the lifts – behave with competence and charm, the enjoyment and behaviour of the people who go there is enhanced.

Maybe that is easier in a resort town than in, say, an industrial city. Maybe it is easier in Canada than elsewhere. It is a huge country with massive resources and a relatively small but well-educated population. But to view the achievement as easy is to miss out on its lessons, and in particular that key one: if people are well treated, they will behave better.

- **Do the detail well**
- **Invest in infrastructure**
- **Make something identifiable**

3. WHAT COULD GO WRONG?

There are three main things that can go wrong with Whistler as a resort. But while I can also see things that may go wrong with Canada as a society and indeed a country, I cannot envisage any danger to Canada as an ethos.

First, the resort and the issue of the skiing itself. Human beings will go on seeking releases from their work and their home lives for as long as our civilization exists; you can walk round the villas at Pompeii and see how it was a resort town for the prosperous citizens of the Roman Empire nearly 2,000 years ago. But there is an issue about the activity that makes Whistler exceptional. True it is not just about skiing and in the summer it has fishing, golf, hiking and mountain biking; its summer population is higher than its winter one. But were skiing to go out of fashion, and there are genuine environmental concerns that might cause it to do so, then the biggest skiing resort in North America would count for little.

The question then would be whether the town would be nimble enough to realign its facilities, rebrand itself and become something else. I am sure it would and maybe the lesson then would be how to become a different sort of resort. But there can be no doubt that a retreat from skiing would be a disaster for the town.

The second thing that might go wrong is that it is simply too successful for its own good. 'And all men kill the thing they love,' wrote Oscar Wilde, and as more and more people go to Whistler, the serene emptiness of the mountains has come under threat. One of the arguments that locals cite against the Peak 2 Peak gondola is that it will give greater access to a finite ski area. This is something that Whistler has to try to manage. Should it expand to embrace other mountains? Remember that by Alpine standards, it is only a medium-sized ski centre; in the Alps there is typically a string of linked towns and lift systems enabling people to ski from one place to another, even one country to another. Western Canada does have plenty of space so expansion is possible, but how you preserve solitude while pulling in the punters – well, that is an insoluble problem.

The third issue, unlike the first two, Whistler can do nothing about. Might the weather change? We already have a shift in attitudes in that there is rising concern about the environmental footprint of skiing.[9] There are also the more general concerns about global warming.[10] But if there were to be some more specific environmental change affecting snowfall on Canada's coastal mountains, Whistler would suffer terribly. Yes, there is artificial snow, but you need freezing temperatures.

It is possible that Whistler might simply be too warm and too low. If that were to be the case, it would be small compensation that other resorts, including many in the Alps, would suffer too.

The bigger issue, though, is Canada. Here I suggest the story is not what will go wrong but what will go right.

To write about the future of the country would be to go far beyond the confines of this essay. There is a host of issues, including the tension between east and west; the heavy dependence on energy and hence the large carbon footprint; the language issue; and the extent to which the country defines itself as different from the USA. I have tried to demonstrate that this one particular ski-resort exemplifies the special qualities of the country itself. Why is it that Canada manages to top the league of human development? Why is Vancouver ranked alongside cities such as Zurich and Geneva as the most desirable places to live? It cannot just be that they all have good access to skiing. What Whistler does is to illustrate some elements of what you might call the Canadian proposition – that a country can be successful in economic terms but take the edge off the harsher elements of market capitalism and tie the whole package up with flair and charm.

Middle East

CHAPTER TWELVE

Property Development in Dubai
The bumpy desert boom

I. WHAT IS THE STORY?

'In the world' – this is the suffix that Dubai likes to attach to all its enterprises. So it is the fastest-growing city in the world. It has the largest indoor shopping mall in the world. It has the first seven-star hotel in the world.[1] It has the tallest building in the world. It has 'the world' itself – the set of offshore developments built on reclaimed islands in the shape of the countries of the world. But the reason for including Dubai here is more precise, for the thing that encapsulates all these 'in the worlds' is that it is the most extreme example – in the world – of property driving an economy.

But like so many other property-driven booms, that came to an abrupt end in 2009. You could say that it has become the world's biggest property-driven bust. However, more of that later. I have stuck with the Dubai story as something that works because, given time, I am confident that this amazing city-state will reassert its pre-eminence in the region. Even if that judgement proves wrong, one thing is for sure. It will never go back to the sleepy Dubai of the 1950s and 1960s – or even the 1980s.

For in the space of two generations, Dubai has gone from being a tiny port on the edge of a Middle Eastern desert to a great city-state of 1.5 million people.[2] It has few natural advantages, some oil though not much,[3] but what it has had is a huge, driving self-confidence from its rulers, using property development as a mechanism for developing an economy. It is the most extreme example of the philosophy of 'build it and they'll come'.

So far they have. Most cities, most new cities, exist because there was an economic function that they grew to meet. With Dubai it is the other way round: it created its own economic function.

Nothing prepares the visitor for Dubai for there is nothing quite like it … in the world. It is a huge construction site, boasting one quarter of the world's cranes in 2007. But it is also a huge construction site without the economic hinterland: there are no suburbs as such, no farms or market gardens, no industrial estates. There is the small old town, Deira, built round the creek – old, that is, in the sense it was largely built between the 1950s and 1980s – and going there is a bit of a relief after the shock of the new. There is also the smallish old residential quarter of Jumeirah with its posh villas – but these, too, have been engulfed by the new developments. And beyond the endless tower blocks is either desert or sea.

A network of highways, with Sheikh Zayed Road cast as the main boulevard of the new Dubai, pounds across the desert, flanked by offices, hotels and malls. Sheikh Zayed, started as a four-lane dual carriageway, is now up to eight lanes and still it is jam-packed with cars – a mini instant Los Angeles.

Famously, Dubai is now extending into the sea, with that same 'world' signature but also with three palm islands – artificial islands in the shape of palm trees.[4] You might imagine there is plenty of land to build on, and up to a point there is. But people want to be on the sea itself and the way to achieve that is to create more foreshore, which is exactly what these artificial islands do. Property development drives not just the economy but also the physical structure. You want to be on the seashore? We will create more seashore for you. The market gets what it wants.

How did all this happen? The basic tale is well known: how a series of visionary members of the ruling Al-Maktoum family – Sheikh Rashid and his sons Sheikh Maktoum and Sheikh Mohammed – created this great modern city from a pretty unpromising base. But quite how they managed to do so is harder to grasp. Why do not other city-states in equally tiny places manage to achieve such success?

My own introduction to Dubai was through one of its builders: the Indian head of an enormous construction company called ABM. Back in the 1970s Krishna Pathak arrived in what was then a tiny emirate with a population of a couple of hundred thousand. He was himself from a relatively modest background (his father was a prison governor in the Andaman Islands) but he became friendly with Sheikh Rashid, the then ruler of Dubai. What could he do? Krishna Pathak said he wanted to start a construction company.

'But you do not know anything about construction,' said Sheikh Rashid, 'and you are not even an engineer.'

'No, but I can find people who do, and you will need good construction companies,' Krishna Pathak replied.

They rode out to the foreshore and looked out to sea. Sheikh Rashid wanted a port built there. Krishna Pathak's company duly built the largest man-made harbour in the Middle East, called Jebel Ali Port, the first free trade zone in Dubai. As for ABM, it now employs nearly 15,000 people, mostly Indians, and is one of the largest construction companies on the world's biggest building site.

This leads into a key issue about Dubai. Nationals account for less than 20 per cent of the population, and so, proportionally, it has the largest expatriate community in the world (that phrase again).[5] People from the Indian sub-continent make up some 60 per cent of the total.[6] The construction crews typically come for two-year stints, with two months off at the end. They live in dormitories, leaving their families behind, and send money home. Eventually they move back, maybe using their savings to start a business, but also with a pension.

It is a very different life to that of a much smaller community of British expats, who reside in luxury flats with staff to look after them and whose children are usually educated in British boarding schools.[7] I did not see the conditions in which the hundreds of thousands of Indian workers live, but there was a series of strikes in 2007 in protest against these conditions. Human Rights Watch has described their treatment as 'less than human',[8] and for some, that comment must be a fair judgement. Some builders have expanded very swiftly without the management to carry out proper supervision. Corners are cut and the workforce suffers. There were nearly 900 construction fatalities in 2004, according to Human Rights Watch, including deaths from heatstroke. There are stories of workers not being paid and being unable to afford a fare home.[9] And when the downturn hit, many workers were summarily dismissed without their contracts being fulfilled.

The defence of the migrant labour system is that for most workers to go to Dubai is a choice made freely. That they are prepared to work there is a function not just of the opportunities in Dubai but also the lack of opportunities back home. However, as the Indian economy has achieved economic take-off, it has become harder or at least more expensive to recruit labour from India. Critics of the migrant system have to acknowledge that such workers not only move mostly out of choice but do make a great contribution to their home economy by sending money back.

Krishna Pathak said that some of his people had worked with him for twenty years or more and that a normal pattern was for the money sent home to be used to build dwellings for the rest of the extended family and to help set up a business. As for the way in which his own workers were being treated, well, I walked round some of his building sites and insofar as one can make any judgement, these sites were as spruce and well organized as any equivalent European operation.

There is, however, one similarity between British and Indian (and indeed all foreign) workers: you cannot become a permanent resident of Dubai. Your visa may be rolled over indefinitely but there is always the power for that not to happen. And, of course, non-nationals have no political power at all. Control is tightly retained by and for Dubai citizens. Every foreigner, at every level however exalted, is a hired gun.

I was told that if people transgress, they are out on a plane immediately. There have been some high-profile cases involving drinking or sexual behaviour where people have gone to jail. If there is a legal disagreement – or even a traffic accident – involving a national and a non-national, the national wins. This is not a Western liberal democracy, even if the trappings of Western consumerism and culture are Dubai's most evident features.[10]

All that said, an implicit social contract exists between the expats and the locals.[11] Dubai hires the best, paying the market rate for the skills it is buying. In return, people do their jobs as well as they can, take the money and go home. I do know of one British enterprise that was cheated on a deal by a Dubai publishing company, and I am sure there are others. But by and large business ethics are strong, within the overarching rule that in any dispute the foreigner is always wrong. If you do not like that, you go somewhere else.

At least until the end of the boom, Dubai's formula has worked wonderfully well in terms of economic performance. It has become the great communications hub of the entire Middle East. It has the largest airport[12] (and is building another,[13] which may eventually become even bigger) and the largest port[14] in the region. It attracts money not just from the rest of the Middle East but from Europe, particularly the UK, most of which is ploughed into property.[15] It is already the prime medical centre[16] of the Middle East and is seeking to become a media and financial hub. A media city[17] and a financial centre[18] are being built and it is seeking to open up higher education: the London Business School opened a branch at the end of 2006.

So its aim is to go beyond property and communications to build a base in all the fastest-growing sectors of world business. The question, which we will come back to later, is whether a top-down society, run by a tiny elite that preserves jobs for its own people, can continue to attract the international talent it needs to fulfil its ambitions.

Among the British expats that I met there, I found a real affection for the place – a deeper affection than Britons abroad feel for, say, France or Spain. To create a society where foreigners are excluded from all power – are kept, so to speak, in watertight compartments – yet actually love the place is an extraordinary achievement, almost as remarkable as the economic success. But if your local population is less than 20 per cent of the total, probably dropping further over the next generation, it is the only way for a local community to run the society. As long as they have control, or feel they have control, the place works.

2. WHAT ARE THE LESSONS?

One lesson is already blindingly obvious: inspired property development can create huge prosperity. It was this proposition that made me single out Dubai for this study. There are other models of economic development in unpromising locations. Singapore is perhaps the best other example, and the development policies of Lee Kuan Yew, its prime minister from 1959 to 1990, were an inspiration for Sheikh Rashid when he first set about creating his vision for Dubai. But the Singapore of the 1950s was already an established communications hub and Singapore's growth came the other way round: the port and the airport drove the property development. And unlike Singapore, Dubai was not a natural communications hub; it became one by an act of vision.

Within that vision is the drive to build the best. Whatever view you take of the result, the physical fabric created by Dubai is remarkable. The concepts of the palm islands and the map of the world are outstanding.

The tower buildings could doubtless have been value-engineered to be cheaper – to offer more floor space or to have lower ceilings. The apartment blocks could have cheaper finishes – less marble, more concrete. You have only to look at the cut-price developments around the Mediterranean to see how corners could have been cut. But the people who can afford it like the best; they recognize quality when they see it. And this carries a further message that should go for all developers: we are in an age, not unlike the Victorian era, when people are prepared to pay for quality. Many of the buildings that are going up now in Dubai will probably be pulled down in thirty years' time, but they are built as though they should last for ever.

There is a further lesson, which is that you can use developments to create service industries. This is obvious in the case of a port or an airport, assuming there is sufficient underlying demand. It is also obvious in the case of shopping malls, and here there is clearly plenty of underlying demand in the region. The mall I visited is very much top of the global range. For example, many shopping centres now sell raffle tickets where the prize is an exotic sports car. Dubai goes one stage further: this mall was raffling an executive jet.

But the more novel concept behind some of the other buildings is to use property as a way of creating themed services. Thus Dubai is constructing a medical city, a financial city and a media city. There is an internet city, a knowledge village, a Gold and Diamond Park and so on.

Already it is pretty clear that the medical city will be a success. There is a large unsupplied need for top-end medical services in the Gulf and this is an obvious place to locate these. Meanwhile, the Gold and Diamond Park fits in well with Dubai's entrepôt status – a form of go-between for the import and re-export of goods. But a knowledge village? Where is the comparative advantage there?

The big new prize, however, is finance. It is too early to be completely confident that Dubai can build itself up as a financial centre. This is a hard industry to create, not least because top-of-the-range financial people are already paid so much that it is hard to lure them to a place such as Dubai by paying them yet more. You can understand why a rich Saudi would prefer to travel to Dubai for medical services, rather than go to London. But he might prefer to have his money managed in London rather than Dubai. Given that the main cost is people, it might also be cheaper to do it in London anyway.

We will see. Some financial business will undoubtedly migrate to Dubai; indeed that is already happening. There is a gap in the global times zones for a successful financial centre in the Middle East, a role formerly played by Beirut and to a lesser extent Bahrain, and Dubai is certainly seeking to establish the best regulatory regime in the Middle East,[19] following its principle of doing whatever it is doing as well as it possibly can. The question is whether it will become a really significant financial centre, the main one for the entire region, handling the investment of much of its oil wealth. If so, this will be a triumph, but even if not, Dubai will be a significant niche financial centre similar perhaps to Dublin. That would not meet its ambitions but it would not be a bad achievement.

Becoming a media hub will be tougher still, largely because the media require a freedom to operate that may clash with the political direction of the Dubai state. But the principle that you build the infrastructure and the business will come still holds, even if some types of business come slower than others.

If those are the main economic lessons, there are also social ones. You could say that Dubai is pretty much a police state, ruled by a benevolent despot. For some in the West, that is uncomfortable, rather in the way that the success of Singapore makes the European and American liberal elites uneasy. But at a practical level, it is surely something of a triumph to have created a society of immigrants who get along together despite the huge differences in background, wealth and religion that one might expect to drive them apart. Dubai is safe and, as far as its residents are concerned, largely drug-free. It copes with the different Muslim, Christian and Hindu approaches to alcohol with a benign practicality, and with a sight less hypocrisy than many other parts of the Muslim world.

There is one other benefit that is immediately obvious to the visitor: the complete absence of hassle on the streets. Vendors offer their wares but do not press them on you; there are no beggars; everyone is courteous to everyone else. The streets in Deira have preserved to a remarkable extent the lively Middle Eastern market atmosphere without the unpleasantness. People do not seem to be living on the edge. They have work – indeed until the end of the boom there was a structural shortage of labour – and they respect that work.

Behind this, I suggest, is a fundamental truth: a society that is both successful in economic terms and manages to spread its wealth to anyone who works hard is going to be a contented society as well as a rich one. Of course, there are many tensions in Dubai and like most visitors I found the scale of the social divide uncomfortable. As the global recession deepened those tensions became more evident. But under the circumstances, in particular the explosive growth and the melding of many different nationalities and cultures, Dubai has surely coped remarkably well.

- **Inspired development can create huge prosperity**
- **Build the best – don't compromise**
- **Use development to create service industries**

3. WHAT COULD GO WRONG?

It has gone wrong. At some stage the boom was always going to hit the buffers; anyone could see that. The city-state has been on a wild, wild ride and we have enough experience of economic cycles to know there would sooner or later be a big bump. It is easy to foresee the economic circumstances. When the world economy hit recession in 2008/9 amidst a global property crash, Dubai was directly in the firing line. As investors generally have become much more averse to risk, property sales have slowed and funding has dried up. Many of the building sites have been abandoned, possibly never to be completed. In the end the Dubai authorities seem likely to be bailed out by the fellow United Arab Emirates member, Abu Dhabi, but at a price. That changes the balance of power within the UAE, with oil-rich Abu Dhabi asserting itself over its brasher and poorer neighbour, but it means that Dubai has time to rebalance its economy until it has coped with its property overhang and global growth resumes.

Politics are another threat. On the political front, greater unrest in the Middle East might in the short term work to Dubai's advantage, for it would appear an island of calm in a region of troubles. But in the medium term an unsettled Middle East would, of course, be very destructive; there is no point in pretending otherwise.

That, however, is not within the ability of Dubai or any of the other Gulf states to control. Dubai would not, so to speak, carry any responsibility for regional unrest but in the long run it would surely suffer from it. What is within Dubai's control is how well it copes with the shift from seemingly endless construction to a more broadly based economy. At some stage that has to happen. The only point in building the various service industry centres is for the financial centre, the medical centre and so on to become successful entities in their own right.

This is important because otherwise Dubai simply becomes a place to spend money earned elsewhere, a superior holiday resort, and there are limits to the appeal of that. To the visitor, much of the development appears unbalanced: the old town of Deira has great charm; the new developments are just new developments. As far as residential accommodation is concerned, so many of these flats seem to be built for buying and selling, rather than for living in. Occupation levels in the newer buildings seem low. The 'build it and they'll come' approach is successful at one level; the problem is that they come and go. This is understandable in that nothing in Dubai is permanent, including the foreign residents. This is a place where people stay for a bit, not settle down. You have to wonder for how long this economic model will endure.

And there is a darker side to the model. If you create a successful entrepôt trading centre, its very success makes it hard to control quite what is traded.[20] So quite aside from any criticisms of the construction business, and in particular the way in which some migrant workers have been treated, Dubai has its shadier aspects too. It has become a centre for the Middle Eastern arms trade, its business greatly boosted by the tensions of the Iraq war. It is one of the main routes along which Afghanistan exports its poppies for the European drugs trade.

Meanwhile, the wealthy and shifting population of expatriates creates a big market for prostitutes[21] – you see the top end of that market in the smarter hotels.

Any prosperous, fast-growing economy is going to generate social problems; it is also going to bring environmental ones.[22] It is hardly surprising there is evidence of damage to coral reefs from the run-off and pollution created by the world's largest building site. Apparently there has also been damage to turtle nesting sites. Meanwhile, desalination plants ensure there is sufficient water not just for people's needs but also for the watering of the golf courses and gardens of the rich. This is not an entirely wasteful use of water as there is some evidence it has led to a change in the micro-climate: because there is now so much lush greenery around, winter rainfall seems to have increased in what appears to be some kind of feedback mechanism. However, desalination itself creates problems of its own in the brine that remains and has to be pumped out to sea.

Beyond that, there is the sheer inconvenience of the place: every journey, except perhaps in the middle of the night, involves sitting in a traffic jam. Some help will come from the Dubai Metro, a light-rail network along Sheikh Zayed Road that opened in 2009. But the heat means that getting in an air-conditioned car will remain vastly preferable for most people to walking to a railway station. Dubai may not be quite the environmental nightmare it is sometimes painted as, but it would be hard to pretend that plonking down all the infrastructure of a Western economy in the desert is an environmental dream.

Growth creates problems but it also generates the resources to help tackle those problems. The issue seems to me to be whether the Dubai ruling elite has got the balance right. Should it have tried to rein back the rate of growth and divert more resources into coming to terms with the social and environmental issues? The answer must be yes: it would have been both wiser and safer to have done so. It would have been wiser because slower growth would have made the country somewhat less reliant on importing foreigners to do everything for it. And it would have been safer because it would have made the economy more resilient and therefore better able to cope with the inevitable reverses. (Krishna Pathak told me that he deliberately restricted the expansion of his company to about 18 per cent a year as he felt it was too difficult to manage faster progress than that.)

Eventually the market will decide the outcome of this extraordinary economic and social experiment. It will determine which attributes of Dubai's offering will succeed and which will not. My own guess is that, barring some catastrophe that damages the entire Middle East, Dubai will continue to be the main financial and commercial centre of the Gulf. It will become the largest single financial centre for the entire region. Even if Dubai recovers well from the 2009 property crash, there will at some stage be an even more fundamental adjustment, when Dubai has to switch from bounding forward to moving at a slower and more sustainable pace. There is a cyclical issue, which is all too apparent. But there is also a structural issue. It will have to go from its present big bang to something more of a steady state.

When that time comes, and it will come within a generation, Dubai will have to try to figure out what its long-term competitive advantages really are. It certainly cannot live on property development alone. If that transition fails, boom will be followed by a much deeper and more destructive bust than the one that followed 2008/9. That bust would be a social catastrophe as well as an economic one: a lot of quite poor people depend on the income they earn working in Dubai.

For the next few years, though, Dubai will remain an extraordinary phenomenon. And for me, the most extraordinary aspect of the whole place is the way in which it manages to be – on its own terms – a social success as well as an economic one: it offers opportunities to people, at every level of financial status, that they could not get at home. This is why they come. And to create a society that is robust enough to ride the ups and downs of its wild boom in reasonable harmony is a triumph indeed. Krishna Pathak cites three things that make Dubai work. It has vision, of course. It has organization in the sense that decisions are taken swiftly with no bureaucratic delays. And it has punishments for non-performance – you have to be good at what you are doing. With those qualities I am hopeful the Dubai success story, battered though it is by the global recession, can continue to work for a while yet. Whatever reservations people might have, it has certainly brought something special to the world. There is no other place quite like it.

Africa

CHAPTER THIRTEEN

Mobile Telephony
Changing the face of a continent

I. WHAT IS THE STORY?

In 1996 Thabo Mbeki, the then deputy president, told the Information Society and Development Conference[1] in Midrand in South Africa: 'Half of humanity has not yet made a phone call.' It was a comment that had been made before, but since then technology has rendered it obsolete – and most notably in Africa itself. Within a decade of that conference, Africa had become the fastest-growing mobile phone market in the world,[2] and by 2009 some countries had almost as many mobiles per person as the USA or Japan.[3] The technology has transformed the African economy[4] and Africans are now the most innovative users of mobiles anywhere in the world.

You could almost say that the mobile phone is to Africa what the computer is to the rest of the world. The continent has been plagued by a lamentable fixed-line service and uneven power supplies. This has crippled economic activity, making it very hard for businesses to operate efficiently. But thanks to a handful of pioneering companies working often in very difficult conditions, it has an excellent mobile network. Africa is the poorest continent but it has some of the most innovative and enterprising people, and the mobile phone has set them free.

My own insight into this came from talking to MTN, the largest mobile phone network in Africa. Based in Johannesburg, this is a tremendously successful company, growing fast[5] and investing a huge amount in infrastructure. It has to, because among the practical difficulties facing operators is the fact that in many locations where they need to put base stations there is no mains electricity to drive them. So they have to put in and maintain diesel generators. Another distinguishing feature is that Africa has the highest proportion of pre-pay customers, nearly 90 per cent of the total,[6] of any region in the world. This simplifies billing but it means there has to be a competent network of sales agents as the relationship with the customer is through these middle men rather than directly with the company. So operators have to make sure their sales agents are successful – that they invest in promotion, that they do not undercut each other and lose money, as they found had happened in Nigeria.[7]

So in a way mobile telephone companies are teaching the continent good business practice as well as doing their job.

However, the most interesting issue is not how the systems are put in and operated but how they are used. Sometimes it is a case of people figuring out how to do their business better by using communications: fishermen being able to check prices at different markets so they know where best to land their catch is a well-cited example. In Uganda, farmers use their phones to check crop prices so they can make a judgement when best to go to market. There is a further effect. Once one person in an area has a mobile phone, he or she can sub-let to other people, making a small charge on the price of the call. So having a mobile can become a small business.

At any rate, all the evidence is that Africans rate their service very highly, because they are prepared to pay what is for them a lot for it.

In the developed world telephony typically takes about 3 per cent of household incomes. In some African countries, including Namibia, Ethiopia and Zambia, it takes more than 10 per cent.[8] This spread of mobile telephony seems to be of particular importance to rural areas, where people feel disconnected from the society around them. For them it is a liberation.

There are many other small applications – small but important to the users. One, for example, is hospitals using text messages to remind out-patients to take their medicines. But perhaps the most dramatic application so far has been the use of mobile phones for transferring money. To start with, this was just another service offered by banks to their customers, but then a number of people realized there was a huge latent demand for simple banking services from people who were not customers. Two entrepreneurs calculated that half the population of South Africa, some sixteen million people, did not have bank accounts but one-third of them did have mobile phones. They founded a company called Wizzit,[9] which in 2005 rolled out the service to those people. It was quickly followed by other companies, including MTN, and now the concept is spreading right through the continent.

The idea is very simple: people have a bank account on their phone, which they can top up or draw down at local agents, banks and shops. They have a debit card with which they can pay bills or withdraw cash from a machine and they can transfer balances to other people at very low cost.

This changes everything. If companies of all sizes have to operate on a cash basis, they are at a huge practical disadvantage. They can operate but it is clumsy and expensive. Everything slows down. One of the great problems of the continent is the lack of a financial infrastructure: people have no way of putting their savings in a secure place or of gaining access to loans. If, on the other hand Africa can create a low-cost banking system without the need to build branches, then the hobbles come off. At the moment the system is principally one of money transfer but expect that gradually to be extended to other banking services.

The exciting thing is that this story has hardly begun. We can visualize the business implications of mobile telephony in Africa, turning a continent where in many places it is hard to run an ordinary business into one where it is as easy as anywhere else. As the capabilities spread, and helped by the advent of hardware innovations such as ultra-low-cost handsets, African people will continue to figure out ways of adapting mobile telephony to other economic functions. But I suspect that the social and democratic implications will be even more important.

A small story to illustrate this: a young art school student in the Democratic Republic of Congo, Kiripi Katembo Siku, wanted to make a film about life in the capital, Kinshasa. But filming was not allowed without permission. So he put a mobile phone in a toy cardboard car, set its camera in cine mode and trailed it around the city. The resulting film, *Voiture en carton*, became a hit on YouTube. It did not show anything untoward, just life in a big African city, but it showed that with very simple technology ordinary individuals could tell their story to the world. So the new technologies do not just bring better information about everything, from politics to sport, to the masses; they enable people to spread information about themselves to the rest of the world.

This is, of course, a common feature of the information revolution. It spreads power. In that sense Africa is no different from anywhere else in the world. But since this continent has greater problems of governance than others, mobile telephony will have a greater impact on the way governments perform. True, this will only be at the margin. The mobile phone, however innovatively deployed, does not of itself create a better system of rule. But it does tip the balance of power, initially just slightly, away from elites and towards ordinary citizens.

By 2012, more than half of Africa's population will have a mobile phone.[10] So within sixteen years of that comment by Thabo Mbeki, we will have gone from a world where making a phone call is a novelty to one where it is commonplace. By then, thanks to their ingenuity and enterprise, Africans will have worked out many more ways of using this simple but astounding technology. I would not want to say this is the technology that saves Africa, for that would be too stark and indeed too dismissive of the contribution of its people in this revolution. But I think you could say that this is the technology that catapults Africa into the modern world and the one that will ensure the continent performs much better in every way during the early part of this century than it did in the latter years of the previous one.

2. WHAT ARE THE LESSONS?

Some lessons from Africa's mobile phone revolution are already there to see. But because the networks are being rolled out so swiftly, we should expect to learn a lot more in the coming years as people devise new applications that fit the special needs of the continent.

For that is the key – applications. The technology is global standard. The best companies developing the networks and fostering the innovative applications are global standard. That is worth celebrating. But equally interesting, surely, are the 'bottom-up' uses that people figure out for themselves and the consequences of those.

Start with the basics. If there is one paramount lesson, it is that communications are the key to economic progress. Each age has transforming technologies that help drive growth: rail, roads, water systems, electricity. Because Africa has relatively poor infrastructure for all sorts of reasons, mobile communications have proved particularly transformational. In most parts of the world there are other ways of communicating, including, of course, fixed-line phones. In Africa there are not.

Between the 1960s and 2000 African growth lagged behind that of the rest of the world. There were bright exceptions, of which Botswana is the most-cited example, but the continent as a whole was losing ground. But since 2000 the picture has reversed and sub-Saharan Africa in particular has begun to grow more swiftly than the developed world, and in some instances as fast as the rapidly expanding countries of East Asia.[11] There are many reasons for this, of which probably the most important is investment from China as part of its drive to secure access to natural resources. But the growth has also been associated with the mobile boom. That will continue. According to research by the investment bank Goldman Sachs,[12] some 40 per cent of the total investment in infrastructure in sub-Saharan Africa to 2050 will be in mobile telephony. Just 3 per cent will be in landlines, 11 per cent in internet services and 12 per cent in roads. The only other aspect of investment that comes close will be electricity generation, 34 per cent.

This leads to a further point. Mobile phone companies have become a beacon of private sector competence. They put in infrastructure that works. They maintain it. They train networks of agents and so spread accounting practices and management techniques. The kit they put in is qualitatively different from other forms of infrastructure, where a company or consortium comes in, builds whatever it is building then goes away again. (In the case of some foreign investors, particularly those from China, even much of the labour is brought in too.) The mobile phone operators are in effect teaching the continent how to run a business: the pricing, the marketing, the management, the human resources, the training. They are, in essence, a practical business school. They also pay a lot of tax and so support government services; MTN is the largest taxpayer in Uganda.

In terms of the applications themselves, the money transfer one is the most notable to date. That probably does not carry many lessons for the developed world because it already has an established banking structure – the weaknesses of which are not of technology or reach but of management and governance – and if you have internet banking, you probably do not need it on your mobile. And we do not know where this application will go in Africa. Money transfer is a real benefit at the moment, but as things become more complex a mobile phone may no longer be the best bit of hardware on which to deliver a banking service; making and managing a loan is much harder.

The 'bottom-up' lessons will be more instructive, even if what they teach is not always strictly ethical. We have the case of farmers checking crop prices but there are also the less encouraging examples of business acumen. I was told of fishermen using lookouts with mobile phones to warn them that the inspectors were on the way. They would have time to switch from illegal small-mesh nets to legal larger-mesh ones. Oh well.

A lot of innovation comes in plain old voice calls. Senior African figures typically have several mobile numbers. One is the general number, which always goes onto voicemail and will be picked up by an aide; another is for business associates who need good access; another is for close friends and family; and finally there might be one solely for one's spouse. In a world where people are always on the move and email access may be intermittent, you can still get things done and the people who need to reach you can.

Perhaps the best way to get a handle on the innovative uses is to start from the point that people are prepared to spend such a large proportion of their income on the services. They would not do it if they did not value them. Within Europe a vast variety of applications has been developed for mobile phones, from paying parking charges to locating nearby restaurants. Some take off and some do not. It does not matter how people use their phones – whether they want to vote to evict celebrities in reality TV shows or send a text message to a radio talk show. But it matters to Africans; as far as they are concerned, the services make a difference.

This suggests Africa will differ from the rest of the world – where mobile phones are as much a leisure purchase as anything else – in that the principal uses will be for business. You could say that Europe, North America and indeed parts of Asia use the technology frivolously, whereas Africa takes it seriously.

If, as a result of venerating the possibilities of mobile telephony, the burst of African economic development is sustained, then maybe this is the biggest lesson of all. The rest of the world may say it to wants to help the continent but in that case it should pay attention to what its consumers choose to do with their own money, rather than impose external policies on them. The roll-out of the most important form of infrastructure in Africa is financed by the people themselves, not some aid agency on the other side of the world. It is almost always run by the private sector, not a state-funded utility. It is entirely in response to consumer demand, rather than being planned by a government bureaucracy. And it works.

- **Communications are the key to economic progress**
- **Private sector competence can act as a practical business school**
- **Pay attention to what consumers do with their money**

3. WHAT COULD GO WRONG?

Nothing really. To be more precise, the issue is not so much what might go wrong with mobile telephony but rather whether a single technology can really transform the economic direction of an entire continent, as suggested above. There are lots of things that can go wrong in Africa. The real question is whether some sort of turning point has been reached and, if so, can telecommunications help sustain this momentum?

No one can know the answer to that. It is not difficult to become depressed about the corruption of African capitalism or the incompetence of African Marxism; the continent can do both. But it really is presumptuous of outsiders to feel they have an answer that the people who live there cannot find for themselves. I have found visits to the two largest economies of sub-Saharan Africa, Nigeria and South Africa, quite inspiring. They are at opposite ends of the continent and have utterly different cultural and political backgrounds, but the people in both have the common qualities of energy and ingenuity, not to mention the ability to cope with adversity. The great thing about mobile telephony is that it builds on all these qualities. It is flexible and adaptive. It responds to market signals. It does not need too much long-term planning (though maintaining the networks is a logistical triumph). And people want it.

So the threat is no so much one of failure but rather one of limited success. The networks will continue to do their job very well and the market will continue to grow until Africa reaches and maybe passes European levels of use. That would be pretty astounding but not at all impossible. However, the continent as a whole may fail to take off. Sure, it will gradually become richer but not to the extent that its physical and human resources should enable it to do.

Maybe this turns on whether mobile telephony is just an economic tool, which is fine in its way, or whether it can also become a social and political driver for change. This leads to huge questions. Is it a device that will help spread democracy? Will it empower ordinary people to make more of their human capital? Will it indirectly at least improve governance? Will it improve education? Will it improve health? Will it stop wars?

It will to some modest extent do all of the above, with the possible exception of the last. It really is possible that the humble mobile phone, used with the intense ingenuity that Africans have developed, will bolt down the change of direction that Africa may have already taken. There will inevitably be setbacks and when these occur they will be widely reported. Those of us who work in the media know that this is the nature of news. But we need to remember, too, that Africa has much to teach the world and the way the continent has deployed mobile telephony carries a huge lesson for us all.

India

CHAPTER FOURTEEN

The slums of Mumbai
Much more than *Slumdog Millionaire*

I. WHAT IS THE STORY?

You see it on your left on the way into Mumbai from the airport: the scruffy low-rise buildings on either side give way to a great grey marshland. Except that this is a marshland full of people living in shacks. It is Dharavi, home to somewhere between 750,000 and a million people – Asia's largest slum. It is also, I suggest, the best slum in the world.

Dharavi was made famous by the film *Slumdog Millionaire*, directed by Danny Boyle and launched in 2008. The film has been hugely successful commercially but has met with mixed reviews as to its accuracy and inevitable criticisms that it glamorizes something that should not be glamorized. Make of that what you will. My own introduction came a couple of years earlier and I do not think I saw glamour, more simply something that should be respected in its own terms.

The word 'slum' carries all sorts of horrible connotations. The World Bank definition is: 'a heavily populated urban area characterized by sub-standard and poor housing and squalor'. Dharavi certainly does spectacularly sub-standard housing and, to the eyes of a Westerner, it looks a huge mess. It is also certainly heavily populated, for its inhabitants are crammed into one square mile.

But squalid it is not, or rather it is not if you look at the way in which the inhabitants make their lives there. Indeed I found it rather uplifting – an example of a society operating in a very difficult environment but organizing itself to provide decent and fulfilled lives for many of its people. No one should try and romanticize bad housing conditions – the 'we were poor but happy' myth of the past. But if good housing is indubitably better than bad, we also need to recognize that people matter more than places.

Governments can bulldoze slums and herd the inhabitants into high-rise blocks – that is what has happened all over the world. What we find much harder to do is to create communities. And for all its most obvious difficulties, Dharavi is a community that works. I find it more helpful to try to think of it as a city in its own right, one that instead of being surrounded by fields happens to be located within a larger special city. Dharavi is much more than a collection of substandard homes.

One measure of success for any place is whether people chose to live there. Of course, Dharavi has a shifting population, as do all such areas: some people move in from the country, find jobs and move on. But for many it has remained a home for a generation or more. For these long-term residents, it is a location of choice.

I began to understand why when I walked round it. My guide was Dr Mithu Alur, a long-standing friend best known for founding one of the country's largest educational charities, the Spastics Society of India. The society pioneered the provision of services for people with cerebral palsy and more recently has been promoting the policy of inclusion of people with handicaps into the mainstream educational system.[1] But the particular reason for Mithu showing us round Dharavi was its role in providing primary schools for the poor.

You leave what passes for a road and walk along a narrow alley between the corrugated iron sheds. You duck under leaking water pipes and electric cables strewn across the alleys at head height. Dharavi seems to have managed to get piped water in and it leaks out into open drains that criss-cross the city. It also seems to have reasonably reliable electricity, which either comes from small generators or is, more dubiously, tapped from the mains. Every home seems to have a television.

You step past people washing their clothes, cooking, doing all the normal activities of daily life. You duck to the left as the alley twists, step over a drain, then head on again, and after a few minutes you arrive at the school. But this is not a school with its own physical building; it is a classroom in someone's home – a living room rented each morning by Mithu's charity, with the furniture, clothes and personal belongings of the owner piled up in a corner. It is, I guess, twelve feet by fifteen feet in size and, of course, it is scrupulously clean.

There is a circle of children sitting round the teacher; a few evidently handicapped in some way, most bright and obviously eager to learn, all of them shining. This is the first of two shifts of children and this particular class is infants. They are being taught the basic skills of reading, identifying objects, using their hands – the usual curriculum of any more conventional primary school. If you shut your eyes to the surroundings and just kneel down with the children, talk to them and play with them, as Mithu made us do, you could be anywhere in the world. Primary school kids are the same everywhere.

For many of these children, this is probably the only education they will get. The parents pay for it. While the charity employs the teacher, hires the classroom and provides the teaching materials, all the parents are asked contribute something, many a tiny amount, towards the costs. They pay what they can manage and so they value what the school is doing. They make sure the children arrive on time. They have a say in what is taught. For example, I was told that parents want their children to be taught English, particularly if they do not speak it themselves, because they know this is a pathway towards better jobs. So the schools teach English. This is not an operation guided by some distant education ministry that sets policy targets and guidelines telling teachers how and what they should teach. Were it not for the charity, it would not happen, but fundamentally it is bottom-up, not top-down. That important bit of any city's essential services, primary education, works.

As indeed does the city of Dharavi as a whole. It is a hive of activity. Nine out of ten people there have jobs, some of them within Dharavi itself, working in thousands of small 'factories'. Others commute out to jobs elsewhere in the Mumbai region. Some people have quite well-paid jobs and could certainly move out to a more conventional part of the city should they wish. Apparently, one of the attractions of living here is that it is a short commute to the main centres of employment, compared with what many of Mumbai's citizens have to endure. Looking at those crammed trains, I can understand why. Some people indeed choose to live in Dharavi even when they own property elsewhere.

If public services are minimal, as they mostly are, the private sector finds a way of filling the gap. Take law and order. I understand there is concern that crime levels are higher than they were a decade ago. There are gangs, which extort local businesses. But there seems to be very little violent crime against the person and the city in fair measure polices itself. There are medical services, probably no worse than those of the other poorer parts of the city, and naturally a multiplicity of markets cater for people's daily needs.

That leads to what seems to me to be the key to understanding Dharavi: it is a great industrial centre – it produces a huge amount. It is a place where people work as well as live. Estimates of the size of its annual output range up to $1.5 billion, a GDP of more than $1,500 per head. That may not sound a lot, but in purchasing power – what the money buys in real services – this is obviously worth far more than $1,500 in a developed country. There are some 15,000 small businesses, run by micro-entrepreneurs with little workshops that churn out hand-crafted products – jewellery, clothing, furniture, leather goods. There are foundries smelting brass and making ornaments.

There are food businesses, potters, soap makers and so on. This is a tremendously hard-working place.

It also carries out an environmentally friendly function: it recycles much of the waste of Mumbai's nineteen million inhabitants.[2] Bundles of plastic, cloth, metal, paper, glass and so on are processed into something useful.

So its raw materials are things other people do not want. Out of waste come useful products and, naturally, jobs. Something like 250,000 people are employed in the Dharavi recycling businesses, with some 10,000 in plastic recycling alone. It is almost certainly the biggest such operation in the world. As Friends of the Earth has pointed out, there is a lot that the West can learn from India on how to increase the proportion of goods that the rich world recycles rather than dumps.

There is, unsurprisingly in any city of close to a million people, a darker side. The working conditions in these small enterprises would shock anyone from the developed world. For example, a lot of the scavenging and sorting work, I am afraid, is done by children. And while, for adults at least, wages are far above those of agricultural labourers, who flock in from the country to take the work, the incomes are not matched by proper health or safety controls. There is no point in trying to correct this by passing laws because more than three-quarters of the businesses are operating illegally.

The public services are pretty well non-existent. There is no hospital and only a handful of public, as opposed to private, schools – though there is a good municipal hospital just outside the boundary. Water supplies for drinking come in on tankers once a fortnight. The sewage is open drains. Not surprisingly, there are serious health problems.

In the absence of municipal authority, the property in Dharavi is managed by 'slumlords'. At one level they function as providers of what would normally be municipal services, but the issue is whether these are regular commercial companies operating within defined legal and ethical standards or mafia-style organizations operating beyond them. Insofar as an outsider can judge, the slumlords seem to organize accommodation in an orderly way. There have been heartbreaking stories of people in other parts of the Mumbai conglomeration being turned out of homes they have bought, with no legal title and with the land then being sold at a higher price to a new band of migrants.

No one, least of all an outsider living in the comfortable West, should seek to play down the deprivation and the sheer unfairness of life in a place such as Dharavi. Nevertheless, the scale of its social problems seems to me to be rather more manageable than that of many cities in the Western developed world of similar size. Dharavi is not a 'bad' area in the sense most Western cities have pockets of deprivation, with high levels of drug abuse, criminal activity and human misery. Its problems are principally physical, not social, and physical problems ought to be easier to fix. So the rest of the world has a lot to learn from it.

2. WHAT ARE THE LESSONS?

There seem be three overriding lessons that Dharavi has for the world.

The first and most obvious is that what people do signals what they want – or more precisely, what they want within the options available to them. Some people choose to live and work here for the reason that it is a better option than the others available. That may be because there are so many jobs in those thousands of workshops, whereas there are many fewer jobs in the places from which some of its inhabitants have migrated. It may be because they find it convenient – anything being better than a three-hour commute. Economics clearly plays a big part, but in a way we do not need to know why people move here, and stay when they could perfectly well move on. If people are making a genuine choice then it would be presumptuous of a visiting journalist, politician or whoever to criticize that decision.

The second lesson is that economic activity helps create stable and self-reliant societies. If there were no jobs and Dharavi were just a commuter city, the case for bulldozing it and building higher-standard housing would be very strong – though were that to happen, as it well may, it would be vital to protect the property rights of the people there. But creating small businesses is something that can never be done top-down. What Dharavi has become, thanks in part to its location and the availability of cheap labour, but also to the spirit and economic freedom it gives its residents, is a haven for entrepreneurship.

There are many other examples in world cities of zones that are relatively free from regulation – offering low-rent locations that attract artists and providers of specialist services – becoming a focal point for would-be entrepreneurs. But these are usually quite small. Dharavi is unusual in the extent to which it is an economic success and this carries lessons for other cities that would wish to build up employment and entrepreneurial activity. It is not a model for development as such, for its flaws are all too apparent. But other cities could benefit a great deal by studying the detail of its business community – who owns the businesses, what connections these have with the rest of the region, what they produce, how they market their output and so on.

That leads to the third lesson. The most effective way to assist a deprived but vibrant economic region is to attend to detail. One such example, and I am sure there are many more, is the work of the Spastics Society of India – work of which I felt so privileged to catch a glimpse. One of the key points of its operation is that it is not a 'Lady Bountiful' charity. Yes, it is a charity, but thanks in part to the fact that the educational services it provides are in part paid for, it is an economically sensitive provider. It gives people the things they really want, which among other things is education for their children.

The broader message here is that anyone seeking to intervene in the hugely complex economic interactions that take place in a complicated, if informal city must listen to the signals of the market to show what people really want, rather than impose some theoretical solution to perceived problems. If you listen to what people want, you may get it right. If you impose an external solution, even if it seems to have been successful elsewhere, you are liable to get it wrong.

There are many ways in which the condition of the residents and businesses of Dharavi could be improved, but the solution is in the detail. Provide basic public sanitation services and the place would work a lot better. Pull down and rebuild and it might work a lot worse.

Already there are many signs that the wealth being generated in Dharavi is being spent there. Parts of the city now have bars, beauty salons and boutiques. In 2007 it got its first ATM from a major bank.[3] But this piecemeal, private sector-led development may be blocked if the city is torn down and redeveloped in a radical and insensitive manner, as indeed seems quite possible.

- **What people do signals what they want**
- **Economic activity helps create stable and self-reliant societies**
- **Attend to detail**

3. WHAT COULD GO WRONG?

Something will go wrong. In fact, that is already happening, for the economic pressures for using the land area more intensively are too strong. Dharavi ought not to continue to exist in the state it does because it could be so much better; it could maintain its present virtues while massively improving the living standards of its people. But this may not happen for a simple economic reason: its location is too good. The land on which this city sits is too valuable to have the low-grade, low-density buildings it has now. It was rejected as unsuitable for building on because it was a marsh, but that was when the Mumbai region had less than 10 per cent of its present population. Then the land was not needed; now it is. Moreover, we now have building techniques that make it possible to construct successfully on reclaimed land at high densities. But to do that would be to destroy the economy and the society of this city.

There have been many ideas about what should be done to Dharavi. Currently, the state government has a $2 billion plan, drawn up by the Mumbai architect Mukesh Mehta, to redevelop it, with apartment blocks, shopping centres, schools, parks, markets, clinics, industrial parks, even a cricket museum and an arts centre.[4] It will, if this plan is fully implemented, become a middle-class neighbourhood. Rationally, seen from a land-use perspective, that is the right thing to do. Already buildings are being demolished in preparation for the new ones.

The approach to implementing this plan is to split the city into five areas and auction off each to private developers, who will have to rehouse dwellers and their businesses on the same site for free. Profits will come from luxury developments and commercial buildings built on the edges of the site.

As of this writing, it was not clear whether this version of the plan would be enforced, or indeed whether the whole redevelopment would go ahead on the scale envisaged. There is, understandably, huge opposition from the local people. This is partly a perfectly understandable resistance to change, but there is also a fear that land of great value will be snatched, people and businesses will be displaced and that those who live and work there now will end up worse off. If the redevelopment plans were bottom-up, it is argued, they might work to their advantage. But if they were imposed from above, they would wreck a thriving community.[5]

I do not think it is right for a foreign journalist to have too rigid a view on such an issue. What should happen is for the people of Mumbai to decide. What can be said, though, is that with light but basic planning, it ought to pay the owners of the land to build much higher-quality stock. It also should be possible to hold down rents while doing so, and thus maintain the social and business structures. There is no reason why the present dilapidated structures should survive; since they are built with a pretty short design life, they should not. The place could and should be much nicer for all.

It could also function more efficiently as an economic producer — good-quality modern factories are better than workshops with tin roofs. Wages are rising and it will increasingly make sense to automate a lot of the functions that are at the moment being done by hand. But there are sound reasons for wanting to try to preserve the ethos and industry of the place. Because things look a mess, that does not mean they are a mess, and vice-versa.

So I suppose the obvious answer to the 'what might go wrong?' question is: inappropriate redevelopment. But some sort of development has to happen.

That leads to what I feel is the great question for Mumbai, the largest city and the principal financial centre in what will become the world's most populous nation.

The parallel is Shanghai. Both are of comparable size. Both have had strong European influences. Both are great ports and trading centres. Both are also financial hubs now. But whereas the municipality of Shanghai has followed a decisive, if brutal, scheme of redevelopment, turning into a modern shining metropolis, Mumbai remains chaotic.

'We are bad at maintenance,' an Indian banker explained, as we looked out from his modern office just a twenty-minute cab ride from Dharavi, over a dilapidated set of apartment blocks. He could have added that they were bad at putting in the infrastructure as well as keeping it going. So in a way Dharavi is a not just a test case for Mumbai but for the nation as a whole. Will India really rival the economic powerhouse that China is becoming? Or will inadequate infrastructure and insensitive planning hold it back? Above all, can it create better conditions for its most dynamic asset: its entrepreneurs?

So much of what is written about the Indian boom concerns the high-technology industries, the computer wizards, the new service providers and so on. But there is also a deep embedded strength in the country's myriad small businesses. These provide most of the new jobs, for the hi-tech sector is tiny in relation to the economy as a whole.

Look at that former marshland, where there used to be nothing except a small fishing village at the edge. Now you see a community that has generated at least a quarter of a million jobs in very difficult circumstances. It is providing essential services to the metropolis around it.

You have to admire the energy that created this hive of activity. That is why I so admire the spirit of the city of Dharavi. All cities have to evolve and Dharavi is no exception, but I very much hope its sense of enterprise and endeavour will survive whatever changes take place in its physical make-up.

There is something bigger here than the future of this strange city within a city. It is the economic future of India. In particular, it is the extent to which India can compensate for poor public services by allowing the private sector to step in, yet within some sort of regulatory framework. Perhaps the most stunning aspect of India, one that hits every visitor, is the multitude of contrasts – contrasts of wealth, of course, but also of education, of health, of opportunity. From an economic perspective, however, the greatest of all contrasts is between the competence of the private sector at every level and that of the public sector. Much has been written about India's great private companies; much less about the myriad tiny ones. What you see in Dharavi is Indian commerce writ small. Its companies show just the same adaptability and drive that is evident in Tata or Infosys, and just the same sensitivity to market needs.

India began its economic leap forward at the end of the 1980s, when it had an economic crisis, reformed its finances and abandoned many of its economic restrictions. Its industrial giants were able to take advantage of these changes and drive growth upwards. But at a local level the business community still faces many restrictions. Bureaucracy still undermines company performance.

The businesses in Dharavi succeed because they are largely beyond bureaucracy. Incompetence they can cope with, the lack of municipal services they can endure, though these make life tougher than it needs to be for the community as a whole. But were Dharavi to be redeveloped insensitively, its business vitality could be gravely undermined, just as forty years of controls at a national level undermined the performance of the Indian economy as a whole. Dharavi has to make the transition to a regular city, with decent infrastructure, rather than remaining in the chaos it is now. But then so, too, does India as a whole. Fingers crossed they both make it. I would bet on their success, as I think would anyone who is privileged enough to catch a glimpse of this fascinating part of a fascinating city – in a fascinating country.

CHAPTER FIFTEEN

The High-Tech Industries of Bangalore

Turning disadvantage to triumph

I. WHAT IS THE STORY?

Think hi-tech India and you think Bangalore. If Mumbai is India's New York and New Delhi its Washington DC, Bangalore is its Los Angeles. Bustling, sprawling, low-density, full of cars, it is also full of green spaces. Full of immigrants too. And it is a city of suburbs, for though it has a pleasant, leafy centre thronged with Indian yuppies, the real action takes place in the technology parks on the periphery. Like Los Angeles there is hi-tech manufacturing and like LA, too, a single 'people' business has catapulted the city to global fame. In LA it was entertainment in all its forms; in Bangalore it has been computer software services, and now far beyond that.

With a population of some 6.5 million in 2009,[1] it has become India's third-largest city[2] as well as its fastest-growing[3] and one of its richest.[4] By any measure it is a huge success story. But its success is a tale of triumph over adversity. And this is the strange paradox that makes Bangalore so fascinating: it has found a way not just to prosper but to prosper in the face of serious headwinds.

My own moment of epiphany, the moment when I grasped the importance of Bangalore to the world economy, was in 2005 on my first visit there. We were on holiday but had been invited to have a look at the offices of one of India's great hi-tech companies, Wipro.[5] We drove out for half an hour from the centre, past the typical mixture of small shops, people pushing handcarts and cows wandering around, to find ourselves in a cluster of shiny new buildings surrounded by lawns, fountains and shrubs. It looked like the campus of a prosperous American liberal arts college.

We were shown into one of the operations centres. We were standing on the balcony of a room about the size of a squash court, with people at workstations down below and large screens round the top. Every now and again one of the people would tap something into his computer – and it was explained to us that they were making small adjustments to the computer system of a British power utility. Now, of course, I had realized that tech jobs were being outsourced but I had not actually seen it. That job had gone from Britain. It could be done from anywhere in the world and computer staff in Britain now had to compete with people on the other side of the globe.

However, if a job can be done from anywhere, why in this particular Indian city? The first thing to appreciate about Bangalore is its location. It is 200 miles from the nearest seaport, Chennai, and until 2008 it had only a tiny, congested airport, a former Second World War military base, with few international flights. So it had no obvious way to export its output – unless that output could be exported electronically. It was the first large city in the world to build an export business in virtual products and services.

The second thing to understand is that it has not been very well run, even by Indian standards. People there complain bitterly about the corruption,[6] about the non-existence of many public services, about the congestion[7] and about the damage that its growth has been allowed to do to the environment.[8]

And the third thing to appreciate is that has an abundance of talented, well-educated, energetic young people – indeed it has arguably the highest quality of human capital in India.[9] Somehow these wonderful people have coped with the most daunting practical difficulties and so ensured the city's success. Why? Well, Bangalore has one thing on its side: it is a place where clever people choose to live. Some 40,000 of its residents have a PhD.[10]

My own introduction to Bangalore came from some dear friends who run an architectural practice there, Mohan and Nina Bopiah. It is a small one but large enough to have designed some of the huge office blocks that surround the city, as well as similar projects in other hi-tech cities. To help me get a physical perspective, we naturally looked at the hi-tech campuses, the new elevated highway, the estates on which the executives lived and their fine club in the centre. But even more helpful was the group of friends they gathered for me to give their perspective on the phenomenon.

Bangalore's history goes back to the ninth century, but it really turned into a substantial city when it became the British military's southern headquarters, chosen partly because of its central location, partly because it was healthy. Since it is 3,000 feet above sea level, although only 800 miles north of the equator, the nights are cool and the days not too baking. When the British forces left at independence in 1947, the Indian military naturally took over their huge parade grounds in the centre and the training grounds and parklands on the surrounding plain. At the time it only had a population of about 500,000,[11] but because armed forces everywhere like to hang onto their land, it still has large tracts of woodland and parkland near the centre – unusually for an Indian city. It calls itself 'the Garden City' and in a way it still is.

After independence, the fact it was a military centre made it the natural place to develop the main Indian defence industries.[12] It was put to me, only slightly mischievously, that India wanted to make sure its defence research was located as far as possible from China in case the country were invaded. Thus India's space and nuclear programmes were both developed from Bangalore.

The key educational establishment has been the Indian Institute of Science, popularly known as the Tata Institute because the industrialist J. N. Tata[13] was the key mover in founding it in 1909. It is now one of only two Indian higher-education establishments in the world top 500, as ranked by the Shanghai Jiao Tong University.[14]

In addition, the old airport moved on from being a wartime servicing and repair centre for military aircraft to become the main aircraft manufacturing centre, which it still is.

Put all this together and by the 1980s Bangalore had become India's main hub for high-tech industry, research and education.

Then the internet came along.

The communications revolution hit Bangalore in a number of waves. During the 1980s it was mostly large US companies, such as General Electric and Citibank, that tapped into the mass of well-educated but not too expensive Indian graduates to write basic software codes for them. Home-grown companies, such as Infosys, Wipro and Tata Consulting, grew on the back of foreign software contracts. Then, during the 1990s, came a wave of call centres and back-office services such as accounting. Next, after the Millennium, Bangalore started to move further up the skills chain, with companies including Intel, Oracle and Microsoft building up genuine R&D capacity. The latest wave has been biotechnology.

Part of the workforce comprises the huge output of Indian software and computer engineering graduates. Bangalore itself produces some 25,000 a year, almost as many as the whole of the USA put together.[15] But the most recent phenomenon has been US-based staff, mostly of Indian origin, coming to Bangalore to do their work.[16] As a result, there are clusters of gated communities between the city and the science parks that look just like the communities in Silicon Valley. We looked round a mini California called Palm Meadows, with its clubhouse, sports centre, library, supermarket and so on. Aside from the density – the homes were crammed together much more closely than they would be in the States – you could think you were in the USA. In a strange way, these new Bangalore residents are creating an Indian version of the American lifestyle, separate from those of the rest of

India – in much the same way the British had created for themselves an Indian version of the British lifestyle 100 years earlier.

Any city that goes from half a million to six million in sixty years becomes a city of immigrants.[17] In the case of Bangalore, it is mostly immigrants from the rest of India rather than the rest of the world. This has worked remarkably well, giving it a cosmopolitan and toler-ant flavour. On the one hand there has been a willingness to accept inward migration, and on the other a willingness of the immigrants to pitch in and do their bit for the community.

I suppose there is an element of chance in almost every success story – the combination of a set of circumstances, the right institu-tions, a group of like-minded people and so on. But there is still a puzzle to Bangalore's success. Why this city and why not other, better-established ones?

To try to calibrate the importance of the various elements of the story, I asked a group of leading residents gathered by my friends. Among them there were a famous author and journalist, a transport consultant, the founder of a hi-tech business and a yoga teacher. We sat round the table of a Mediterranean-style restaurant, packed with the young, stylish professionals who abound in Bangalore, having a champagne brunch.

The first point of agreement was its diversity. Bangalore happened to be on the boundary of three main language areas: Telugu, Tamil and Kannada. There was a comfortable relationship between the reli-gions, with mosques, temples and churches side by side.[18] There had not been a riot, or indeed any war, for the past 200 years. There was something of the coastal trading culture of south India, so although it was not on the coast, it was a natural place for people to do business.

The next element was education. The Tata Institute, of course, has been crucial, but there was also the wider point that this has been a place where the state has invested in science, by making it the largest single complex in India for government-funded scientific activity.

The third was physical location – the weather, though the nights are not as cool as they were a generation ago, but also the availability of land and, so far at least, adequate water supplies. It is a shame to lose good farmland but for the time being Bangalore can sprawl outwards in every direction. As for water, you do have to insert a caveat, for the main supply is pumped up 1,000 feet from the Kaveri River,[19] and that may become a serious constraint on growth in the future.

The one element, it was explained to me, that was not part of the city's success was the government. Yes, national government had made it the country's premier centre for state-owned hi-tech industry. But neither it, nor the state government, nor the municipality have had a significant role in boosting the city as a centre for private industry from India or abroad. There has been very little investment in infrastructure: roads are inadequate and the first stage of a rapid-transit system is still to be completed.[20] Power supplies frequently fail. Municipal bus services are being upgraded but have lagged far behind demand. And the airport saga – the new Bangalore International was fourteen years in the planning, the postponements, the red tape and the construction – became a national scandal.

Why? Well everyone seems to agree on this: corruption is a serious barrier to getting large projects done. However, I think there is a deeper flaw in the Indian public sector that goes far beyond the failures to provide good services. It is the compartmentalization of responsibility within the public sector – that each part only does the things it is legally required to do. Since providing high-quality infrastructure requires an enormous amount of co-operation between departments, things just do not get done.

What is astounding is the way in which private companies have got round these barriers, basically by setting up parallel services for their employees – electricity supplies, transport, healthcare, sometimes even accommodation.

But while they can patch some things, they cannot patch everything, giving a certain fragility to the city's success.

2. WHAT ARE THE LESSONS?

Bangalore's stellar progress to becoming India's capital of the information industries has been largely unplanned. It was the result of contributions from both public and private sectors that happened to combine and have an unintended consequence. It was the mix of being both a military quarters and a centre for scientific education that led the Indian government to locate its nuclear and space research there. But military high-tech industries are quite different from commercial hi-tech industries and I think it was partly luck that a number of companies, foreign and domestic, chose to locate there.

But not entirely luck. Higher education and high-tech industries require talented people, and to attract these people requires a place that can make them feel happy and fulfilled. Being a military centre alone would not have triggered this. Being a base for state-owned industries might have done, but only if the educational facilities were there too. My own first big lesson from Bangalore was that the best thing that can happen to a city is to have top-end university and other educational establishments located there. If you bring in enough clever people, they will figure out how to make the place hum.

The next lesson follows from that: critical mass matters. One of the paradoxes of a world of hugely capable and near-free telecommunications is that while in theory this enables online services to be located anywhere, in practice those services will tend to be clustered together. That same telecommunications capability enables centres of excellence to deliver their output anywhere. Yes, the economic playing field has been flattened, but the same forces that flattened it have also created new peaks – and higher peaks than would have been possible before the communications revolution.

Clever human beings need other clever human beings. They need them to co-operate with, sometimes to compete against, to socialize with, maybe to have families with. So they cluster together. A world where human capital is the key form of capital is a world of peaks and plains.

This puts a premium on places becoming and remaining attractive places to live. A city cannot do much about its weather but a city can try to make sure that its economic growth does not damage its attraction. It is true Bangalore's growth has led to a deterioration in its quality of life in a number of ways. Obviously there is the traffic congestion, not helped by the tardiness in building a ring road and a highway to Chennai. Both of those projects are now happening, though slowly, and Bangalore is at last putting in a mass-transit system, which will help further.

But, and this is the central point, the fact remains that the city is an easier place in which to have a middle-class lifestyle than other large Indian cities. The quality of the private sector services, both those provided by the large companies and those that have sprung up in response to demand, is high. The infrastructure has to be acceptable but if the other services people need – housing, schools, shops, restaurants – are good, people will put up with traffic jams.

A central ingredient of places that are attractive to mobile talent is diversity. This is not one of the elements that the pollsters include when they are researching their league tables of the top cities. They measure hard variables, such as the time taken to get to work, not soft ones such as the variety of people in the streets. To a Londoner, Bangalore does not appear diverse because nearly everyone there is Indian. But to an Indian, it does, because they are different sorts of Indians, speaking different languages and with different cultures and religions. Somehow they make it feel a welcoming place to newcomers, which I suppose is unsurprising as it is a city of newcomers.

Last, there is the most obvious lesson of all. It is that one of the key elements of economic success is a spirit of openness among the people. Other things are 'nice to have': Bangalore could cope better with the infrastructure problems if it had better governance: better planning (and less corruption) would have ensured that its new airport was opened on time, for the road links would have been in place; the municipal bus service would have been improved earlier. Other cities, for example Hyderabad, have started to challenge Bangalore, using better infrastructure as a principal weapon.

But resourceful private business can get round these troubles.

There are, however, things that are absolutely 'must have' and Bangalore seems to have them. These include physical safety and low crime. They include cultural diversity. They include good education. And they include welcoming incomers. If people are paid enough, many of them will put up with a lot of discomfort and maybe even some danger. But that increases the cost of doing business and renders an economy vulnerable to competition.

There are challenges to Bangalore, of which more in a moment, but for the time being the success story rolls on.

- **Bring in clever people – they will make the place hum**
  - **Critical mass matters**
    - **Diversity attracts talent**

3. WHAT COULD GO WRONG?

There is a huge question and a number of second tier ones.

The huge question is whether India's extraordinary economic growth run, to which Bangalore has contributed significantly, can continue. You have to remember that certainly until the early 1980s, arguably until the early 1990s, India had failed to achieve its economic potential. People spoke dismissively of the 'Hindu rate of growth' – the notion that India might grow at around 3 per cent a year, enough to maintain the standard of living of the increasing population but not to make any real inroads into poverty. That all changed, particularly from the early 1990s onwards, and Bangalore became a standard-bearer for the new successful India. That seems set to continue. For what it is worth, the early signs are that India is coming through the 2009/10 global downturn in relatively good shape, and certainly much better shape than any major developed country economy.

Whatever happens to the Indian economy as a whole, it is pretty clear that Bangalore's momentum will not fade for a while yet. It has achieved critical mass and that will continue to attract new foreign enterprises to the city, as well as fostering the growth of domestic ones. There is capacity to grow – the office campuses being built in the new science parks and the (slowly) improving infrastructure will ensure that. But obviously were the Indian economy to slow down, perhaps as a result of the sort of bureaucratic restrictions that held the country back until the 1990s being reimposed, then Bangalore would take a hit. It would continue to be successful in Indian terms but this is a global game. There are certainly plenty of other cities in Asia that would take advantage should Bangalore's growth falter.

But it would be very hard for any one city to escape a national economic reversal, and I would wager that Bangalore would figure out some way to keep itself ahead.

However, it will face serious challenges – secondary issues when set against the issues faced by India, but serious nonetheless. This is two-way: because Bangalore is a beacon for the country, what happens there will influence what happens in India. So it does matter to every-one that the city can cope better with these challenges. Talking with our friends in that restaurant, three main problems kept coming to the fore.

The first was infrastructure – obvious but unrelenting. Pressure on the city will mount as growth continues and the question seems to me to be whether, by sprawling yet further, Bangalore can become, like Los Angeles, a true multi-centre city. But it has to be one where, unlike LA, people do not have to travel from one end to the other from work to home. Imagine LA without the freeways; people would cope because they would have to, but their lifestyles would be quite different. If other cities offered similar employment prospects and a better quality of life, then businesses would move.

This leads to the second challenge – that from other cities. A number of places are making a credible attack, chief among them Hyderabad, Pune, Chennai and even Kolkata. None has the unique combination of qualities that has propelled Bangalore to stardom, but each has particular advantages. Thus Hyderabad is almost as large a city as Bangalore, is cosmopolitan in the sense that it is a meeting point between north and south, and has a pleasant climate and much better infrastructure. It also has ambition: it is constructing the tallest building in India and its airport has the longest runway. Pune benefits from being part of the wider Mumbai commercial complex, is an education centre, has a good climate – and is now pushing five million in population. Chennai, the former Madras, has history, scale and already is the second largest exporter of software in India, after Bangalore. And then there is Kolkata, the former Calcutta, until 1911 the capital of British India and, until the 1980s, still the largest urban conurbation in India. It is at last recovering from the period of economic decline from the 1960s onwards and, while it has struggled to attract much foreign inward investment, its revival since the 1990s has in fact been led by the IT sector. It is not to be written off.

Industries do not move easily but these other cities can and probably will chip away at Bangalore's lead in IT. They have in a way been inspired by Bangalore but there is also a certain jealousy: if it, why not us? And they can offer lower costs, which, as the industry matures, will become a more and more important advantage.

The third potential problem is that Bangalore might miss the next hi-tech industry that comes along behind IT. We cannot know what this will be. Maybe biotechnology – that would be the obvious candidate and it is certainly being talked about as the next boom. Some biotech firms will undoubtedly be located there, and in 2009 the signs were encouraging. But it may not become the key centre – that role is still to play for – and other cities such as Pune may have the edge.

I like Bangalore. One long-term resident of Mumbai complained to me that there was not the drive she was used to – people did things more slowly. But there is a fizz to the street scene on Bangalore's Mahatma Gandhi Road – the boulevard along the south side of the British army parade ground, where the fashionable shops and coffee bars cluster and the fashionable young shoppers throng in and out of them. It is a city where a lot of young people are doing well for themselves, better perhaps than they could anywhere else in India. They want to celebrate their success and to be seen to do it. This sense of youthful achievement gives a bounce to the city that is very attractive. This is not a place that feels fragile.

So I guess this city's growth is assured for another decade or two, maybe longer. If this proves right, it will be the ingenuity and energy of the people on MG Road, as everyone calls it, that make it succeed. It will not be the high-ups of local politics. You see, Bangalore does not have old money, like Mumbai or Delhi. It has young professional self-made couples seeing it as place to be successful, to raise their families and have a happy life. A lot of families have double incomes and a good support system. They love it. And while they continue to love it, the city will love them in return.

China

CHAPTER SIXTEEN

The
Municipality
of Shanghai
Driving the emerging financial capital

1. WHAT IS THE STORY?

If you want to catch a feeling for what drives China's largest city, go down of an evening to the Huangpu River that runs through it. Stand on the bank, either on the raised parapet on the Bund side of the city or the walkway on the new Pudong side, and look at the traffic on the river. If you catch the tide right, it is a mass of boats, their diesel engines pounding them upstream or down: large prosperous cargo vessels, ferries scurrying backwards and forwards, tugs towing barges, small dark lighters so low in the water that it looks as though each wave might swamp them. And then look around at the young couples beside you, well dressed and prosperous, maybe taking photos of each other or just watching the boats go by. And look at the early twentieth-century commercial palaces that line the Bund and the soaring skyscrapers in Pudong. There you have the twin aspects of Shanghai

– the commerce and industry that drive it – and the young professionals who are seizing its opportunities – and the physical representation of its two great bursts of growth, that of the early twentieth century and the one happening right now.

The Shanghai phenomenon astounds everyone who goes there. There are many other fast-growing cities in China, other cities that are driving the Chinese economic boom. There are many other municipalities with great ambitions. There is Beijing, 650 miles away, with its new airport, tower blocks, ring roads and 'birdcage' stadium, a legacy of the Olympics. But there is nothing on the scale of Shanghai in terms of wealth generation – no other place where thoughtful and determined top-down planning combines so well with local bottom-up entrepreneurial zeal. Indeed Shanghai's relationship with Beijing is one of the great tensions of Chinese politics: as Shanghai citizens say, Beijing spends the money that they earn.[1]

It was international trade during the second half of the nineteenth century and the first of the twentieth century that catapulted Shanghai from being a sleepy fishing town to a great global metropolis, the country's main window on the world. The city was forcibly made to look outwards by having large chunks taken over by foreigners, who created concessions, enclaves where local laws did not run.[2] You might say it must have been humiliating to have what was to become your largest city controlled by outsiders, and indeed it was, but in economic terms it worked – as you can see on the Bund, a testimony to Shanghai's wealth in the early years of the last century.[3] It suffered during the Second World War when it was occupied by the Japanese, but it recovered, though as it turned out only briefly. In 1949, on the eve of the Communist takeover, it had the third-largest stock exchange in the world after New York and London.

Then came a generation and a half of slumber. The bankers and merchants fled to Hong Kong, making it the most important finance centre in the time zone. The city missed out on the initial reforms of Deng Xiaoping in the 1980s, when Shenzhen, the mainland village close to Hong Kong, was chosen as the experimental special zone where capitalist ideas could be tried out. It was only from 1992 onwards, after a visit to the city by Deng, that Shanghai started the climb back towards its former glory.[4]

Then came an astounding decade. After an investment famine lasting more than fifty years, Shanghai completely renewed its creaking urban infrastructure. In the space of ten years it built new ring roads, new elevated highways, a mass-transit underground system, new tunnels, new bridges, an opera house, new Western-style hotels, hundreds of new office blocks and a new airport. The most astounding thing of all was the development of Pudong, which had been a quiet residential and farming area, into the hi-tech city that now features on every brochure about Shanghai.[5]

How? Why? If Shanghai were just riding on the Chinese boom, then it would be a straightforward enough story. Of course, to some extent that is exactly what Shanghai has been doing. It is the country's largest city,[6] its largest port, the mainland's largest financial centre and its main communications hub, and it has the largest stock of hard-working, entrepreneurial and ambitious people. So, of course, it was going to do well out of the country's economic growth. But there is something more. Shanghai has had a municipal government whose grand vision was to restore the city's status as the principal financial centre not just of China but the entire East Asian time zone. And it has shown the determination and attention to detail to make a good fist of achieving just that.

There is a dark side to Shanghai's boom and there have been sizeable investment errors, of which more later. But in terms of its achievements in a small space of time, the city's municipal government must rank number one in the world.

I spent a day with local officials talking about the way they had approached the city's development. Four things emerged from these conversations. The first was the sense of looking to the very long term. Although the actual municipal plans were only done on a fifteen- to twenty-year horizon, there was a sense that the decisions would shape its future for a century and more. So you plan big, even too big, because eventually the economy will catch up. The Pudong development is the great example of this 'think big' mentality.

Second, there was no nostalgia, only pragmatism. The city's economy would inevitably shift away from manufacturing to service industries, and it would have to cope with that. Old buildings that no longer fulfilled their economic function would be torn down, even if it meant displacing people. If there were aspects of the city's heritage that pulled their weight, such as the historic buildings on the Bund, they should be preserved.

Third, there was a recognition that any great city has to develop artistic and educational clout. Most cities realize this but Shanghai has been as single-minded and committed here as it has with its investment in infrastructure. It has built a world-class opera house and theatre; there are new art galleries and new museums. It also built new campuses for several universities, including the Jiao Tong University. This is arguably one of the nation's best and certainly its best-known, having pioneered the global ranking of world universities – a league table that has spawned many imitations and struck fear or delight into universities around the world. Jiao Tong dates back to 1896 and is jointly administered by the government and the Shanghai municipality. But since the 1990s the money that has driven its growth has come from Shanghai; the city has invested in its brains. Aside from Jiao Tong, there are sixteen universities in the city and its suburbs.[7]

And finally there was the attention to detail. For example, the plans for the city's economic development have been thought through exhaustively, right down to the proportion of jobs that might be expected to develop from particular sectors. In the medium term, Shanghai has to shift from being principally a manufacturing city to principally a service one, with financial services as the main driver of growth. The point is not whether this will happen – it will – but rather that the planning shows up where pressure points might arise.

Of course, things do not always work out as planned. Anyone who flies into the new airport in Pudong will wonder why the quickest way to the centre is still to take a taxi or a minibus, and not the Maglev train that runs at up to 270 miles per hour. The reason is that the journey takes longer by train because its end is a suburb in

Pudong; you still have to make your way in from there. The plans to extend the Maglev to the centre and on to the old airport on the other side of the city have been dropped, at least for the time being and instead the regular underground system is being extended to the airport.

Another example of poor planning is the stock exchange. It opened in 1990 with the largest trading floor in Asia, and it is huge – bank upon bank of dealing stations stretching out into the middle distance. But there is hardly anyone there: when we looked out from the viewing platform, there were half a dozen people on the floor, sitting and chatting. What has happened is that trading migrated from the floor to online dealing at about the time the floor was opened, so the entire investment has in effect been wasted. Maybe from a symbolic point of view there is some value, but to the outsider it is hard to see it.

There are many other examples of badly planned investment. Changing trains at the central subway station at Renmin Square, where the underground lines intersect, involves a long hike because the stations are on different sides of the square. It has been improved but it is still confusing, even apparently to locals. There is also a dinky little 'sightseeing tunnel' under the river between the Bund and Pudong that serves very little function and very few people.

So it would be wrong to pretend that every decision the city has made has been for the best. But the defence, surely, is that some waste is inevitable in any giant city, particularly one that has to play catch-up. There are plenty of examples in the West of cities overbuilding and taking years to fulfil the dreams of their planners. The extraordinary thing about Shanghai is that, so far, this is a dream that has broadly come true. And the dream works its magic on visitors. Every time I have left Beijing, I have felt a sense of relief; every time I have left Shanghai, I have wanted to go back.

2. WHAT ARE THE LESSONS?

The first thing to be clear about is that there is a certain continuity in the life of great cities, and any new administration has to build on that. My argument on Shanghai is that its municipal government has been dealt an interesting hand of cards – and played it with skill and flair. Within that hand there are several long suits. One is scale, not just of population but also of economic activity: even during the dreadful days of the Cultural Revolution, it looks as though Shanghai's economic output continued to creep upwards.[8] But beyond scale there was embedded entrepreneurial competence, which the years of oppression from Beijing had not entirely crushed. I am told that even when the population of China was required to dress in blue overalls, the cut and cloth of the Shanghai people's overalls was just a little smarter than that of other cities. These people have long wanted to do it right.

There are other examples of a city's citizens working successfully with their municipal government to bring it back to what they might see as its rightful place in the world after some kind of economic, social or military disaster. St Petersburg has recovered its role as Russia's cultural capital, Tokyo as Japan's principal generator of wealth, steadily outstripping is old rival, Osaka. But equally there are instances where cities do not really recover properly. For example, Berlin's progress since the reunification of Germany has been disappointing: two decades after the Wall came down, it is still an economic backwater, still a city too large for its present population. And arguably it took London two generations before it fully got over the destruction of the Second World War. Why are some cities able to bounce back from disaster while others find it harder?

Part of the answer is that any city's economic prosperity will depend on the performance of the economy as a whole, and Shanghai has been boosted by China's extraordinary growth run. But success, I suggest, is also dependent on two other elements: infrastructure and glitz.

Great cities have to be places where people can get about easily, of course, but beyond this they have to create a buzz about themselves – a sense of glamour, a feeling of being a city where hard-working, ambitious people should try to make their mark. And one without the other does not work: you need to have both.

Infrastructure does not have to be perfect but it has to be good enough. In Shanghai it had been so neglected that a huge investment programme was essential: new roads, bridges, tunnels, the start of the metro system and so on. But the most important single element of that programme was one of town planning rather than just investment – the extension of the city from the west bank of the Huangpu River across to Pudong. Shanghai was lucky in that it had the possibility of that great leap eastwards, but the way in which this has been executed bears the imprint of a grand vision. The idea was that you would not be able to claim the city had recovered its status as the principal financial centre of the entire time zone if you simply rebuilt it on its early twentieth-century footprint; you had to take the city further. But that extension would not do the job of inspiring the world unless you built on a scale that would convey the magnitude of your ambition.

You can see this by travelling around Pudong – not just the glittering towers on the riverside but the hinterland, with country clubs, executive housing, golf courses, swish office parks. The flat, featureless landscape is being turned into a suburban parkland, giving the new middle class the lifestyles their peers would expect in the West.

To be sure, this is happening all over China: on the outskirts of every city there are executive estates, and entire new dormitory towns are being built as copies of Western ones. In Beijing the entire metropolis has been ripped up and rebuilt with giant office tower blocks and enormous (and perpetually clogged) ring roads. But what Shanghai has done is more visionary. When you look across from the Bund, it is not just another set of modern blocks such as you might see in every fast-growing city in the world. What you see is ambition, for there is nothing quite like that iconic view anywhere else on the planet.

So the lessons for other municipalities seem to me to be threefold. First, the vision of the planners should be consistent with the history and ethos of the city. Second, the infrastructure they put in must be good enough. And third, there has to be a sense of the special – that what is being done is in its way going to be world-class. Shanghai scores on all three counts.

- **Vision must be consistent with history and ethos**
- **Infrastructure must be good enough**
- **Convey the magnitude of your ambition**

3. WHAT COULD GO WRONG?

Every large city in China is suffering growth pains, most obviously pollution and congestion, and Shanghai has its share of these. To some extent they will curb its growth. But to focus on this point is to miss the city's biggest challenge: within a generation Shanghai will cease to grow – China's one-child policy will see to that. Already the city has one of the lowest fertility rates in the world, around 0.7 babies per mother in 2008,[9] with population growth being maintained by inward migration – young people flocking into the city to take up the jobs that economic growth has generated. But inexorably, as the population ages, the city will come to feel different. All of China will feel different for the same reason, but the transformation will be most marked in its largest city: Shanghai's population will become the oldest anywhere on earth.

So a first question must be: how will the Shanghai authorities manage this transition? It is a challenge that will require a quite different mindset from the present driving ambition, and the people who run Shanghai may not be suited to the task. Who these people are, of course, has changed over the years, but the change has been particularly marked as the city has been caught up in national politics with inevitable casualties. Beijing needs the revenues from Shanghai but resents the power that this gives its rival. Among the casualties has been its high-profile mayor, Chen Liangyu, who was jailed for eighteen years for corruption in 2008.[10] Anyone who delves into corruption in China would hardly be surprised by the story. This is something that the whole of China has to tackle and doubtless Shanghai has its market share of that.

The transition it has to make is not only towards more ethical standards of official behaviour; it is equally towards a way of making decisions sensitive to the wishes of the ageing population. The people within the municipality who have been driving change have had the same broad ideas about where they would like to see Shanghai go. The issue now is whether the next generation of leaders can help make the city a kinder, gentler place – one that can still generate economic growth but also create the welfare system needed to help support its growing army of elderly citizens.[11]

It is neither kind nor gentle now. It is not hard to catch sight of the dark side of the city. For me, the most poignant glimpse of the disruption that its bounding growth has caused came when riding out through the suburbs to the nearby city of Suzhou on a train. As we began to pick up speed after leaving the station, I glanced to my left to see we were passing an area that had been cleared for redevelopment. Only one house, a grey brick one, was still standing. And just at that moment when we swept by, an elderly women, clearly in some distress, was being carried out of the building by what I presumed was her family. Another couple of seconds and we were past. There was no way I could know the full story and I am sure much worse things happen than an eviction – all over the country and often, probably, in more brutal circumstances. But that image of misery, that tableau of troubled people set against the grey tooth of the home, will remain with me.

For the next few years the bulldozers will continue, the skyscrapers will rise, the masses will flock in and this great city will keep growing. But the nature of the growth will change from making things to providing services, and the municipal authorities need to be sensitive to that too. I was much impressed by their planning, in particular their acceptance that manufacturing should become less important;

this is not something that is easy for politicians in the West to acknowledge, let along encourage. But service industries require a different approach to manufacturing; they are more fragmented, more subtle, more surprising. They need to be nimbler in response to twists of demand. They do not need so much investment in physical capital; instead they need investment in human capital. A Google needs a different form of investment from a General Motors and the Shanghai authorities need to adapt to that.

Errors have already been made, like that construction of a huge physical trading floor for the stock exchange just as trading went electronic. You build financial services by encouraging talent to move in, and by creating the conditions where it can thrive; you do not do it by building a factory. That requires a much more 'hands off' approach than Shanghai is accustomed to. The authorities must provide the legal and administrative framework to international standards.

But here lies another problem, because the phrase 'international standards' may raise a hollow laugh among any locals familiar with Shanghai's not-so-distant past and the controlling nature of the businessmen who arrived from abroad. If the second coming of Shanghai's economy in 1992 was made at home then it is fair to say that it could have been no other way, accompanied as it was by severe restrictions on foreign investment, foreign ownership of companies and any multinational groups seeking to float on the stock exchange. That sense of exclusion has not been so marked since China's accession to the World Trade Organization in 2001, and gradually these restrictions have been lifted, if tentatively and amid a welter of bureaucracy, so that cross-border joint ventures have proliferated and overseas companies have moved closer to a listing on the Shanghai market.[12]

But now the authorities must take the next step. They must welcome foreign enterprises and give them real freedom – rather than seeing them as some sort of partner in a joint enterprise from which the foreign secrets can be stolen. Stolen? That is a harsh word to use and Shanghai residents bristle at it. From an outsider's perspective, though, it seems fair for we are rooted in the notion from our schooldays that you should not take other people's ideas and pretend they are your own. From a Chinese perspective, it is simply being a quick learner, surely a prized quality everywhere. An example: if you look at the cars on the streets in Shanghai, you will see a lot have VW badges and seem pretty much like their European counterparts. They are made locally in a joint venture dating back to 1984, the Shanghai Volkswagen Automotive Company. This has been very successful. However, there are also cars that look like VWs but are badged differently. They are virtually identical and apparently of high quality, except that they sell for one-third less than the originals. Now in Shanghai there have been complaints that VW did not share its technology.

In manufacturing it is possible to reverse-engineer products, and in China there are copies of BMWs, even something that looks like a Rolls-Royce Phantom. But it is much harder to reverse-engineer a financial services company, where the output is not a physical thing that can be replicated but rather a service to the customer. Japan found it very hard to build up a competitive global banking system and the country made huge errors in its international investment programme. Japan's slump in the 1990s hangs over Chinese economic planning, for there are obvious similarities between the long post-war Japanese boom and the present Chinese one. Part of the Japanese problem stems from financial inexperience and China needs to avoid that. This is a matter for the country as a whole, rather than the municipal government of Shanghai, but Shanghai would suffer more than anywhere else.

So the transition the city has to make is not just a shift from manufacturing to services but one towards an international outlook, building up and when necessary importing Western-style financial skills. If it is to become a global financial centre, it must be a magnet attracting global players. Western banks and other institutions are there but find limits on their activities.

A bit of symbolism. The initials of the British bank HSBC stand for Hongkong and Shanghai Banking Corporation and its former Shanghai headquarters is a magnificent domed palace to commerce on the Bund. After moving its Chinese base to Hong Kong at the time of the Communist takeover, it is now back in the city, but in an unremarkable tower on the other side of the river in Pudong. Its former HQ, beautifully restored, is occupied by the Pudong Development Bank. You can gaze up to the dome of the banking hall, with its murals of the great commercial centres of the world as perceived in the 1920s, but the subliminal message is that China is in charge now and foreigners must know their place.

Yet if Shanghai is really to achieve the ambitions of its leaders to become the main financial centre of East Asia, it will have to open up and offer the same sort of welcome to international finance that Hong Kong has established and maintained post the end of British rule in 1997. Opening up will be particularly difficult for Shanghai, given its history. Any visitor does not need to listen hard to hear tales of the indignities that the foreign powers heaped on China during the nineteenth century. But foreign control was explicit in Shanghai, with its various foreign concessions where local laws were subsidiary to foreign legal systems and where foreigners had in effect taken over the administration of much of the city. That is what transformed it from being a small fishing village to a great trading metropolis, but it is not easy for the Chinese to admit that now.

This is not just a matter of losing face. As Shanghai becomes more successful as a financial centre, so it will become more international, and to some extent that will mean its local politicians lose control. The next stage will be different and in some ways harder.

This is a hard-working and hard-driving city. What it has achieved over the past two decades is astounding and has profound lessons for other cities with any ambition for themselves. It already represents a pinnacle of human achievement and its success story has such momentum that it has many chapters yet to come.

CHAPTER SEVENTEEN

The Hong Kong Jockey Club
Much more than gambling

I. WHAT IS THE STORY?

If you have not been to Hong Kong, do go. The view across the water to the island is one of the great urban sights of the world. You arrive at one of the great airports of the world. You are whisked in on the high-speed train or the network of motorways. You have the choice of some of the best hotels in the world. Even a simple meal showcases some of the best cooking you can find. And you have the people: successful, of course, hard-working, of course, and rightly self-confident. There is, though, something more than this. It is a sense that this is a society that is honourable, honest and free.

The seven million residents of Hong Kong enjoy a greater degree of economic independence than any other people on earth: the city-state regularly comes top of the world on this measure and did so again in 2009, ahead of Singapore, Australia and Ireland – with the USA, UK and Canada just behind. Consider these statistics taken from the Index of Economic Freedom compiled by the Heritage Foundation in Washington DC and the *Wall Street Journal*. First, fiscal policy: there is a standard rate of 15 per cent for income tax in Hong Kong, while the top corporate rate is 16.5 per cent. Then business freedom – and the absence of red tape: it takes less than half the world average of thirty-eight days to start a new company there. Or you could look at how low the barriers are set to trade – a tariff rate in 2006 of zero per cent – or the way in which Hong Kong encourages foreign investment by not applying any ownership restrictions.

All this, if you consider its historical background, is astounding. Neither British colonialism nor the People's Republic of China is noted for generating such freedom. The colonies had to organize their economies to generate wealth for the home country, while Communist China, for all its recent progress, has not been a haven for individualism. Yet together they have produced – on the admittedly narrow measure of economics – the freest society on the planet.

That last statement, of course, begs a series of questions about the relationship between economic freedom and political freedom. Which matters more? Can one be durable without the other? But as a visitor to Hong Kong over the years, another question seems to me to be more intriguing. It concerns a government that controls some things extremely closely, much more closely than in a typical European liberal democracy, yet allows huge freedom elsewhere. The obvious example is that the state owns all the land. Imagine that in 'big government' countries such as France or Sweden: it would be unthinkable for the farms to be nationalized or for people not to be allowed to own the land on which their homes were built. Yet owning the land is crucial to Hong Kong's public finances and in a way underpins the economic freedom noted above.

There is, however, another example that is probably more interesting and certainly more fun. The Hong Kong authorities run the world's best gambling organization, the Hong Kong Jockey Club. Really the world's best? Well, that is open to debate, of course, and may depend on whether you regard horse racing as the supreme form of gambling, or whether you prefer the gaming tables or slot machines. My vote would be for the horses. The point, though, is that the Jockey Club not only has some of the best facilities in the world but, and this is the crucial point, provides 6.5 per cent of the revenues of the Hong Kong government.[1]

That is some contribution – and to a very large pot. If you think of it as a real country, which in a way it is, Hong Kong has the seventh-highest GDP per head in the world.[2] And the money is used well: it is second only to Japan in terms of life expectancy[3] and, even more impressive, it has the fifth-lowest infant mortality rate,[4] after Singapore, Bermuda, Sweden and Japan. As this rate is generally accepted as a good test of the quality of healthcare, the Hong Kong government scores well against other advanced countries in terms of the provision of high-quality services. Yet it finances a significant proportion of this spending from a gambling monopoly – and aside from the tax contribution, the Jockey Club is also the largest giver to charity in Hong Kong.[5]

Gambling is also big business in other parts of the world, Monaco being the best example. But Monaco is tiny, a population of 32,000. Las Vegas runs on gambling but it is one medium-sized city in a giant country. In Hong Kong the sector may be a small proportion of the whole economy, but it is a big contributor to the development of infrastructure.

A gambling monopoly only brings in the revenue if it is well run and can manage, in the absence of competitive pressures, to maintain quality of service, adapt to changing market preferences and not take its privileged position for granted. The Jockey Club has been doing that since 1884, though racing at one of its two courses, Happy Valley, goes right back to 1846 when the British took over some swamp to create a venue for the sport. Once outside the settlement, it has now been enveloped by high-rise buildings and is ten minutes' walk from the harbour. The happy result is that people can drop in for an evening's racing after work every Wednesday.

The other course, Sha Tin, is in the New Territories, half an hour's drive from the island. It has more space, is surrounded by greenery

and feels lush and manicured by comparison. It holds its races at the
weekend and is the place where you feel you have escaped from the
pressures of the city. We went there one weekend to marvel at the
plush facilities and the order and calm of the proceedings – all the
beauty of the horses you will find at any top-flight meeting, but none
of the scruffiness or edge of a course in Britain.

Racing in Hong Kong is calm because it is a monopoly. All betting
is on the tote. There are no bookies; no one making the odds; everything is electronic. All off-course betting is run by the Jockey Club, as
is any sort of gambling in the city-state. No other gambling is allowed
– no casinos, no machines – because Hong Kong seeks to minimize
social problems by limiting the number of both places and activities
where its citizens can chance their arm.[6]

Naturally, though, people might want a flutter on something other
than horses; they are, after all, Chinese. So the club also runs betting
on football matches around the world and a lottery. Fancy a punt on
Hull City versus Tottenham or AC Milan versus Juventus? Or want to
pitch in for the lottery prize of HK$5 million? You know where to go.

There are two reactions to this. In one sense it is all too easy to have
a monopoly, enforced vigorously by the law, over such a basic human
urge as gambling. You do not need great commercial acumen, merely
reasonable competence, to be a success. Hong Kong could certainly
let private sector companies in. It could tax them and regulate their
performance. That is the successful model used around the world.

The other reaction, though, is to celebrate that it is possible and
maybe preferable in this most entrepreneurial of world cities to run
gambling as a state monopoly. It may seem anachronistic but it works.
Were gambling run by the private sector, there would surely be more
excess, probably more corruption, maybe more human misery, for
gambling can indeed lead to that. The contrasting experience of
neighbouring Macau shows the other way of running the industry,
because gambling there has been franchised out to private companies.
In terms of growth Macau has been much more successful, in 2006
passing Las Vegas to become the greatest gambling centre on earth.[7] It
accounts for 40 per cent of the former colony's GDP[8] and has

undoubtedly taken business from Hong Kong. But there has been a price in crime and corruption,[9] and in any case, there is always that threat of excess and the human toll it can exact. For the good of society as a whole, you can make a strong case that Hong Kong is a better model.

In fact, the Hong Kong Jockey Club has responded to the challenge of Macau. It has increased the number of race days,[10] gone into other events such as making its clubhouses available for weddings and exhibitions, and generally tried to make its pitch more attractive to younger people. It is flexible, pragmatic and appropriate to the ethos of Hong Kong.

That leads to the much bigger story. Just as the Jockey Club gives freedom within defined limits for people to enjoy themselves, so Hong Kong's government does the same for people's livelihoods. Economic freedom is about doing the things you want to do but within the limits that society has to set out. This concept, as noted above, has been developed by the Heritage Foundation, which is normally described as a conservative think-tank. So some might feel that its enthusiasm for market solutions encourages it to underplay the weaknesses of the things it espouses, most notably small government. But in the case of Hong Kong, the facts speak for themselves. You might expect it to score highly on business and trade freedom – the speed and ease with which businesses can be set up and the few restrictions over importing and exporting goods and services. You might also expect it to perform well in terms of size of government and the low level of taxation. But you might be surprised at the very high scores achieved by Hong Kong for lack of corruption, as assessed by the independent organization Transparency International, which ranked Hong Kong fourteenth in the world in 2009, ahead of the USA and Germany. The level of protection for employees is quite high too,[11] for though the regulations are flexible, they are strictly enforced and declaring workers redundant is expensive.

Perhaps most notable of all is the direction Hong Kong has taken since it became a special administrative region of China. You might have thought it would start to slip down this league of economic freedom. Actually it has, if anything, improved its position since 1997, which is a considerable tribute to the Hong Kong government and indeed the authorities in Beijing. As a result, the former colony has maintained its economic progress, despite its high cost structure and despite the inevitable swings in the world economy.

Like so many Britons, I find the Hong Kong story thrilling. To look out on that waterfront from the Star Ferry is awe-inspiring. To have created an economy combining that level of GDP[12] with such excellent health outcomes, out of zero natural resources, is a massive tribute to the people who have done it. However, they have been able to achieve sustained growth by operating within a supporting legal and administrative framework. I am not trying to say that the Hong Kong government, either before the handover to China in 1997 or subsequently, is an ideal model for the rest of the world. Rather, there are elements in the Hong Kong system which do carry messages for the rest of us, as the next section seeks to highlight.

2 . WHAT ARE THE LESSONS?

Hong Kong's attitude to governance is almost Victorian in its self-confidence and sense of morality. It is at one level highly authoritarian. I have chosen its management of gambling as a microcosm of the way it runs the whole economy, controlling some things very closely though seeking to deliver quality and value in the facilities it provides. Its control over land use is similarly authoritarian. It is also very tough on drugs,[13] ironically so since the British colony's original wealth was derived from selling opium to the Chinese. (The Jockey Club, incidentally, now funds clinics that treat drug abusers.)

However, in terms of government spending as a percentage of GDP, Hong Kong's is very low at around 15 per cent[14] – much the same as that other authoritarian former British colony, Singapore. How does it manage to provide the social and other services at that level of spending? The answer is that people pay a contribution, even for services such as healthcare that are state-supported.

The result is that in serious economic downturns, and Hong Kong is as vulnerable to these as anywhere else, people who lose their jobs suffer serious distress. Those who fail to save for their old age suffer too. There is some safety net, probably a better one than in almost all other Asian countries bar Japan, but not at the level of Western Europe or North America.

So this is a different deal from the one presented to the citizens of the democracies of the West. The state pushes responsibility to the people, requiring them to provide for themselves as far as they reasonably can, and only steps in when absolutely necessary. In return for taking that responsibility for themselves, Hong Kong citizens have greater economic freedom than their counterparts in the West and also seem to manage to sustain better health and higher overall levels of educational achievement.

As far as health is concerned, for me the stand-out statistic is that Hong Kong has half the level of infant mortality of Aberdeen, the booming city of northern Scotland. Of course, the latter is much smaller but the two cities have a similar level of GDP per head and Aberdeen has much higher levels of public spending per head on healthcare. Yet on that mortality measure, Hong Kong is far ahead.

It is also ahead on secondary education. Hong Kong students rank in the top five countries in the OECD's huge PISA (Programme for International Student Assessment) study, which examines the abilities of 15-year-olds. It is far ahead of the USA and well ahead of the UK. In the 2006 study it was second only to Finland in science scores, which is self-evidently excellent. Better still, compared with previous years, it seems to be improving its overall performance.

At a time when most countries in the West are seeking to push more responsibility back to their citizens, there is surely a message here. Western governments are doing this because they find themselves unable to generate sufficient tax revenues to sustain the state infrastructures they have created. Demographic change has made the arithmetic even more alarming, as each generation of older people has to rely on a smaller and smaller cohort of people of working age to pay for their pensions and healthcare. The Hong Kong government faces all these pressures too. In one regard the problem is even greater, for the fertility rate there, at an estimated average of 1.02 children per mother in 2009,[15] is lower than in any Western European country. But its government model is ultimately more robust.

That is going to matter more and more as this century unfolds. How do governments meet the aspirations of their people without getting bogged down in the conflicting charges that they are not providing good enough services, or providing them at too high a cost?

You might say it is rather eccentric that the Hong Kong government should supply a service most people would not regard as essential – gambling on the horses – but be rather thin by developed world standards in its provision of state support for education, healthcare and pensions. Put that way, it seems a strange ordering of priorities.

But this seems to me to be the wrong response. Governments often take commercial activities under their wing if they feel their people need particular protection. A good European example is that of Sweden's monopoly over the retail sale of most forms of alcohol. So if a society judges that its public needs shielding – be it from excessive drinking or excessive gambling, be they Scandinavian or Chinese – then in both cases the government's response is rational and right.

There are surely some broader conclusions. One is that there is no universally appropriate boundary between the state and the private sector, either in the provision of services or in the financing of them. Lots of different models work perfectly well.

On the other hand there is a case for nudging people to take responsibility as far as is practicable for their education, healthcare, pensions and so on, rather than have the state take that responsibility away. Insofar as this can be done, you preserve state resources for helping the people who really cannot help themselves, and you also make it easier to deliver economic freedom.

Those freedoms, or at least most of them, surely matter – especially if they help deliver greater growth and hence higher living standards. They do seem to do that. But they also matter in themselves. It must surely be worth making it easier for people to start new businesses, or to protect their savings, or to spend more of the money they earn in the way they want to.

My point is not that Hong Kong is the right form of government for the world. Rather it is that there are elements of the Hong Kong model, both its restrictions and its freedoms, which other governments should take very seriously. This system has performed effectively under such different political umbrellas as British colonialism and Chinese Communism. So it must have something going for it.

- **Lots of different models work**
- **Nudge people to take responsibility as far as is practicable**
- **Freedoms matter**

3. WHAT COULD GO WRONG?

The story of Hong Kong is inevitably bound up with that of China itself. The Chinese economy is as buffeted by the swings in the world economy as any, and Hong Kong, which acts to some extent as an economic gateway to the mainland, is arguably more vulnerable than most cities or regions of the country. So as and when China's great economic run slows, Hong Kong will have to adapt, finding other ways of earning its living in the world.

This is an obvious challenge and, of course, what happens in China is beyond its control. The key, though, will be how nimble it can be in finding new things to do. There are lots of reasons for confidence, including the flexibility of the business community, the legal and regulatory framework and the 'good value' government – all the things that drive the city to the top of that economic freedom index. You cannot predict with any great confidence how Hong Kong will adapt because you cannot know, except in the broadest outline, how the challenges will develop. There must, however, be two broad concerns. One is the relationship with Beijing; the other the changes that are taking place to Hong Kong's population.

So many predictions have been made about the development of Hong Kong post-1997 – and so many of these have turned out to be wrong – that anyone adding to this pile has to step carefully. For me the seminal conversation was in the early 2000s, with a friend who at that time was editor of the main newspaper, the *South China Morning Post*. It was, he thought, extraordinary that China had not only fully observed the conditions of the formal 'One country, two systems' agreement under which it took control from the British, but that it had lived up to the spirit of it too. No other country in the world would have allowed one of its provinces the degree of autonomy that Hong Kong enjoyed. And China not only allowed it but supported it. At some times, he understood, Beijing would have liked the Hong Kong authorities to show more independence, rather than trying to second-guess what Beijing wanted.

Since then the relationship has settled down even more and it is now quite hard to see how the former colony's sense of independence might be challenged. This is a big point, for the independence is crucial to Hong Kong's openness to the world. Not-so-small point: the citizens of most of the developed world do not need a visa to visit Hong Kong, whereas they do to mainland China. Meanwhile, the mainland Chinese need a permit to enter Hong Kong. So while it is perfectly possible that the relationship between China and Hong Kong will deteriorate, it is hard to see any reason why it should.

My greater concern is what happens to the human capital of Hong Kong – the people who have made it a beacon for the rest of the world.

One obvious issue is the ageing of the population. Now the fertility rate is not as low as that of Shanghai[16] and at the moment its population is still increasing. Nevertheless it means that the city is relying on inward migration to maintain population growth and in another few years, as the population ages further, the size of the working population seems set to fall. That must affect its sense of dynamism. There will not be a sudden collapse of the economy and Hong Kong will probably be good at coping with the shift, but there will inevitably be some change of mood. It will become a less vibrant place.

The other issue is what happens to the education system; the secondary schools are indeed excellent but after that there is some way to go. There are encouraging signs. One is that a much greater proportion of students now receive their higher education in Hong Kong itself, rather than travelling abroad, than was the case a generation ago. Another is that three universities – the Chinese University of Hong Kong, the City University of Hong Kong and the Hong Kong University of Science and Technology – are ranked in the world's top 300 in the league table published by the Jiao Tong University of Shanghai.[17] That is impressive given the size of the population. There is, however, no really top-flight university, nothing in the top 100, and that should be an attainable target.

There is another concern you often pick up when talking with English-speaking residents – the use of English among the general population has slipped, in contrast to Singapore, where it has increased. The reason is that English is discouraged in Hong Kong, whereas in Singapore it is the official language. This is not picked up by the PISA study because English in Hong Kong is deemed a foreign language and these are not assessed.

Does this matter? Well, probably yes, not so much because of the language issue itself but for what it says about the place's attitude to globalization. Should it look north to Beijing or out to the rest of the world? Of course, it must do both but there is an inevitable tension. However optimistic one is about Hong Kong, and there are many reasons to be extremely optimistic, there is a certain fragility to it. The city-state can run things supremely well and the Jockey Club is an example of that. It provides a great platform for global businesses and has become a significant financial centre in its own right. But fragility gives edge. The knowledge that you have to try harder, have to drive on, has created a society that attracts admiration from around the world. Hong Kong's only resource is its people and those people have much to teach the rest of us.

Japan

CHAPTER EIGHTEEN

Public Safety in Tokyo
The world's safest giant city

I. WHAT IS THE STORY?

The world's biggest city is also its safest. The Tokyo conurbation has the largest collection of human beings on the planet. Take Tokyo itself, add in its port of Yokohama and the other surrounding cities that stretch across its plain and there are some 35 million people crowded together.[1] But they live in extraordinary harmony, for Tokyo is also the safest mega-city in the world. On all measures, bar one, it has the lowest crime rates: the fewest murders per head of population, the fewest rapes, lowest burglary rates, lowest levels of street crime and so on.[2]

Come to the exception in a moment; first focus on the achievement. The level of public safety is particularly evident to the visitor for you feel you are being looked after, cared for, as you walk around. Now, as opposed to in the early 1970s when I first visited the city, a foreigner is not an object of curiosity³ – people are almost surprised you *do not* speak Japanese, for so many non-nationals living in Japan now do. What has not changed is the sense that the community has responsibility for the individual, even if that individual is obviously foreign. Everyone who visits will have stories of the common courtesies, even if it is simply people putting themselves out to give directions. Those who lose something – leave their wallet on a train, say – will experience the supreme honesty of the city and its people: there is every likelihood they will get it back intact, with the finder going to considerable inconvenience to make sure that happens. Naturally the city is not totally crime-free, for no place ever is. But the chances of being attacked? Well, such events are so infrequent as to be almost negligible.

Such a benign atmosphere gives huge freedom to the city's citizens. Children can go on their own to school by public transport, or travel around at weekends. Young people can go out at night in perfect safety. Office workers who find themselves worse for wear after an evening bonding with colleagues in a bar can get home securely in the middle of the night.

It is also profoundly egalitarian. There are wealth differentials in Japan, but they impinge less on daily life than in Western Europe or the Americas. Richer people do not need to buy personal safety by, for example, taking a taxi home at night. They can use public transport, which given the distances and the traffic would probably be quicker anyway. There is no need for gated communities. There are, as in all large conurbations, poorer areas and wealthier ones, but the differences in safety between them are minimal.

So how does Tokyo do it? There are two broad strands to the answer. The first lies in Japanese society; the second in the way in which this society interacts with its policing system.

Japan's complex web of reciprocal obligations and mutual support is renowned and we caught a glimpse of that ethos ourselves many years ago when the house of some Australian/British friends, who lived on the outskirts of the Tokyo conurbation, burnt down. It was a gorgeous traditional house, some hundreds of years old (we had stayed there some months earlier), but it was completely gone. Mercifully they and their children were unharmed but they lost everything except the clothes they were wearing. The next day their neighbours made ready another house in the village which happened to be unoccupied; it was full of all the things they needed, from cooking equipment to clothes for the children. Everything was done for them, they were back in business and there was no question of payment at that stage. In fact, nothing was written down. But, of course, there was an obligation: in the months that followed, they were expected to return the objects they had been lent and make other reciprocal gifts or payments in line with the help they had been given.

The point about this story is that this sort of unspoken arrangement within a community can only exist if there is a very high level of trust and a sense of obligation. Other societies have this too; it is a survival pattern and one not necessarily confined to close communities. The basis of the Arab tradition of hospitality to strangers, for example, is that you never know when your own life might be at risk and dependent on the actions of other people. But Japan can be a harsh environment by the standards of other developed economies – earthquakes, tsunamis, fires – so it needs this strong social glue to hold it together.

These community bonds are reinforced by community policing. As long ago as 1874, Japan began developing the 'Koban' system of small community police boxes, often just an office set in a wall but staffed round the clock by three or four officers working in shifts.[4] Separate from the regular police stations, the scheme has evolved to the extent that there are now around 6,500 Kobans across the country and 1,200 in Tokyo, where much of the function of the attached officers seems to be to help strangers navigate their way through the city's impenetrable street system. Some 20 per cent of the city's police serve in these mini-stations so they are a visible reminder of police presence, rather like the foot patrols in London. Like the bobby on the beat, their job is to know the neighbourhood, but this operation differs in that the officers at each Koban visit every house in their patch twice a year, taking note of who lives there, their ages and their possible vulnerability. So the system is somewhere between the conventional idea of policing, to stop crime, and a wider social service to help the community in whatever way it needs.

The Koban system has its weaknesses. It has proved hard to adapt the traditional street corner box to an environment of tall buildings. Communications with residents tend to be through the managers of the estate rather than directly with the people who live there, which apparently does not work so well. It is also undoubtedly intrusive in the sense that its officers have a much greater knowledge of what goes on in every household or business than the police in most other developed countries. But in a society of shared aspirations and similar perceptions of the common interest, many would accept that intrusion is a price worth paying if it makes Tokyo the safest large city in the world.

There is, though, a dark side: the very high levels of gangster activity among the notorious yakuza. If street crime – 'disorganized crime' – is very low, the organized version is very high, much higher than in Europe with the exception of southern Italy, and probably higher than in North America too. Indeed it may be that the gangsters are part of the reason for the low rate of crime generally. As a top Japanese official told me: 'Without yakuza activity, we cannot explain Japanese security and economic and political activity.'

Much of the commercial activity of the city is in some loose way associated with the yakuza. One example is that large companies have sometimes had to pay the crime syndicates to avoid having their shareholder meetings disrupted, though that has recently been made illegal and such disruption has declined. Another is the protection money paid by small businesses to local yakuza groups. Still another is the occasional exposure of politicians who receive illegal funding. Further activities are the usual specialities of organized crime, including prostitution, drugs and gambling.[5] Certainly they are remarkably pervasive, and there are an estimated 80,000 to 100,000 people involved in the gangs in one way or another.[6]

Why so pervasive? This is not the place for a history of the movement but it is worth noting that the yakuza carry on a deeper tradition, that of feudalism: people pay their dues and in return are protected. This happens at an individual level but also at a national one. After the Kobe earthquake, much of the support operation was carried out by the yakuza and there was favourable comment that they acted far more quickly and effectively than the official relief effort.[7] To an extent unknown in the USA and even Italy, the yakuza have a semi-official status. They may not be generally admired or respected but they are accepted as a part of society, and while it is impossible to defend them, it may well be that overall crime is low because some of the 'policing' is done by the gangs.

To many people in Japan, that would seem rather shocking. It is all the more so because the yakuza are a considerable drag on many commercial activities, quite aside from the often brutal way in which they enforce discipline. Given their ability to disrupt normal business life, some companies find it more sensible to pay to keep things quiet.

This is both illegal and morally indefensible, yet still we may have to acknowledge that organized crime does exert a social discipline.

2. WHAT ARE THE LESSONS?

There are at least three broad lessons from Tokyo's experience in improving public safety. One is that policing has to be done at a local, even an individual or family level. A second is that cohesive societies with a strong collective identity can provide a higher level of security than their more individualistic counterparts. And the third is that Japan regards criminal behaviour almost as something to be cured, rather than simply putting the perpetrators in jail to keep them out of mischief.

The policing point is much the simpler. The Koban system has been tried elsewhere – for example, in Singapore, Indonesia and Brazil – and all with the involvement of the Japan International Cooperation Agency, which does show the readiness of these countries not just to import the idea but to do it well. Underscoring this enthusiasm, over 250 of the police boxes have been established in the sprawling Brazilian state of São Paulo since the scheme was introduced in 1997, and there are around 100 in the far more compact city-state of Singapore.[8] However, the results are not conclusive for a couple of reasons. First, the Indonesian experiment, in Bekasi, east of Jakarta, has only been up and running since 2005; as with São Paulo, to pass judgement on the effectiveness or otherwise of an initiative, and the extent to which it has embedded itself in the culture and changed attitudes, needs a longer view. Second, while Singapore's Koban system dates back to 1983, the state is a semi-authoritarian, low-crime one anyway, with the 'prevention' of community policing co-existing with the 'cure' of very tough sentencing, so it is hard to gauge exactly how much difference the Kobans have made.

Of course, that the system has been adopted so vigorously elsewhere is in itself a demonstration of faith, but I suspect that part of the reason why the system works in Tokyo is that the physical layout of the place makes it easier to police. This city is a series of many small villages that just happen not to have any land in between them, and Japanese houses are relatively small – most are on two storeys – and thin-walled. In many continental European cities, by contrast, people live in apartment blocks, while in North America the general pattern is suburbia. Accordingly people in Tokyo know much more about what is going on around their homes than is the case in a city where people live ten or more storeys above the ground or where all their transport is done by car rather than on foot. It may be that Japanese cities have as much to teach the world about designing the physical environment for safety as they do policing as such.

But we also know that policing does matter because there was a surge in crime between the late 1990s and 2002, with serious offences nearly doubling. This was met by a seven-point plan developed by the National Police Agency, of which the most significant point was much better information sharing between police and communities at a local level. Clear-up rates improved, with those for murder reaching 96 per cent in 2006. Clear-up rates for burglaries and robberies were lower, at around 60 per cent, but this is still very high by international standards.[9] Effective prosecution further discouraged criminals and though the figures for most crimes were not back down in 2007 to the level ten years earlier, there is, in the opinion of many Japanese, a reason for that: the number of immigrants is significantly higher.

That leads to the next point, the cohesive nature of Japanese society. You do not need to listen very hard in Tokyo to know who gets the blame for the rise in crime: it is foreign gangs targeting the city's citizens.[10] The influx of Chinese students is often cited, the point being that China is – or at least is perceived to be – a lower-trust society than Japan. Whether this is right or not, that Japanese people feel this way means perceived security has fallen as immigrant numbers rise. What can the rest of the world learn from all this?

It is difficult. We cannot all turn ourselves into being more Japanese in our attitudes, even if we wanted to. Moreover, there are many strains within Japanese society – strains that have increased as economic growth has fallen. One of the things that troubles people I have spoken to in Japan is the growing gap between young and old, with the young no longer feeling they should take responsibility for their parents' and grandparents' generations.

There are, however, some things that can be said. One is that there will always be a tension between individualism and collectivism and many Western societies feel the pendulum has swung too far towards the individual. There are signs that it is starting to swing back: the tougher policing and zero-tolerance policies in the USA (particularly New York), for example, and the UK's anti-social behaviour orders and other measures. What you cannot get away from is that insofar as it is possible to reinforce a sense of common community, one of the prime benefits is likely to be a reduction in crime.

Another point here is the notion that criminal behaviour is almost an illness that needs to be cured rather than an activity that needs to be punished. The self-image of the Japanese as a high-trust society in a way makes it easier to treat crime as an aberration and is therefore an effective weapon against recidivism. You can shame people; you can threaten to exclude them from wider society if they do not mend their ways; and you can persuade criminals that they need to be cured.

This does not always work by any means. There has been a rise in what the Japanese regard as abnormal crimes, including those where there might be some form of mental illness involved. And people can only be cured if this is what they want. But if you start from the position that the prime function of the judicial process is to treat people rather than punish them, well, maybe you find it easier to cut crime levels. One thing reinforcing this is that Japanese people are very sensitive to crime; they want to feel safe. So any action that seems to serve this aim will get a tailwind of popular support. You could almost say that Japanese people in general, and Tokyo residents in particular, have low levels of crime because that is what they demand. Other societies, maybe more concerned with the rights of the accused, cannot say the same thing.

As societies get older, there are two good reasons for expecting crime to fall. One is that there will be fewer young people, and it is young men who commit most crimes. The other is that voting power will be with the old and they are particularly vulnerable to crime. So they will vote in the politicians who are most effective at tackling it.

Maybe the purest lesson Tokyo has for the world is that citizens should demand less crime – in which case they might get it.

- **Policing must be done at a local, even an individual level**
  - **Cohesive societies provide a higher level of security**
  - **Is criminal behaviour something that can be cured?**

3. WHAT COULD GO WRONG?

There are two great threats to public safety in Tokyo. One is from organized crime; the yakuza; the other is from some kind of disaster, natural or otherwise, that overwhelms the authorities, leaving society vulnerable to a wider breakdown. In other words, public safety is partly about cutting crime at all levels and the emphasis up to now has been on that. But it is also about the flexibility of society in responding to unforeseen events.

Some people in Tokyo believe that the yakuza constitute the most serious threat to Japanese society. Their activities are interwoven with politics, parts of the commercial world, in particular construction, and to some extent the police. If that last point sounds disturbing, the reality everywhere is that for the police to function effectively, they must have some sort of relationship with the criminal community because that is where they get much of their information.

Maybe this should indeed be the greatest concern but my own instinct, as someone who greatly admires Japanese social organization but is not part of it, is that the questionable ability of Japan to cope with the unforeseen is even more troubling.

The Kobe earthquake was a warning, though not so much the earthquake itself, nor the errors in construction that the collapse of so many buildings revealed. No, the warning was in the uneven response by the authorities to the disaster – slow, ill focused and in some cases overly bureaucratic. As noted above, the swiftest response in relief work came from the yakuza.

Of all the world's great cities, Tokyo is surely the most vulnerable to another giant earthquake, sitting as it does close to the point where two fault lines meet. Since everyone is aware of that and a huge amount of effort has gone into designing buildings to be earthquake-proof, the city can believe with some confidence in its likely resilience; this is a known problem, expected and planned for. My concern is that there might be some combination of events – perhaps involving a natural disaster, a terrorist attack, perhaps some public health catastrophe – which the authorities would be unable to meet adequately.

To take a very different example, they responded poorly to the financial disaster of the early 1990s, condemning the country to more than a decade of lost growth. Japanese society was extremely resilient in the face of that: people pulled together, accepted a lower standard of living, rebuilt their savings, looked after those who had been particularly hard hit. The reaction of ordinary people was much more impressive than that of their leaders. But there was great misery, often concealed, among those who found themselves destitute through no fault of their own.

There have been various incidents in Tokyo, of which the subway gas attacks in 1995 were the most serious.[11] The response of the authorities to that act of terrorism was uneven and although the death toll was much lower than in the London underground attacks of 2005, there was a general perception that this owed everything to good fortune rather than careful planning.

So public safety in the world's largest urban conurbation seems and indeed is wonderful and deserves to be celebrated. True, it has not been tested under severe conditions and let us hope fervently it is not. Meanwhile seek to pick the bits of the Tokyo system, in particular the local policing, which could be applied elsewhere. Let us try to bring Tokyo's safety, and hence a key element in its quality of life, to the citizens of other great cities around the world. The world has a huge amount to learn from Japanese society.

Australia

CHAPTER NINETEEN

The Great Sporting Nation

How Australia trains the world

I. WHAT IS THE STORY?

Australia is the greatest sporting nation on earth. That is a statement to be challenged, of course, and at a number of different levels. Yet it has undoubtedly had a great record at successive Olympic Games since some very poor results in Montreal in 1976, rising high up the country medals tables to placings that have been exceptional given the size of its population. It also manages to get a relatively high proportion of its young people engaged in some form of physical activity. But more than all this, a sporting ethos gives identity to the nation – an ethos that at best manages to combine keen competition with the notion it is the game itself that matters, not just the winning. And this imbues Australia with a quality of openness, egalitarianism, directness and decency that any visitor quickly picks up. You feel it in the air. It is what makes this country such a special place. I have been to the five capitals of the mainland states and aside from the fact they are all by the sea, they are completely different. But they do have one thing in common: the interest and participation in sport. This is the glue that holds the country together.

This is a story that comes in two halves: excellence in official organized sport, including the hosting of probably the world's best Olympic Games; and the heritage of its less organized sibling – what ordinary people do outdoors. The first dates back to the Montreal Olympics, the second much earlier. But there is also a shadow, of which more in a moment.

Montreal was a disastrous games for Australia, since it sent 182 athletes there and did not win a single gold medal.[1] That shock led to serious soul-searching, for achievement in sport was something that many people felt defined the country. Australia did rather better in Moscow in 1980 and reached number four in the medals table at Athens in 2004.[2] True, it slipped back to sixth in Beijing,[3] behind the UK in fourth position, which was not something its citizens took lightly. But by any standards, sixth place for a nation of twenty-two million people – one-third of the UK population – is a terrific performance. That the UK did even better was actually a compliment to Australia, for Britain had adopted many of the processes of selection of elite athletes, as well as the training techniques, developed there.[4]

The focal point for Australian success was the creation of the Australian Institute of Sport in 1981,[5] which has become the model for elite sports training just about everywhere in the world. This is the showpiece for the body in overall charge of sport in the country, the Australian Sports Commission. The AIS has a 160-acre campus in the lush suburbs of Canberra and a total staff of nearly 200, with facilities there and in other cities. It funds a network of coaches on campuses all over the country and scholarships for particularly promising athletes. It supports some 700 athletes with equipment, science and medical facilities, accommodation, meals, travel and help with education and career planning. In the Canberra campus there are two arenas, an indoor swimming centre, a gymnastics hall, soccer and hockey fields, indoor training and a sports science building. In 2008 it had a budget of A$56 million.[6] Excellence does not come cheap.

Nor is excellence inclusive. The general public are encouraged to use many of the facilities, reasonably enough since they are paying for them. They can go for a swim in the pool. But a student cannot get accepted just because he or she is good at sport or interested in a career in it. The most important thing about the AIS is that is not some sort of specialized university teaching sports to large numbers of students. Its job is to help the elite – to pick the very best and push resources behind them to make them even better.

So how does it do it? The first thing is to spot them. The AIS has a National Talent Identification and Development Squad but the various states also have similar teams, seeking out talent locally.

You can see this best by looking at what happens in the less-populous areas. Obviously the big states such as New South Wales and Victoria have massive resources to throw at sports excellence. But those with relatively tiny populations mirror the national network in a thorough way. Take Tasmania, which only has 500,000 people. The Tasmanian Institute of Sport has a three-stage talent-spotting programme, starting in the schools where physical education teachers pick out promising youngsters and submit their results to a state identification co-ordinator. The scores of the best students are checked and then they are put through other, more scientific tests. The best of these students then choose the sport they want to go for and train under the eye of expert coaches, who select the best (again) to go into the talent development squads. At this stage they get more coaching, equipment if they need it and so on. The very best then step up and do the same thing at national level.

Or go to the Northern Territories, population 220,000. In Darwin, more than 1,000 miles from any other sizeable city, there is the Northern Territories Institute of Sport, with a staff of twenty, the same orderly talent identification programmes, the same coaching help and the same scholarships for outstanding athletes.

Starting age? Well in some sports, such as diving, they are looking for children as young as 9, but the more usual age would be 12.

Money? There are various levels of scholarships depending on whether the athlete is in the national squad, a national development squad or a junior squad. The key point is that no one with the potential to perform at a national level need abandon their sport because of a lack of finance. If you are really good, you will get the backing you need.

You will also get the facilities. That is one of the things at which Australia excels. You could measure this by the number of swimming pools and athletics tracks, or by the way sport is everywhere. There are no other great cities of the world where the outdoors is so evident: the sailing in Sydney Harbour, the rowing on the Yarra River in Melbourne, the beaches in Perth – the list goes on. But the quality of the facilities and more generally the status of sport were really brought home to the world by the successful staging of the Sydney Olympics in 2000.

The president of the International Olympic Committee, Juan Antonio Samaranch, declared the games 'the best Olympics ever',[7] while the writer Bill Bryson put it slightly differently: 'The Australians would rather win a gold medal than a Nobel prize.'[8]

Unfair that may be on Australian Nobel laureates but the games were exceptional not just in their objective performance – records in ticket sales and television audience figures[9] – but in the way they galvanized the country. There were 70,000 helpers who worked unpaid to support the event, in many cases giving up their holiday allowance to do so.

Unlike some other games, there was a decent legacy at a reasonable cost: the Olympic village was built on reclaimed land and the main facilities are being used heavily nine years after the event. The Olympic Park in the western Sydney suburbs clocks more than eight million visitors a year, with over a million going to the Sydney Aquatic Centre to swim and dive in the pools used for the games.[10] The former Sydney Superdome, now the Acer Arena, has become the city's top indoor hall for concerts and sport. It is one of the most popular indoor entertainment venues in the world in terms of visitor numbers, sharing top ten status with the likes of the O2 Centre in

London and Madison Square Garden in New York.[11] The main stadium, which at 110,000 seats was the largest Olympic stadium ever built, even bigger than the Beijing's 'bird's nest', has been slimmed down to a little over 80,000 and, thanks to a sponsorship deal, has been renamed the ANZ Stadium.[12] After a slow start (just ten events in the year after the games) it is now hosting an event a week. Among other things it is the main ground for the National Rugby League and for major soccer matches.

So it is all in use, unlike the facilities for Athens 2004, most of which are crumbling.[13] The main downside is that to keep top-notch facilities going is expensive. The park is huge, more than 10,000 acres. It is naturally the home for the New South Wales Institute of Sport but also a bank headquarters. It already has hotels but it is a long way from being self-sustaining financially. So there is a twenty-five-year development plan to turn it into a whole new town with a 17,000 population, offices, homes and shops. The aim seems reasonable, given its location in a prosperous and fast-growing city: to try to cut the cost of running the show but keep the legacy going.

As for the games themselves, various calculations have been done on the expense, of which the most authoritative came from the auditor-general of New South Wales. He reported in 2002 that the Olympics had cost A$6.6 billion, with a net cost to the public of between A$1.7 billion and A$2.4 billion. As noted earlier, excellence does not come cheap. That figure, however, is much smaller than the bill for the Athens games and far, far smaller than Beijing in 2008,[14] even allowing for the inevitable inflation in between.

In any case there are the intangible benefits. Like most of the world, Australians watch a lot of sport, and not just on television: roughly half the population go to at least one sporting event every year.[15] Unlike people in so much of the developed world, however, Australians play as well as watch. Something like two-thirds of the population – more than thirteen million people aged 15 years and older – take part in some sort of physical activity.[16] Further, some four million say they exercise at least five times a week. No other country can claim such high participation in sport.

If the story were to end there, it would be one of unrivalled success. Unfortunately there is a darker side, not so much to the sporting scene but to public health.

So before going any further, the country is confronting the troublesome fact that like other developed countries it has an obesity problem. On some tallies it is an even greater one than in the USA, with half the population classified as overweight. More of that later. Meanwhile ponder this strange paradox: the most sporting nation on the planet is also the most obese.

2 .   WHAT ARE THE LESSONS?

The first and most obvious lesson is that if a country focuses its resources on a goal, it will go a long way towards achieving it. Australia has taught the world how to do elite sport right. It stands in massive contrast to other high-achieving nations of recent years, especially the former Soviet Union and its satellites and in some measure China too. Australia's triumph has been to train athletes decently – without drugs, without harmful health effects, without oppressive coaching, without coercion. It is the way a democratic liberal democracy should operate, working to reach the highest standards but retaining its humanity, sense of proportion and respect for the individual. That is worth a cheer.

The more surprising thing is that what Australia is doing is not very difficult or even expensive to replicate. Britain adopted many of its ideas (and recruited several of its coaching staff) in the run-up to the Beijing Olympics. Other countries could very easily learn the same lessons; they just need to follow the same orderly, sensible process mapped out by Australia. First, you comb the country, going into the schools and identifying the youngsters with the most natural talent. Then you create a structure for developing that talent, including scholarships, coaching, access to training facilities and so on. Then you look after the young people, both during their training and in their subsequent careers.

The result is that you not only discover the best talent; you create a climate where the talent is attracted to the programme. You make it good for the people themselves. They are signing up for the good of the country to be sure, but they are also signing up for their own future.

Of course, this needs resources, but in the broad scheme of a modern nation state the costs are not so big. Australia has to some extent gold-plated its programmes, doing them to a higher standard than is needed, and there will be increasing pressure for the sports programme to deliver a bigger bang for its buck.

There is, I suggest, a lesson that goes beyond sport. It is about achieving excellence. Surely general educational achievement matters much more than sporting prowess. It really would be better to win Nobel prizes than gold medals. So why should resources go into helping people jump higher than others instead of, for example, ground-breaking medical research that will save millions of lives?

The short answer is that you can do both. Indeed the total resources Australia puts into elite sport are quite small compared with what the country directs into medical research.[17] But carping at spending on sport misses the point, because the Australian experience teaches us that this model can be applied to other endeavours. The world can learn from this.

Suppose a country, any country, wants to improve the quality of its scientific education – a goal that everyone should surely aspire to. How does it go about this? Well, it should start by finding the best people in the world at training scientists. It should set up a programme loosely modelled on the structure of the AIS, with regional units picking promising students and providing the backing they need to develop their talents. It should create an elite scientific centre, or maybe promote one or more existing institutions. And it should measure performance internationally.

A university wanting to improve its standing in the world league could do the same. So could a commercial company or a not-for-profit foundation or a police force – any form of social or economic organization. No one would suggest that the AIS model should be followed slavishly. That would be ridiculous. My point is simply that there are elements in Australian sports training that have applications far beyond sport itself. For although the aim and drive of the AIS is for excellence, it also takes into account the needs and desires of individuals. It wants people to win, but it wants to look after them too.

- **Focus your resources on a goal and you will go a long way towards achieving it**
- **Discover the best talent, then create a climate to attract it to the programme in question**
- **Measure performance internationally**

3. WHAT COULD GO WRONG?

There is one obvious question that needs to be answered. It is not so much what can go wrong but whether the country has got value for its investment over and above the winning of medals. Australian sports training focuses on excellence but in one respect the nation is far from excellent: it has this severe problem of physical fitness. So the question is whether the strides in elite sport made by the country since the early 1980s have contributed to the overall well-being of the community.

It is impossible to give a definitive answer, but we do know a lot about the scale of the problem. The definitive report on this was produced by the Baker IDI Heart and Diabetes Institute in Melbourne. It was called, provocatively, *Australia's Future 'Fat Bomb'*, and when it was published in 2008 it caused something of a storm. The report calculated that nearly four million adult Australians were obese and a further five million were overweight, a considerably higher proportion than previously estimated and more than half the adult population. For the middle-aged the situation was even worse: seven out of ten men and six out of ten women were either overweight or obese. The institute calculated that over the next twenty years an extra 700,000 people would suffer cardio-vascular disease as a result of being overweight, of whom 123,000 would die, many prematurely.

Add in the effect of being overweight on type 2 diabetes and the case for slimming down Australia was overwhelming.

So what was to be done? The report called for overweight Australians to lose five kilograms of weight in five months – 'five in five'. That, it calculated, would cut those deaths to 81,000. If Australians managed to lose another five kilograms, deaths would fall to 54,000. You could question the precision of the numbers but you could not dispute the scale of the problem or the benefits from such an outcome, if it could be achieved.

Whether it can is another matter. The Baker Institute made a number of suggestions, of which the core was that people should eat less and exercise more. But just how you achieve those objectives is terribly difficult. A subsequent report for the National Preventative Health Taskforce, prepared by the Obesity Working Group,[18] called for tax breaks on fitness products and incentives for food companies to regulate the amount of fats, salt and sugar in their products – worthy enough ideas but unlikely to have a radical impact. The government is, however, taking this seriously and is putting together a programme to try to tackle the problem. The first stage of fixing a problem is to recognize that you have one, so it deserves support.

The obvious question is whether this is a 'Montreal moment' – a time when a country is so shaken by what it sees that it is determined to take action. This may all seem a long way from sport and the Olympics and in a way it is. But if the most sporting nation on earth cannot use that legacy to become fitter, and tackling obesity is key to that, then there is a problem for all of us. It should be easier – given the sports facilities, given the high participation rates in sport, and given the experience of failure at Montreal – for Australia to figure out how to tackle obesity than for other countries to do so. It is far too early to know whether its first faltering steps are likely to work. Certainly there is a really active debate going on there because the country has become troubled by a reality that clashes with its self-image. To be the fattest nation on earth is not what you put in the brochure. All of us should wish it well – and raise a low-alcohol glass to its success.

I want to end with another point. In any human sense of values what matters most in sport, more even than winning gold medals, is that the young people who join in should enjoy it. A friend whose daughter represented Canberra in the women's under-16 basketball team noted that the level of ability and drive was awesome. But he added:

'What is striking about this elite women's basketball … is its dedication, its professionalism and seriousness of purpose, but at the same time the girls' ability to keep having fun together no matter how high they go in the sport.'

Teach young people to strive for excellence but also to have fun. That is a powerful message for the world.

Global

CHAPTER TWENTY

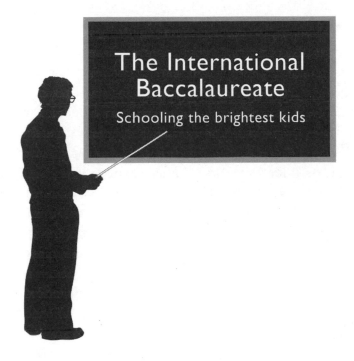

The International
Baccalaureate

Schooling the brightest kids

I. WHAT IS THE STORY?

The International Baccalaureate (IB) is the world's fastest-growing
school curriculum and examination system – and the only truly international pre-university diploma. But it is more than that: it is a set of
ideas about how young people should be educated to become effective, successful and honourable global citizens. If, in this ever more
global world, the most important form of capital is human capital,
the IB is the most important common force shaping the ideas of the
next generation of people who will help run the world.

Virtually every country has some form of national examination
system for its schools. It has to, for you cannot run a country
without it. You must have some way of benchmarking how well
schools and the children they teach are progressing – some way of
making sure that young people have the core skills they will need to

become grown-up citizens. It is also a great convenience, almost a necessity, for a country to have some common exam for university entrance.

We think of this as completely normal – that each country should have its own exams. But while national education systems operate in a series of watertight compartments, the world economy does not. Families move around from one place to another. Companies establish subsidiaries abroad. Even at an undergraduate level and very much at a postgraduate level, students move between countries, sometimes studying in universities on the other side of the world.

So the need for some sort of global examination for school leavers is obvious. How and why the IB came to fulfil that role is much less so because it has done much more than just create a curriculum and an exam; it has devised an approach to education that is broader, more humane, more rigorous – well, I suppose just better – than any national education system in the world.

There were in 2009 more than 750,000 IB students in 138 countries. It is true that nearly half were in North America and nearly three-quarters in the rich developed world, but it seems growth is increasingly coming from the developing countries, where schools are clamouring to join its programmes. The rate of expansion is phenomenal: just in 2007 there were around half a million students in 126 countries and even then the number of schools was rising by 17 per cent a year compounded. In 1990 there were around 300 IB programmes; by 2008 there were 3,000.[1]

And that is happening not because some government or company is promoting it. The momentum for growth is supplied entirely by the demand from schools and parents, spread largely by word of mouth. In market terms it is the most successful education programme in the world, but, of course, it would not have become that had it not also been driven by a sense of mission.

I came to realize what an extraordinary phenomenon the International Baccalaureate was by accident. I was speaking at a conference for the IB's team of long-term planners in 2007. As we talked about world economic growth, and in particular the passing of the baton to countries such as China and India, it dawned on me that the IB ethos was really the ideal one for our increasingly global economy.

The services it offers are ideal, of course. It is a world where the top universities not only scour the planet for their postgraduate intake but also their undergraduates. What started as a mission to create a global examination that was appropriate for a handful of international schools has become a tremendously useful benchmark of academic achievement for universities seeking to boost the number of foreign undergraduates. So in practical terms this is a winner. But it also seems to me to be a winner on ethical grounds, for it builds in a sense of values and an approach to learning that is free of national assumptions and prejudices.

To understand why, you have to go back to the start, well described in the book *Schools Across Frontiers* (1983) by Alec Peterson,[2] one of the founders of the movement and in 1968 its first full-time director-general. The story begins earlier, though, in 1924, with the founding of the International School of Geneva for the families of employees of the League of Nations.[3] This was the first of what is now a string of international schools around the world. It survived the Second World War and in 1951 helped to set up the International Schools Association as an umbrella group for what was becoming a loose network of establishments that had taken Geneva's lead.

It became clear during the 1950s that preparing different groups of students for the various national examinations was both inefficient and also against the spirit of the schools – in the sense that students were segregated into different national groups. In 1962 a small conference organized by the school in Geneva discussed the idea of founding an International Baccalaureate – using that name.

In 1964 the group got a grant from the Twentieth Century Fund[4] to look at the feasibility of such an exam, and then in 1966 another larger grant from the Ford Foundation,[5] which enabled Alec Peterson to take a year off from the Department of Education at Oxford University to become the IB's director-general. There was a series of conferences among a group of like-minded educationalists throughout this period, with the core IB curriculum being accepted by nine schools as far apart as Montevideo and Tehran in 1968. There then followed two years of trials and the first twenty-nine IB students used it for university entrance in 1970.

Told like that, the lead-up to the launch of the IB sounds pretty linear – a clear and steady path towards an agreed goal. Actually it was much less organized, relying on a tiny group of people armed really only with persuasion and contacts – and those charitable grants. The UK had a big role, for though the IB's headquarters were and still are in Geneva, the Department of Education at Oxford University helped in the early days with the administration and examining. The administrative arms of the IB are in Wales and the Netherlands, while the largest number of schools (and students) doing the IB is in North America.

There is a further twist to the tale. The British Royal Family was important too. Those first diplomas were presented by Lord Mountbatten, great-uncle of the Prince of Wales. Why? Well, he was involved because he supported a parallel educational movement, linked by its philosophy: the United World Colleges. These are schools rather than a curriculum and an examination, but the idea is much the same – that young people should have a broad education that stimulates social responsibility and a global outlook. Their ethos was inspired by Kurt Hahn, founder of Gordonstoun School in Scotland and the Outward Bound Trust.[6] The first of the schools was Atlantic College in Wales, and by 2009 there were thirteen such colleges around the world. Lord Mountbatten was the first president of the movement, followed by Prince Charles and then by Queen Noor of Jordan and Nelson Mandela, whose children and grandchildren were educated at one of the colleges.[7]

This movement continues, with a new school being added every couple of years, but while it is in its own terms successful, it is in world terms tiny. But in the early days of the IB, having the drive and contacts of Lord Mountbatten and the people round him provided a credibility that a small group of educationalists would not have had on their own. The United World Colleges network, like the international schools, also needed some form of final examination that transcended national boundaries, and it too contributed to developing the IB system.

So there was, by the early 1970s, an established IB that many universities around the world would recognize. But at that stage it was still very much a niche operation – and a European one in the sense that the majority of schools using it were either in Britain or on the Continent. Then, at the end of the 1970s, there was a sudden huge shift towards the USA and Canada. In 1977 there were twenty-nine schools in Britain and Europe offering the curriculum, and just ten in the whole of North America – and twelve in the rest of the world. Only seven years later, in 1984, there were sixty-six in Britain and Europe but 126 in North America. It was this dramatic shift that really helped turn the IB from being a European niche system to a truly global one.

It was entirely unexpected. Initially there had been three efforts to establish the IB in North America: one in the international schools, one in the elite private schools and one in the community colleges. The first was a modest success, but there were not very many of them. The second was a failure, with hardly any taking it up. And the third saw some experiments but the initiative petered out. Two things changed everything. One was that the public schools (in the US sense of the word) were taking up the IB as a way of helping to improve standards. The other was that there was support from an American industrialist and philanthropist, Blouke Carus, who spotted a short story about the IB in the *International Herald Tribune*, while on a visit to Europe, and realized that it could be used to raise standards in the USA. He became chairman of the IB in North America and with his enthusiasm and financial support in effect 'sold' the idea to public schools across the land. It is another example of US philanthropy changing things in a wholly positive way.

Many US high schools had programmes for the handicapped, or students with learning disabilities, but they did not have them for the highly gifted. These 'magnet' schools – public schools offering specialized courses – found the IB particularly attractive as a way of distinguishing themselves from other high schools, with the IB helping to give their best students a shot at top US colleges, as well as international universities. The International Baccalaureate Organization in Geneva had established a North American 'subsidiary', the IBNA,[8] and that became adept at selling the concept of this different international curriculum and exam. Thanks to the work of Blouke Carus the idea took off. Schools flocked to adopt it and the IB stopped being something largely for the rich kids of international business people based in Europe – and became something for bright ones anywhere in the world. That, of course, was what the whole idea was about.

As I was talking about globalization to the IB planners, I realized why the IB fitted with uncanny precision into the needs of an increasingly global economy. It encouraged young people, of course, to think about a multi-polar world, where good ideas can come from anywhere. But alongside breadth it also encouraged depth, in particular by requiring students to produce an extended essay on a subject of their choice. You do not just need knowledge; you need judgement – and that is much harder to acquire. I came away hugely impressed and wanted to see the IB in action.

So I went to two very different schools, one an upmarket private school in the leafy London commuter belt; the other a public high school on Staten Island in New York.

Sevenoaks School in Kent was founded in 1432, which even by British standards is going back a bit. But although one of the oldest schools in the country, there did not used to be any sense of greatness: for many years it was quite small and even in the 1960s it was not particularly highly ranked. Since then it has transformed itself into, on some measures, the best school in the land. And it has done so thanks to the IB.

Sevenoaks was a pioneer for the IB in Britain. It was among the first schools to adopt it back in 1977, and it did so originally for idealistic reasons – in particular its breadth and international dimension. But more than this, it was the first to use it as a competitive tool. Being international had brought advantages, particularly in the early 1990s recession, because it gave the school an edge in attracting the children of European and other foreign families in the UK. The size of its sixth form grew and more and more students switched out of the narrow 'A' level British curriculum. Disenchantment with the UK exam grew and in 2004 Sevenoaks became fully IB. That really catapulted it to prime status.

It is exceptional by British standards: in 2007 the *Sunday Times* ranked Sevenoaks as the top co-educational independent school in the country, and it topped *The Times* and *The Independent* league tables in 2006. It is also exceptional by world standards: in 2007 more students from Sevenoaks reached the highest possible IB score than from any other school in the world.

Of course, the physical surroundings are impressive: a mixture of eighteenth-century grandeur and hi-tech sports facilities set in 100 acres of leafy Kent in a prime commuter town. The staff are impressive: an inspirational head teacher, Katy Ricks, and a clutch of dedicated specialists. But you would expect all that. What I found most impressive were the students. It is always great meeting the best young but their candour was special. For example, they told me about their difficulties with the IB – in particular that it forced them to focus on their weaker subjects. One who was good at maths struggled with languages; another had the opposite problem. But all, and this was a mix of British and foreign, recognized the value of being required to do something at which they did not naturally excel. This is a system that favours all-rounders, a bit like real life.

And along with the breadth comes the depth – the extended essay, one of the special features of the IB, a study of a subject of the student's choice. One pupil who showed me around was studying the economy of Gaza – she was Palestinian. Another was looking at the US Civil War from the perspective of the South – he was half-American. Yet another was looking in detail at the economics of a football club – he was a Brit. You select what you are interested in and produce a piece of original research on it – a tough one for a 17-year-old.

That leads to a further issue. Does the IB suit the less elite schools? To try to discover an answer to that, I went to Curtis High School, on Staten Island.

You see Curtis on the hill to the right from the ferry as it pulls into the jetty: fine yellow brick and limestone buildings topped by a Gothic clock tower. It was founded in 1904, the first of the series of high schools to be built by the city in the outer boroughs when greater New York came together as a single entity and city leaders wanted to make a commitment to the boroughs. They did well, building a cathedral to education. For many years, Curtis was the beacon school for Staten Islanders, adding a concert hall and swimming pool in the same confident style, and later, and less successfully, a science block. Right through to the 1950s this was the school that parents fought to get their children into.

But Staten Island changed and the school began to struggle. In the early 1980s there was a sharp decline in demand and the school had to do something. One of the things it did to pick itself up was to adopt the IB. According to Dr Aurelia Curtis (a coincidence of name), now the school principal but at the time a teacher there, the IB 'immediately breathed new life into the school'. But it was eventually dropped, partly on grounds of cost, and it was not until 2003, when Dr Curtis took over, that plans were hatched to reintroduce it. Her case for doing so was not just to attract academically brighter students but to imbue the entire school with the ethos of the IB. As she put it to me: 'The prize is not the diploma; it is the shaping of the person.'

Curtis High has had its disciplinary and safety troubles in the past. When you walk in, you are greeted by guards; students were complaining about having to swipe cards when they arrive and leave. But then this is a poor district of New York: officially, half the students come from families below the poverty line, and in reality the proportion will be higher because many immigrant families prefer not to disclose their incomes. Many children come from families where English is a second language, and Curtis has to cope with that too. I watched a young teacher take a class of students with limited English through the shifting US policy on its neutral status during the first part of the Second World War, teaching them both history and language at the same time. It was thrilling to see everyone included, everyone taken forward.

Most exciting of all were the IB students – why they were doing the IB and their hopes and aspirations. You know, their responses were exactly the same as those at Sevenoaks.

So they liked the breadth of the curriculum, though they found it tough to be made to focus on subjects they were not naturally good at; they were inspired by the social aims of the IB and wanted to do good in the community; they celebrated its global view – that it introduced them to ways of thought different to those they were familiar with. They had only just begun to think about the subjects for their extended essay but were approaching it with the same enthusiasm and diversity of options as the students in Kent.

At Curtis, the IB is not just for IB students; it is for the whole school. While perhaps the diploma is only being taken by 10 to 15 per cent of the school, Dr Curtis's aim is to have everyone take some course on it, so that the IB touches everyone.

2. WHAT ARE THE LESSONS?

There are two rather different factors that make the IB experience so appropriate for our global world. One stems from the curriculum and diploma, the other from the decision-making structure of the organization.

The IB is not just a pre-university diploma and a curriculum leading to that diploma; it is an idea of learning. Actually, it has now become a three-stage curriculum, for while the original pre-university stage remains by far its most important 'product', there is also a Primary Years Programme for 3- to 12-year-olds and a Middle Years Programme from 11 to 16. But it is fair to say the diploma still dominates the enterprise. That is what the other programmes build towards and, in hard cash terms, the diploma does to some extent cross-subsidize the earlier stages.

As a non-educationalist, two features of the IB stand out to me as being special. One is the breadth: it requires students to be rounded in their education. The other is the personal development: it requires them to do more than pass an exam. So there has to be an additional language as well as the best language, presumably the mother tongue; there has to be maths; there has to be science; there has to be some form of the arts – music, theatre or the visual arts. You would expect all this, but what you might not expect is that there is also an element about relating individuals to society. This could include conventional disciplines such as economics, geography and history, but it could also take in subjects that most young people would only encounter at university, such as philosophy and psychology.

The other feature is the requirement to do more than pass an exam. This includes the extended essay noted above, study of the theory of knowledge – how human beings learn in different ways (emotion as well as reason, for example) and the different kinds of knowledge (e.g. artistic and historical as well as scientific). Finally, there is an element of action and service. Students have to do something in and for the community – a real task beyond the classroom.

This has to be right. The concept of service is so central to the survival of human beings as a species – doing things for our community that go beyond our narrow self-interest and the social requirements placed upon us – that we should seek to embed this notion in young people as part of their education. What you do matters less than the fact that you do it.

At any rate it works. The diploma is very attractive to schools, which have to make the choice as to whether to adopt it and which then have to satisfy the IB authorities that they can attain the appropriate standards. It is attractive to universities around the world, which increasingly recognize it. It is attractive to parents too – so attractive that some schools have been known to claim they prepare for the diploma when they are not authorized to do so. I saw a story in an Indian newspaper warning parents they should check that schools claiming to offer the IB had indeed got authorization, as some schools were jumping the gun.

And it is attractive to the young people who study for it. I have only caught two criticisms from students. One is the point noted above – that it is tough to have to focus on your weak subjects and hence spend less time on ones you find easy and love doing.

The other is harder to pin down. The point was made to me that the ethos of liberal tolerance that runs right through the way the curriculum is taught can become irksome. The whole idea behind the IB, whose development was influenced by the horrors of two world wars, was to mould good global citizens – hence the emphasis on a global outlook and on service, as well as learning. But to some students at least, this can become as much an intellectual straitjacket as the typical national educational systems.

Such a reaction is probably inevitable, given that there is this sense of mission among supporters of the IB. People with strong beliefs can generate resistance. But my impression is that IB leaders are aware of this and sensitive to it. They are certainly sensitive to what their market – universities, schools, parents, students – thinks and wants. That leads to the second message for the wider world: how the International Baccalaureate Organization runs itself.

All organizations must have a structure that can enable effective decisions, but with a not-for-profit enterprise it can be hard to balance competing objectives. It has to be run as a business but the aim is not the clear one of growing the bottom line. Growth has to be balanced against the need to maintain standards; the freedom that national bodies should reasonably expect has to be balanced against the core ethos of the organization. Of course, all international organizations face these challenges, but you would imagine that something as global as the IB would find it peculiarly tough to cope.

It seems to manage. It reorganized itself at the end of 2007 to cope with its growth, changing its legal and tax arrangements and creating a single strategic governing board. But that is detail. More important, I think, is not the way things are done but the achievement in transforming what began as a European and, to be honest, pretty elitist organization into a genuinely global one that offers a remarkable degree of open access. It is not just a Western system. It is not just for private schools. It is not an elite club. And it has moved on in many ways since it was launched. Thus it keeps reviewing and updating its curriculum free from the interference of any national government, or pressure from any passing educational fad in one particular country.

- **Provide breadth and focus on personal development**
- **Encourage actions that go beyond narrow self-interest**
- **Keep reviewing and updating**

3. WHAT COULD GO WRONG?

I suppose in one sense nothing much can go wrong. The IB is being propelled forward by the globalization of the world economy and that seems likely to carry on for at least a decade, maybe a generation. Were that process to go into reverse, there might seem to be less need for a truly non-national diploma, but even that may not be so. For example, if barriers were erected to international trade, people might feel all the more need for qualifications that go beyond such barriers.

It is, however, possible to see a set of circumstances where students could be forced into a national examination system rather than an international one. Governments could get jealous if their own preferred examinations and diplomas were rejected and people turned to a global standard instead. But whether that is likely to happen on any significant scale is another matter. Besides, were we to move to a world of increasingly rigid national barriers, the problems of the IB would be pretty small compared to the problems of human society.

There are two more practical problems, one that is already evident and one that is likely to become so. The first is the difficulty of coping with very rapid growth, for there is the matter of quality control – making sure that those new schools adopting the programme can pass on the spirit of the IB as well as meeting its formal requirements. It is an obvious problem and the IB team is very aware of it. Growth will inevitably change the nature of the organization, as what began as a tiny group of like-minded people becomes a large global bureaucracy. The trick will be to maintain the ethos that created the IB in the first place, while figuring out ways to extend it on an ever bigger scale.

Coping with growth is a common problem of management, but none the easier for that.

The other problem is more subtle. It is the extent to which the original ethos of the IB – forged in the chaos of post-war Europe and in the determination to teach young people to avoid another great global conflict – will need to be modified. The original purpose, however admirable, will seem less relevant as time passes and growth shifts away from Europe and North America towards the rest of the world. The IB will have to come to terms with the smaller role of the West not just in economic terms but also as a generator of ideas and a stock of values. As universities in China, India and the other emerging nations grow both in size and in competence, the values of such countries will become a more weighty influence on higher education globally. Asian ideas will increasingly challenge Western ones.

This is something the West has to come to terms with and goes far beyond the IB. But higher education is one of those areas where the pressures and challenges will be most evident, and so the IB will be at the centre of a much larger debate – let us not call it a clash – between different ideas and values.

That surely is the most important issue facing the IB … and also its most important mission. Managing a rebalanced world economy, indeed a rebalanced world, is going to be very difficult. The folk memory of how the last great burst of globalization ended will fade as the dreadful first half of the twentieth century passes further into history. We have to understand each other, respect each other, and what we need for that is a generation of young people who think globally, who respect each other and who have a powerful interest in a harmonious world society.

The IB is still a relatively small enterprise in terms of the global education industry but it is operating at a fulcrum point. It is changing things. It already matters hugely and I believe it will matter more and more in the years to come.

Conclusion

Anyone reading through these tales will have found their own messages – ideas that ring true and give clear signals. Most of those I hope I will have identified, but I certainly will not have spotted all of them. People who have travelled with me on the journey will come from different backgrounds and bring different insights. They will grasp things that I have failed to understand, draw lessons that I have not identified and indeed disagree with some of my judgements. But there are, I suggest, a number of common threads that run through the narratives and it might be helpful here to set out ten of the ones I have found most powerful. They are not the only lessons by any means, nor, I ask, should they be applied in a mechanistic manner. This is not, 'Follow these ten rules and everything in the world will be all right.' It is more: 'Here are powerful ideas that can be applied to many situations. If they are applied sensitively and thoughtfully, there will be better outcomes. We can all learn from things that work.'

I. OPTIMISM — BALANCED BY REALISM

Let us start with a defence of optimism. If you travel the world looking for things that work very well, you cannot but be optimistic. There were magic moments when, during the research of this book, I was thrilled by what I was seeing or being told. Such moments included chatting with International Baccalaureate students in New York and near London, watching the mass of boats travel down the Huangpu River on the evening tide in Shanghai, walking round the shining business parks on the outskirts of Bangalore, and many, many more. I have tried to convey that sense of wonder and delight.

Naturally I witnessed misery too – anyone would have to be deeply insensitive not to – and I have tried to be frank about that. Amid every example of something that is working well, there are instances of things working pretty badly. But the trick, surely, is to have some sense of balance. I cannot accept that for every winner there has to be a loser, and I hope these examples show this perspective to be true. In any case, pessimism paralyses, preventing the action needed to fix what has gone wrong. It is profoundly destructive to start out with a belief that nothing can work.

• Pessimism paralyses

Besides, there are many reasons to be optimistic about the state of the world in the early years of this century. The backcloth to this book is the greatest burst of prosperity that the human species has ever experienced, followed by a serious economic reverse in much of the world, though, crucially, by no means all of it. The reverse has taught us the fundamental lesson that progress never follows a straight line – something that, sadly, it seems we need to be reminded of from time to time. However, we should also have taken another message on board. That the two most populous countries of the developing world, China and India, have performed so much better than any of the developed nations should, at the very least, persuade us that Europe and North America have lessons to learn from Asia. The economies of both China and India continued to grow rapidly right through the recessions in the developed nations. From their perspective, the burst of prosperity has pretty much continued.

• **Progress never follows a straight line**

Two conclusions self-evidently flow from this. One, a fundamental tenet of this book, is that important and successful ideas about economic and social management can come from any part of the planet – not just the 'advanced' West but also the supposedly less-advanced East.

The other is that global prosperity has rather more solid foundations than many in the West feared. The baton of growth has been passed from one side of the world to the other but the race continues. While we can maintain some measure of growth, we will have the capacity to improve living standards everywhere – as well as the resources to tackle the accompanying challenges, like the threat to the environment.

So the case for the optimism implicit in this book has in a way been supported by the economic downturn. Of course, there have been serious reverses, as at least four of the case studies show. The Irish economy, the Dubai property market, the City of London's financial services business and the finances of Harvard University have all taken massive blows. The question then is whether they are resilient enough to carry on making progress once economic conditions improve and their own excesses are tackled. I will come to the need for humility and flexibility later, but the general point here is that you learn more from periodic setbacks than you do from uninterrupted success. If I am indeed right that in all these instances the success story will eventually be resumed, then that is a further reason for optimism. And if I am wrong, then it will be for others to carry out the autopsies and figure out what can be learnt.

2. EXCELLENCE — TEMPERED BY DECENCY

There is a great temptation in many walks of life to do things just well enough. Companies produce goods that are good enough to sell at the price at which they can make a profit. Governments try to do well enough to get re-elected. Doing anything too well is wasteful in the sense that resources are being used that could otherwise go to making more goods with a proven record of doing just fine. The very essence of the market economy is allocating scarce resources as efficiently as possible; the best can become the enemy of the good.

But the examples here are, in the main, about excellence – about doing things as well as can possibly be done, in some cases almost obsessively so. So in the cases of Harvard and the International Baccalaureate, the drive is for academic excellence; with Australian sport it is athletic excellence; in Bangalore it is providing the best service to the world; in Copenhagen the best city environment, and so on. It is easy to celebrate excellence, if difficult to sustain it, but those like me who do celebrate it must also admit there are costs – and tackle that issue.

There needs, in particular, to be some sensitivity to the fact that shooting for the stars can cause a lot of disruption. There will always be a tension between elitism and access and this has to be managed with a sense of decency. Take excellence in sport – in Australia or else-where: you are trying to win gold medals at the Olympics, so you create a structure designed to do just that. But along the way there are thousands of great athletes who do not make the final cut. As talented as they are in absolute terms, the bar keeps getting raised as the selec-tion process passes through an ever-narrower series of tests – and if they do not reach the standards set by the very best, they do not get into the elite development squads. It is not quite a game where there is only one winner but it is pretty close.

While life in general is not like that – we do not need a few star doctors, for example, just a lot of competent ones – one of the trou-bling aspects of the modern world is that we do seem to be heading towards a *Winner-Take-All-Society* (the title of the 1995 book by Robert H. Frank and Philip J. Cook that charts the phenomenon). The cult of celebrity, the earnings of sports stars, the salaries of some top business executives and the very competitiveness of global society have all contributed to a tendency to heap rewards on the few at the expense of the many.

• If in the drive to be the best you neglect your wider responsibilities, you are liable to end up in greater trouble when you meet headwinds

The lessons in this book, though, show that a more balanced approach is possible. In Australia, sports education for all has been improved. The quest for excellence has lifted the quality of the country's facilities, which are made available for the population at large. At Harvard, the university strives for 'needs blind' access, meaning that an applicant's ability to pay is not considered until after an offer has been made, at which point decisions on the level of financial assistance can be taken. Harvard does suffer from the charge of elitism and in some measure that charge must be justified. But the moral there is that if in the drive to be the best you neglect your wider responsibilities, you are liable to end up in greater trouble when you meet headwinds. The Museum of Modern Art, in the chapter about New York philanthropy, is unashamedly elitist but its efforts to remain accessible have helped it retain funding through the downturn.

Perhaps the best example of excellence and access sharing the same stage is provided by the Edinburgh Festival, which is in effect totally open to performers: you can just show up and do your thing. Yet the event also remains a showcase for some of the best entertainment and artistic talent in the world.

• Pursue excellence but be aware of the needs and aspirations of those below the elite level

That is surely what matters. You have to strive to do things really well but you have to be aware of the needs and aspirations of people or organizations below that elite level. The most corrosive attitude is to lie about excellence – to pretend that something is wonderful when it is really second-rate, or worse. That is as bad as not valuing the worthy contributions to society from those of us who will never achieve excellence but try to do our best.

3. COMMUNITY WORKS — IF IT IS
ALLOWED TO

Top-down or bottom-up? There has to be leadership but there also has to be community. All the examples in this book have some element of community – a group ethic that binds together the efforts of the individuals who are currently holding the baton. But in several examples here, it is absolutely core. A word about these.

The most obvious case of a working community is Dharavi – a city within a city, built by people organizing themselves into a hard-working society that manages to fulfil, one way or another, most of their basic needs. It is not the ideal way to do things but it does, in its own terms, work.

Now take another, completely different community – one not bound together by any physical space: the schools, students, teachers and organizers of the International Baccalaureate. There is no central mind, just a voluntary association of people who have come together with a single aim. In the case of Dharavi, the objective is to have a better life than they otherwise would; with the IB, it is to give students an education that will help them lead better lives than they otherwise would.

Now take yet another community, the City of London. There is no central mind, no plan – just an aim to provide financial services to the world and make money out of that. As in all walks of life, there are people who do not pull their weight and people who seek to exploit the system. Communities mirror the frailties of humankind as well as its virtues. But as I have sought to argue, there is a collaborative sense too. It is a more complex community than it was a generation ago, or indeed when my two grandfathers worked there, but there is still a group identity.

This leads to a huge and multi-layered question: how do you create and maintain communities that work well?

Well, one way is to fix those problems – gang warfare, corruption, drugs, alcohol – that have destroyed so many other communities. Zurich's approach to tackling drug abuse is a very good example of a municipality dealing with a set of social problems that would, if left to themselves, have undermined what was otherwise a community that functioned very well. It is a slightly different case but policing in Tokyo has helped achieve outstanding levels of public safety in the world's largest urban conurbation, though it has been less successful in containing the city's gangs, the yakuza. In the case of the City of London, effective self-regulation has long been an important part of its success, but as we have seen, that is not always enough; external regulators are sometimes needed to maintain ethical and other standards.

So even communities that run themselves well may occasionally require outsiders to keep them sweet. However, that process can have a more positive slant than policing or regulation. There are myriad instances of where a community under pressure has decided that in order to become stronger, it must look beyond its own resources. The best of Main Street USA is the way in which a competent municipal authority has not only shown it can mobilize the local community but also known when to go outside for help. While the 'outside' might be the state or even federal government, it might also be a company seeking to invest. Look at how communities in the American South have been revitalized by German and Japanese companies establishing car plants there.

- **Mobilize locally, but go outside for help when needed**

The hardest aspect of this question, though, is how you help create successful communities in the first place. I think the answer is that you do not, or at least outsiders do not. It has to be bottom-up, as for example it was when Visiting Neighbors was created in Greenwich Village in New York.

It is about seeing things from ground level. You can wreck communities by insensitive town planning, as has happened in many cities around the world, or support them by thoughtful urban design, as has been done in Copenhagen. All outsiders can do is look at what is there and, where feasible or necessary, maybe give a helping hand. But first, do no harm.

• Look at things from ground level up

If successful communities, almost by definition, form themselves, there is surely something to be learnt from them. People band together because they can achieve more together than they can apart. They give their time and sometimes their money for little or no personal gain, save the knowledge that the group activity, whatever form it takes, is worthwhile.

For me, the big lesson here is not how to create or even support a community, but the need to celebrate it.

• Celebrate community

4. GOVERNMENT WORKS TOO

Communities work but so too can governments. In any crisis, people turn to them. For all the suspicion of the power of the modern state, if something goes wrong then it is the government that is in the front line to fix it. There are, in these early years of the twenty-first century, plenty of examples of this, ranging from the sudden shock of the banking crisis of 2008 to the longer-term environmental concerns about global warming.

The wide-ranging debate about the role of the state is far beyond the scope of this book. It will be fascinating to know if the late twentieth century turns out to have been the high point of 'big government' and the years ahead will see it being downsized – and it is fascinating to speculate about the extent to which power will be pushed up to supra-national bodies, of which the European Union seems a prototype, and down to small communities. However, my aim here is to make a much more limited point. It is that there are examples from all around the world of governments doing things well and we should try to learn from them.

The obvious example here comes from Hong Kong. It is an extraordinary exercise in lean government, achieving excellent results in education and health and, under the usual measure of the share of GDP being spent by it, remaining one of the smallest in the world. But that lean government it is also intrusive: it owns all the land and runs what is on some measures the second-largest industry, gambling. As a result, it quite overthrows conventional stereotypes.

There are other examples. In Shanghai the municipal government has driven the growth of China's largest city, with the Pudong project being the largest urban-building development in the world. The Australian government took the lead in promoting and funding sports education. It was successive municipal authorities in Copenhagen that established its programme for reclaiming the centre of the city for pedestrians and cyclists and promoting its remarkable (for a cool northern city) street culture. It was a combination of the Swiss government and the Zurich municipality that conquered its drug culture.

• Compare like with like

Even where the progress has been mixed, government has still led well. Ireland and Dubai – the two examples of uneven but, I believe, ultimately successful economic leadership – show what can be done in a remarkably short space of time. In the late 1980s both places were relative backwaters: Ireland was the poorest member of the European Union, Dubai one of the less important of the Gulf states. A quarter of a century later, despite all the reverses that I absolutely acknowledge, the progress is staggering compared with what was there before. To expect governments to get it right every time is naïve. The fair way to assess their performance is to measure real progress under one jurisdiction against that under comparable jurisdictions elsewhere. Governments work; they just do not always work.

5 . BECOME A TRUE MAGNET FOR TALENT

One way in which governments work is when they create an environment that attracts talented people. More mobile than ever before, human capital has become the most important as well as the most elusive form of capital. Most manufacturing know-how crosses national boundaries in the time needed to build a new plant or buy a licence; finance crosses national boundaries at the speed of light. The most 'sticky' form of capital are the brains of clever people, and to persuade those who could go anywhere in the world to come to your country, your city, your workplace requires a complex mixture of attractions. It is not just the financial rewards, though they matter a great deal, but also the subtle mixture of opportunity and challenge in the job market. The lifestyle naturally has to be attractive but there is more to this than providing a pleasant environment in which to live and bring up a family, for there have to be cultural and social opportunities too. Above all (and this is what makes it tough), there has to be critical mass: talented people want to be where other people with similar talents are congregated.

> • **Create an environment that gets talent**
> **to attract talent**

Indeed it is more than that: they *have* to be surrounded by people with similar talents if they are going to do their job. That is obvious in a football club, for great players have to play with a great team. But it is also true in other walks of life. The world is now a bit like a medieval city: one street has all the bakers; one has the moneylenders; one has the tailors and so on.

There are several examples here. Thus top academics want to go to Harvard or one of the Ivy League universities in the USA. Top bankers have to be in London, New York or maybe Hong Kong – not yet Shanghai. Software engineers could obviously be on the West Coast of the USA but many of the Indian nationals who emigrated there have been attracted back to Bangalore or Mumbai. Dublin has done a great job in wooing back Irish nationals who had left to work elsewhere. Dubai is the supreme example of a city-state endeavouring to become a magnet for talent, as it has sought to attract the very best in every sphere. If you want to be a ski-instructor, well, the best place in North America to find a job is probably Whistler, and if you want to try your hand as a stand-up comedian then you see if you can hack it in Edinburgh.

There is a paradox here. In theory, software can be written anywhere; in practice, workers with special skills and companies seeking to hire them create clusters of talent. People go to a particular place because that is where they know they can get the best jobs, and companies go there because they know they can hire the best people. It works for both sides.

The practical question is: how do you kick start this process? Sometimes there is a large element of luck. Bangalore happened to have the characteristics needed to become a hi-tech hub, and then reinforced these with an open society welcoming self-made entrepreneurs. Edinburgh happened to have started a festival where uninvited acts turned up, and the Fringe was born.

Sometimes the driver has been government policy. There are two particular examples here – Dublin with its tax-friendly regime for foreign companies and Dubai in actively seeking to hire the best – both of which are being imitated elsewhere in the world.

Sometimes, once a degree of critical mass already exists, the driver is market forces. I suppose the best examples of this are the City of London and Harvard, though in both cases the relevant authorities have reinforced the power of the market. The magnetic draw of City salaries has been supported by the relatively open immigration policy of the UK government, while in Harvard the draw of high academic pay is supported by outstanding facilities and excellent students.

Pull all these together and the big message, I suggest, is that to attract talent you have to put out the welcome mat. You have to state in all sorts of different ways that you do not care what it says on the passport. You want talented, hard-working people and you will respect and cherish them.

• Put out the welcome mat

Cherish them, that is it. Some years ago I spent several sessions teaching on a course for high-flyers at a firm of accountants and management consultants. I was astounded at the resources that this firm put into training and asked why it spent so much money on developing people who might go off and take all these skills elsewhere.

'No, Hamish, you do not understand,' I was told. 'These are clever people. They understand about human capital. They know that while they stay with us, we will go on trying to add to that stock of capital. That is why you are here. It is the moment that we *stop* increasing their human capital that they will take themselves off somewhere else.'

So to be a magnet for talent, the talented have to feel they are getting something back. They are not just going to do a job, pick up the salary cheque and clock watch till the end of the working day. They have to know that they can increase their human capital in all sorts of ways, building soft skills as well as hard ones, being part of the community – supporting it and being supported by it. Then they will stay. You attract talent by adding to it: it is truly win, win.

6. BE HONEST ABOUT FAILURE

It is axiomatic that you learn more from failure than success. These are all success stories but in every example, every single one, there has been failure in some form or other at some stage. The other common feature, though, is that with a few wobbles, all the people involved have been able to acknowledge failure and correct their course.

The economic downturn has been the most common cause of failure. Both Ireland and Dubai ran into a wall. Both had made matters worse for themselves by allowing their exuberance to spiral out of control. 'We had,' as a Dubliner said to me, 'got a bit ahead of ourselves.' In the case of Ireland, there has at least been a recognition that much greater discipline will be required in the future, and I am prepared to bet that Dubai will also acknowledge its errors, if in a more subtle way. Remember, too, that Ireland's economic success story could only begin when the country's political and economic leadership acknowledged past failures and policies were changed in a radical way.

The City of London has also suffered, but the scale of the present downturn looks quite small when set against earlier difficulties – the aftermath of two world wars, for example, and the collapse of confidence in the UK economy during the 1970s. It was because one form of business, providing investment wealth for the world, was a casualty of conflict that the City had to figure out what else it might do. It was because of the weakness of sterling in the 1970s that it learnt to deal in other currencies, reinventing the international markets we still have, albeit in somewhat battered form, today.

• Face failure, and turn it to your advantage

A similar acceptance of failure has been behind the general economic turnaround in both China and India – China from the reforms of 1978 onwards, India from the fiscal consolidation and regulatory reforms of the early 1990s. Two of the success stories, Bangalore and Shanghai, could not have happened without such seismic changes at the top. In the case of the Hong Kong Jockey Club, the reverse has been recent in the loss of business to Macau, and with Dharavi I suppose the difficulties are so endemic that the entire enclave, the city within a city, is a response to failures from above.

Other examples? Well, the Australian sports education system was born out of the failure of the country's athletes at the Montreal Olympics. Mobile telephony in Africa was developed because of the failure of the entire continent to have an adequate fixed-line phone system. The Zurich drug-rehabilitation programme only happened because of the catastrophe of 'Needle Park'. The Tokyo police had to respond in the early part of this century when crime rates rose sharply. True, it did not face failure by the standards of other more violent cities elsewhere in the world, but it was shaken out of its complacency.

We will have to see to what extent the market downturn forces a rethink of how New York philanthropy develops but the signs are already encouraging and I was fascinated to learn how the Museum of Modern Art was reacting. Harvard University has to undertake a radical re-examination of its high-cost (though excellent) model in response to the decline in its endowment income, and while it is early days yet, there is no reason why it should not emerge stronger in the end.

Of the more purely commercial stories – the Mittelstand in Germany, Ikea in Sweden and Whistler in Canada – I think the point here is that the discipline of the market imposes an acceptance of failure and the need to learn from it; unless you learn, you go out of business. That will sadly happen to some Mittelstand companies, though others will spring up in their place. Ikea and Whistler will adapt, or at least they always have in the past.

• Keep learning, keep making mistakes

The message here, surely, is not to be ashamed of making mistakes. I was told a lovely story about a young IT expert who was in charge of putting new software into a large British company's systems in the mid 1990s. After about eighteen months and some £5 million of spending, he had to conclude that the system would not work and they should scrap it and start again. The entire investment was wasted. He reported to the chief executive and finished by saying that he felt under the circumstances that he should resign.

The chief executive was furious: 'How dare you resign! We have just spent £5 million on an extremely expensive exercise in management education and the last thing we want is for you to take that knowledge away and give it to some competitor. Now tell me how we make this thing work.'

You see the point: failure is an essential part of any learning process. The inexcusable response is to fail to learn from failure. Both individuals and organizations alike are unable to acknowledge errors for a host of different reasons, but one thing that stands out in these examples again and again is the need for a certain humility. And that is the next lesson here.

7. THE NEED FOR HUMILITY

I was chatting to an acquaintance in the summer of 2008 – someone who was running a large global business – and I made a remark about feeling a failure over something. 'Don't we all,' he replied. 'Don't we all.'

As it happened, that particular person has faced some serious reverses, but the point goes beyond business. A number of examples here, social as well as economic, chart the need for a sense of humility about achievement. I was very struck when talking with two organizations supported by New York philanthropists, the Museum of Modern Art and Visiting Neighbors, by the perspective they apply: yes, they are doing fine but there is much more they could be doing in the future. Or in the case of the team running the International Baccalaureate and both of the schools I visited, there is a great sense of service to the community but also one of modesty. The IB is successful but it has the problem, albeit a welcome one, of managing that success. There is the practical dilemma: how do you maintain quality control when you are growing very fast? But there is also the more emotional dilemma: how do you continue to learn when things are going well? How do you learn from success?

There are several instances in these case studies of humility being in rather short supply. Had Harvard been a little less bombastic about its achievements and its wealth in the early years of this century, it would have found it easier to adapt when the harsher climate struck. Had

Irish politicians – and even more, Irish property developers – been more sensitive to the good-luck element of the boom years, they would have been in better shape in the bust. Had development in Dubai gone just a little bit slower, then it too would have managed the transition from over-rapid growth to more sustainable progress without the disruption and pain that has occurred.

However, the argument for approaching everything with humility goes beyond the need to avoid getting one's comeuppance when the wind changes; you are likely to be more effective in the good times too. There are several examples here of sensitivity in the midst of success, traffic management in Copenhagen among them. One of the reasons why the city was transformed so successfully was that the changes were incremental and appeared seamless. Copenhagen did not impose the sort of aggressive anti-car policy that some other cities have followed. It listened to its shopkeepers and other commercial interests. It avoided conflict. Gradually it made progress.

• Be as sensitive to success as you are to failure

Other examples include the Edinburgh Festival, which despite its success has always been cautious and self-critical; it keeps on growing because it is constantly worried that one day it will not. This attitude means that when there are glitches, such as happened with the ticketing system for the Fringe in 2008, they are solved as soon as is practicable. Still another example is Billings – the most successful town in Montana and nudging towards the top of the 'best place to live' surveys in the USA. But talk to people there and they are worried about all sorts of things: the schools, the opportunities for young people, the danger of drugs and so on. Brash it is not, which is probably why it is such a beacon for medium-sized towns across America.

Or take Zurich. Outsiders do find it a bit self-satisfied, maybe overly sure of its bourgeois values. But in its approach to drugs it has not been at all bombastic. Yes, it is doing something better than most other places, but not every addict is successfully treated and Switzerland is far from being drug-free. The city continues to make progress because it is cautious about its success.

• Acknowledge good fortune

To recognize humility is not to ask people to wear a hair shirt. It is simply that unless they understand the real reasons for any progress they make – acknowledging, for example, the importance of a lucky combination of circumstances (as in Bangalore) – they cannot learn from success. And that is just as important as learning from failure.

8. BE NIMBLE

A theme running through most of the case studies is that they are good at 'course correction'. When the economic or social background changes, they change too. It is extraordinary that an entity as huge as London's financial service industry should have been so nimble over the years, shifting the nature of its business model and even its physical location as the demand for different types of service has altered.

A large part of the banking business moved from the square mile of the old City – which had unwisely tightened its planning regulations, making it hard to build large dealing floors – to the new Docklands site in Canary Wharf, three miles to the east. The new hedge funds decided to set up in St James's in the West End, rather than in the City, because – well, in my own view because the restaurants were better. If that seems a facetious point, the message is a quite practical one. It is that entire industries, particularly service industries, can move location swiftly. They are extremely nimble. And any organization seeking to attract them – be that a municipality, a national government or a regional development agency – needs to be nimble too.

Other examples here include the way in which Shanghai has projected itself as the Chinese mainland's industrial and financial centre, changing the mix of businesses it seeks to encourage as its development proceeds. It has a plan, but if necessary it can change that plan very quickly. The Hong Kong government has been quick on its feet too, in adapting to the shift from manufacturing to finance and in its change of status from UK colony to part of the People's Republic of China. Billings has been nimble in its shift from railway hub to service-industry centre, growing steadily while other Montana cites have declined. All over the USA, it has been the nimble Main Street cities that have flourished while the slow-footed have retreated.

The Irish authorities have made swift moves to alter their financial policies in the face of recession; arguably they reacted faster than the Dubai leadership as it faced a similar transition from very rapid growth to serious recession. You can have a debate as to whether Ireland moved quickly enough, but by the standards of other EU governments it has been exceptional. Change ought to have been easier for Dubai, given the absolute power of the ruling family, but I am not sure it has turned out that way.

I am more impressed when governments move quickly than when commercial enterprises do so. You would expect Ikea and Whistler to respond quickly because that is what their managements are trained to do. The Mittelstand companies of Germany, meanwhile, live or die according to their ability to adapt. The firms that run the mobile phone systems throughout Africa have been very swift in meeting new customer demands and grabbing opportunities as they arise.

• Be quick to adapt

But it is difficult for politicians to change course quickly, partly because they are running large bureaucracies but also because they have to build political support for their actions.

As for the 'in between' organizations, those that are neither purely commercial nor public sector, there are a couple of contrasting experiences. Thus the Edinburgh Fringe has been good at adapting to electronic ticketing, notwithstanding the glitches, whereas Harvard has been relatively slow in adapting to the fall in its endowment income. It will be all right in the end but the experience has shown that the governance of great universities is a tough task. Power is diffuse, inevitably and rightly in my judgement, but that does mean it takes time to turn the ship around and head in a different direction.

The market will give signals, as the next section discusses, but it takes an acute ear on occasion to pick up those signals and adapt.

9. LISTEN TO THE MARKET

The market sometimes gets a worse press than it deserves. Things are declared to be too important to be 'left to the market' – and, after the financial failures of 2008, it would be absurd not to acknowledge its flaws.

But consider the alternative. This story is probably apocryphal but it makes the point. It is of the Soviet Union visitor to Britain seeing supermarkets full of food. 'Who organizes the bread supply for London?' he asks, and refuses to believe it when he is told that no one does.

This is not some crass assertion that the market can solve every problem. But in all the stories here, there is an element of sensitivity to the signals that it gives.

Start with an improbable example: traffic management in Copenhagen. People like to drive their cars, don't they? So they need to be compelled to get out of them – right? Well, yes in part, for there are restrictions on traffic. But car-free areas were brought in sensitively: parking has been provided at the edges of the pedestrianized zones; there is proper provision for essential traffic; and the whole scheme has had the co-operation of businesses within the zones. As a result, not only have there been evident environmental benefits but many shops have enjoyed an increase in footfall and hence sales. So the market reinforced the process of change, making it much easier politically to extend the scheme.

* **Work with the market to effect change**

Another improbable example is the Zurich anti-drug offensive. The aim was social and medical: they had to try to reclaim an area of the city for its citizens and also to reduce the harm that people were doing to themselves. But there was a strong economic incentive, too, because businesses nearby were suffering as a result. Perhaps even more important, a powerful economic incentive was put before the drug users: if they signed up to the programme, they could get free heroin from the clinics.

Still another example is New York philanthropy. I make the point that in many cases people are giving to things from which they will derive no personal gain. So is the market irrelevant? Not at all. Intangible benefits matter too. If you look at how both the Museum of Modern Art and Visiting Neighbors operate, they are acutely sensitive to what the market wants. The museum is in its prime leadership role because New Yorkers want access to modern art. Unlike many of its counterparts in Europe, it is not supported by the national government and only receives very limited backing from the city itself; it has to pay its way in the world. Visiting Neighbors has to provide the service that people want – both the visited and the visiting. It is extending its reach because people ask for its services, not because of any executive decision to expand. Thus it is responding to a market demand.

That leads to my main point. The market is not just about money. Yes, cash provides a convenient benchmark; it saves a lot of time. But sometimes the signals come in quite different ways. You have to figure out how to measure the welfare of Copenhagen or Zurich citizens, or how to compare the Museum of Modern Art with other museums and Visiting Neighbors with other charities. To be successful, they have to stand the financial test of the market – but the other tests matter just as much.

• Remember, it is about more than money

You can see this in Edinburgh. It is a market, the largest one for theatrical and other creative talent. But people are not performing there to make money. In fact, to stage a successful show on the Fringe costs the performers something upwards of £20,000, with the probability of not much of that coming back in ticket sales. Some people do this to foster their careers, but many do it because it is fun.

So in the more obviously commercial stories here – the City of London, Ikea, the Hong Kong Jockey Club, the Mittelstand, mobile telephony in Africa – satisfying the market in financial terms is the core of the operation. But even in the less obviously commercial, the market matters too, and in all sorts of ways. Bangalore, Dublin and Dubai want to attract talented people who will promote the economy. Harvard needs the best brains from every quarter of the world. Australia is in the market for its elite athletes. Dharavi succeeds because it supplies market services to the rest of Mumbai.

All resources are finite. Economists use the ugly expression 'opportunity cost' to describe the idea that if you apply resources to one thing, they are not available to do something else. That applies to finance, of course, but also to human beings, to commodities, to energy, to water, indeed even to that intangible of political capital.

In most cases, that resources are finite is recognized – all right, not in Dubai's energy use – and factored in. Tokyo uses its police manpower carefully. Whistler is aware of its environmental responsibilities. American towns that do not run a tight budgetary regime soon find themselves in trouble.

• Manage your resources carefully

So you have to listen to market signals on both sides. You have on the one hand to provide the goods and services that people want, but on the other you have to be aware that you must do so as efficiently as possible. There are plenty of mistakes here. Harvard allowed itself to extend a building programme without regard to any possible decline in its endowment income. Shanghai has wasted resources on the Maglev rail link to the new airport, when a conventional rail system would have done the job. And part of London's financial services business, though by no means all of it, got carried away by its apparent success in the boom years and misallocated resources.

It would be ridiculous to claim any of these examples is a perfect manifestation of a perfect market. There is no such thing. My message is simply that, by and large, entities that are sensitive to market signals are likely to succeed, while those that ignore them are bound to fail.

10. HAVE A SENSE OF MISSION

The market alone is not guide enough. In every story here, there is something more: a sense of mission – the desire to be world class. You quite often get people with a sense of mission, some of whom do go on to achieve remarkable things. In a few cases here, it has indeed been an individual, or a small group, who has set things moving. But what seems to me much more interesting is the way in which that sense is maintained in a genuine manner, and how it is passed on over time.

• Keep it real

It has to be real. Many corporations now have a mission statement, setting out their supposed values and aims. However, many of these are pretentious rubbish. It is not just that companies fail to live up to their stated values; it is almost as though the mere statement of those values is a substitute for living up to them. And so periodically someone in the top management of some corporation is forced to resign over some ethical issue. Rarely, maybe too rarely, they end up in jail. Any journalist who has reported on business will know of disgraceful behaviour by supposedly reputable corporations that has for whatever reason not come out. Some of the most revered business leaders are some of the worst offenders.

So let us not confuse mission statements with mission. What emerges here is a much more deep-rooted concept – the idea that there should be a collection of values, maybe never stated, that everyone involved in an operation instinctively understands. In the case of the International Baccalaureate, the mission is very clear: broad, internationally minded, ethical education. In successful US towns and cities, the social order of Main Street is understood by all; there is an unwritten constitution that acts as a glue for communities. The mission does not need to be spelt out and indeed it is probably better if it is not, for the community does not need to impose any particular code of behaviour or any set of values. It simply tries to do the right thing for all its people.

• Do right by those who share your objectives

This distinction between a formal mission and a collective sense of shared objectives becomes clearer if you compare at one extreme Harvard, and at the other Dharavi. Harvard has a mission statement going back to 1650, opening with: 'The advancement of all good literature, arts and sciences …' It was restated in 1997 by the then dean, Harry R. Lewis, when he stressed the need to: 'liberate students to explore, to create, to challenge, and to lead'.

Most of us would find both versions of this mission statement exemplary. There are legitimate charges that the leadership of the university has not always lived up to the aims that were set out, and it would be astounding if it had. But as a statement of objectives, of 'why we are here', it is great.

Dharavi, by contrast, has never set out its aims; the idea would be ridiculous. But I believe – I hope I have convinced you – that it has just as profound a sense of moral obligation and purpose as Harvard. It is to run a community for often disadvantaged people, who can live their lives in safety, provide for their daily needs and bring up their families in conditions of respect.

Whether the mission is set out formally or not is pretty unimportant. What matters is that it is embedded deep down in the minds and spirits of each generation of people who help to keep the entity running. If it is not really embedded then when things go wrong, as they always will, it can be hard for that entity to pull itself back together.

You can perhaps see this best in the City of London. There have been many financial crises over the years and there will inevitably be many more. There have also been periodic scandals, where people have behaved dishonestly or unethically. There will be more of that too. On occasion life has imitated art: Anthony Trollope's bent financier Augustus Melmotte, in *The Way We Live Now*, is uncannily similar to the late Robert Maxwell. That both the fictional swindler and the actual one were outsiders distrusted by the more established City leaders is a small excuse. But often the problem is not a single individual but a more general failure, where no one really believes they are doing anything wrong. For example, the separation of broker and jobber on the stock exchange at the end of the nineteenth century came in response to buyers being cheated after being sold shares at inflated prices. One hundred years later, the Lloyd's insurance market similarly cheated its 'names' – the individuals who supplied it with capital.

After each scandal the rules had to be changed. The City's mission – that financial services must be open and honourable – had been lost. But, and this is the key point, once the scale of the scandal became clear, there were enough people imbued with the mission to pull things back. At one meeting of Lloyd's governing body, one of the bad guys protested that there was nothing in the rules that prohibited a particularly egregious practice. 'I know it is not in the rules,' replied the person put in to clean things up. 'It is in the Sermon on the Mount.'

You see the point. Having a sense of mission does not mean that everyone at every stage subscribes to that mission. What it means is that enough of the community has signed up to enable it to be re-established when standards slip.

We will see more examples of this need to reassert a mission in the future. At the end of 2009, a couple of such instances have come to the fore. Ireland's political and commercial leaders have been responding to the pressures of the downturn by going back to the basic lessons of the late 1980s and early 1990s: responsible fiscal policies, the encouragement of sustainable business, the attraction of investment capital – the actions that created the Celtic tiger in the first place. They are doing it with determination and order. The froth is being blown away and the core values restated.

The leadership in Dubai is similarly rethinking where it goes from here, though the shift of mood (unlike the shift in the economy) is less apparent. How realistic Dubai's vision of the future is, we will not know for several years.

• Keep the long game in view

This is a long game. The ideas embedded in a mission not only have to be passed on to the next generation; they have to be refined and adapted. Policing in Tokyo has had to adapt to larger numbers of foreigners moving into the city – people who have not been brought up with Japanese cultural attitudes. Australia has had to adapt to the fact that other countries can imitate its pioneering methods of sports coaching. Commercial activities have to adapt to changing markets and tastes.

But if you do not have a core aim, you are rudderless. That is why there has to be a sense of mission – the idea that whatever you are doing, you do it as well as you can.

That's it, really. Do your best. And, if you have fun doing it, it might just work!

Acknowledgements

Many books are in some measure a team effort but this one has surely been more than most. The reason for that is partly the breadth of the tales I have tried to tell. Each one has been the result of hours of conversations with friends and acquaintances, people suggesting candidates for inclusion to me – and sometimes dispatching my own early ideas. It would be ridiculous to claim to be an expert on such a wide range of subjects so I have leant heavily on people whose judgement I trust.

It has been a team effort for a further reason. As you can see I have drawn many of the ideas from my own experiences from childhood onwards. Thus the chapter on Ireland would have been written quite differently had I not been brought up there, the chapter on Main Street USA could hardly have been written had I not had cousins in Montana, and the chapter on Mumbai had I not such close friends there. I have tried within each chapter and in the introduction to give some indication of the debt I owe to others but I am very aware that there are many more people who have influenced my thinking in some way or other. To them I am most grateful and I ask them to forgive me for not mentioning all by name. I am also grateful to my colleagues at *The Independent* for the questioning (and debunking) atmosphere of the newspaper and to the many organizations that have asked me to speak at events, from which I always go away with new ideas.

A number of people have read specific chapters, corrected mistakes and on some occasions encouraged me to reconsider my judgements. They include Mithu Alur, Sathi Alur, Mary Anne Arisman, Mohan Bopiah, Nina Bopiah, Katey Cochrane, Sandra Coyle, Howard

Cummer, Ray French, Ian Hill, Tony Kevin, Glenn Lowry, Tadashi Nakamae, Simon O'Hagan, Krishna Pathak, Susan Scott and Qin Shi. Thank you all so much.

There are four other friends to whom I have a special debt. Tim Walker and Taylor Dimsdale helped a great deal in the research. (Taylor took on another role in our family in September 2009, by marrying my daughter Alex!) Klaus Weinzierl, a retired German schoolteacher, checked the entire draft for both its consistency and its English – I rather like the idea that native English speakers need a non-native to correct their grammar! And Matt Rowan has edited the entire book, unearthing new facts, picking up errors, sorting out sources and helping me to tighten my arguments. The mistakes that remain despite everyone's efforts are entirely my own.

At the publishers, HarperCollins, Arabella Pike and Annabel Wright have been encouraging, patient, supportive and kind – and with just enough prodding to make sure the project was eventually completed. Michael Upchurch has helped greatly in the final stages. Rebecca Morrison has designed the cover and the chapter illustrations, Carol Anderson copy-edited the book and Ben Murphy compiled the index.

Finally, I would like to thank my own family, my spouse Frances Cairncross and my daughters Izzy and Alex. All three have not only lived with this book for several years but also helped shape it in various ways, making suggestions for structure and content, introducing me to people and ideas, and assuring me that it would eventually be finished. For that, and for everything else you bring to my life, I will ever be grateful.

HAMISH McRAE
London, November 2009

Notes and sources

The UK and Ireland
Chapter One – Edinburgh Festival: the biggest arts festival of all

1. Underlining the evolution of the festival to 'the world is watching' status – a place where business chiefs and politicians, as well as the performers, feel they have to be seen and heard – the publishing and broadcasting tycoon Rupert Murdoch addressed the television festival in 1989 to predict the future of multi-channel television and to rail at the dominance of the BBC. His son James, the head of Murdoch Snr's News Corporation empire in Europe, made the same attack in the same place twenty years later. J. K. Rowling, the *Harry Potter* author, gave a reading to the children's section of the International Book Festival in 2004.

2. The accolade 'World's biggest arts festival' was bestowed by *The Guinness Book of Records* on the Edinburgh Festival, and in particular its Fringe, in the 1990s and the city has been proclaiming that status ever since. It is not disputed, and some of the festival's counterparts around the world vie only for the honour of being 'second after Edinburgh', with the general consensus being that this description is most deserved by the annual Adelaide Fringe in South Australia. Established in 1960 and run alongside the biennial Adelaide Festival of Arts over three weeks in the autumn months of February and March, attendances for the 534 events at the 2009 Fringe came in at just over one million. This was a record for the event and, just in terms of visitor numbers, the Edinburgh Fringe six months later was only twice as big at around 1.9 million. However, the 534 shows at the Adelaide Fringe contrasted with Edinburgh's 2,098. Adelaide Fringe; Edinburgh Fringe.

3. In essence, the arts programme is the Edinburgh International Festival, the mainstream three-week event with which everything began in 1947. A showcase for classical music, opera, theatre and dance, there were 2,300 performers in 2008, attracting a total audience of 394,000 for box-

office revenue of £2.6 million (around $4 million). Edinburgh International Festival.

4. Introduced in 1979, the jazz and blues programme begins in late July and ends just as the main body of the festival is getting underway. It features nearly 100 shows and in 2009 22,000 tickets were sold and around the same number of people attended free concerts. Edinburgh Jazz & Blues Festival.

5. The Edinburgh International Book Festival began in 1983 as a biennial event and went annual in 1997. It claims visitor numbers of 220,000 each year to 750 events including debates, 'meet the author' discussions and writing workshops. Edinburgh International Book Festival.

6. Now run separately from the rest of the events, over twelve days in June, the Edinburgh International Film Festival (EIFF) began alongside the main festival in 1947 with the original aim of screening the new wave of documentary films. That remit widened to include independent and art-house productions from around the world and its schedule now encompasses new international and UK films from both established and first-time directors. Steven Spielberg's *ET* had its UK premiere at Edinburgh, and other films to have taken off in Britain from the EIFF springboard include *The Full Monty, Billy Elliot, Man on Wire, The Bourne Identity* and *Pulp Fiction*. The event claims annual audience figures of 55,000. EIFF.

7. Although the Cannes festival restarted after the war in 1946, it was not held in either 1948 or 1950 because of financial problems. Festival de Cannes.

8. The Edinburgh International Television Festival has been running since 1976 and is, one level, an industry talking shop involving lectures and debates. However, there are also two talent schemes, The Network and Fast Track, offering contact-building, workshops and master classes to those trying to build a career in TV. Edinburgh International Television Festival.

9. This section of the festival is called Edinburgh Interactive. In essence it is a two-day conference for the industry, but members of the public can also participate by playing video games free of charge and seeing previews of upcoming titles.

10. According to the UK government's Sector Skills Council, Scottish games developers generate sales of more than £200 million ($320 million) a year, with the best-selling *Grand Theft Auto* featuring among their

innovations. The local industry has a cluster of firms in the city of Dundee, employs around 700 workers and benefits from government support for start-ups and research and undergraduate courses at Abertay University. Skillset; Scottish Development International.

11. Founded by members of the city's ethnic minority communities, the three-day festival made its debut in 1995. Mela attracts 20,000 people to its mix of theatre, music, dance and fashion shows. Edinburgh Mela Festival.

12. Fifty galleries participated in the Edinburgh Art Festival in 2009, featuring the work of both new and established artists from around the world. Edinburgh Art Festival.

13. Started in 1950, although there had been informal pipes and dancing from the inception of the International Festival in 1947. An Edinburgh Festival Punter, a semi-official internet guide.

14. The annual Festival d'Avignon is still going strong as a showcase for the 'live performing arts'. It put on forty-two shows during its run in July 2009 and sold 125,000 tickets. Festival d'Avignon.

15. Helping to establish the Edinburgh International Festival in 1947 was Rudolf Bing, then the general manager of Glyndebourne, the grand old English operatic festival. Edinburgh International Festival.

16. The eight groups were all theatrical, going under names such as Pilgrim Players, the Glasgow Unity Theatre and the Christine Orr Players, the last of which performed *Macbeth* at the Edinburgh YMCA. Nowadays, theatre accounts for 28 per cent of the Fringe's activities; comedy leads the way with 35 per cent. An Edinburgh Festival Punter; Edinburgh Fringe.

17. The journalist's name was Robert Kemp of the *Edinburgh Evening News*. He commented: 'Round the fringe of official Festival drama, there seems to be more private enterprise than before … I am afraid some of us are not going to be often at home during the evenings!' Edinburgh Fringe.

18. Fringe performers had started to form a loose collective when students opened a drop-in centre for them in the city's Haddington Place. At an inaugural meeting of Fringe groups in 1954, one producer remarked: 'We are cutting each other's throats.' Edinburgh Fringe.

19. From the start, one of the central principles of the society was that there should be no artistic vetting of performers. Edinburgh Fringe.

20. *Beyond the Fringe* was the stage revue that launched the careers of Peter Cook and Dudley Moore, regarded as two of Britain's most influential comedians.

21. The Edinburgh Fringe.
22. At the last official Census, in 2001, the city had a population of 448,000. An estimate in 2008 from the General Register Office for Scotland put the figure at 471,000.
23. Fringe venues include churches, a Quaker Meeting House and even the Sweet Grassmarket Swimming Pool – for 'a nightly damp and steamy mix of water-based spoken word, comedy and music'. EdinburghGuide.com
24. Richard Demarco, holder of a CBE in Britain and the Chevalier des Arts et Lettres de France, has been a passionate supporter of Scottish art and, more generally, contemporary works across Europe through his Edinburgh gallery, the Demarco European Art Foundation and, more recently, the Demarco Archive Trust.
25. The German avant-garde performance artist, sculptor and installation artist (1921–86) is regarded as hugely influential and hugely controversial in equal measure. In 1980, invited to define the spirit of German art, he put on an exhibition in the Demarco Gallery but also achieved a degree of notoriety in Scotland when going on hunger strike in support of the artist and novelist Jimmy Boyle, then a gangster in prison for murder who had been refused permission to practise art. Demarco European Art Foundation.
26. Formed in 1963, the modern-day Traverse is repertory theatre staging twelve shows a year, with an accent on new Scottish writing. Sources: An Edinburgh Festival Punter; the Traverse Theatre.
27. The Cannes festival is held in May, Venice and Toronto in September.
28. The Fringe claims that public funding accounts for just 1 per cent of its annual turnover.

Chapter Two – The City of London: the world's international financial centre
1. The Canary Wharf complex was developed on disused dockland in the East End of London, with full construction beginning in 1988 and the first tenant arriving in 1991. As of 2007 it was host to 93,000 workers, mainly in financial services, employed by multinational institutions such as Barclays, Citigroup, Credit Suisse and HSBC.
2. For rankings, see the Global Financial Centres Index, 2009, produced by consultants Z/Yen Group for the City of London Corporation. In terms of international transactions, the UK accounted for 18 per cent of all cross-border bank lending at the end of 2008, compared with 8 per cent

in both the USA and Japan; for foreign exchange turnover (October 2008), the figures were 35, 16 and 6 per cent respectively; in turnover for over-the-counter derivatives (April 2007), the UK's share was 43 per cent, while the figures for the USA and Japan were 24 and 4 per cent respectively. In 2008, London accounted for 70 per cent of the trading in international bonds. (International Financial Services in London; calculations based on figures from the Bank for International Settlements, London Stock Exchange, Bank of England, Futures Industry Association, International Securities Market Association, World Federation of Exchanges.)

3. The pound had been worth $4.85 before the start of the First World War and, in spite of the cost of the conflict, the British authorities restored it to that level in the 1920s before sterling unravelled during the Great Depression of the 1930s. In 1940, though, an agreement between the USA and Britain pegged the pound to the dollar at a rate of $4.03, where it stayed until 1949 when, confronted with the wartime legacies of debt and a manufacturing industry that had been turned over to the military effort, the UK government finally devalued it to $2.80. Sterling was devalued again in 1967, by 14 per cent.

4. During this period, it was estimated that a new foreign bank was coming to London – opening either a branch, a subsidiary or an office – at a rate of roughly one every two weeks. In 1967 there were 114 of these operations, in 1970 there were 163. *The Banker* magazine, 1986.

5. The levy, the 'interest equalization tax', was imposed by President John F. Kennedy on foreign securities at a rate of up to 15 per cent to offset the much lower returns offered by domestic securities. Designed to stem an outflow of dollars from the USA, the move compounded the effect of the long-established 'Regulation Q', which curbed the interest paid on American savers' deposits, in coaxing more money to the London market. The tax was abandoned in 1974. International Monetary Fund (IMF); *Time* magazine article, July 1963.

6. Big Bang also swept away the old system of face-to-face dealing on the trading floor, replacing it with electronic dealing – though there was an attempt to retain the floor trading, which was subsequently abandoned.

7. Among the venerable names of British finance delivered into foreign hands in the years after Big Bang were the following: Kleinwort Benson (with roots dating back to 1855), bought by Dresdner Bank of Germany; S. G. Warburg (around since 1946 as a merchant bank), taken over by

SBC of Switzerland; Smith New Court (founded 1924), which fell into the hands of Merrill Lynch of the USA; Barings, 233 years old when it was bought for £1 in 1995 by Dutch bank ING in the wake of a billion-dollar fraud; Schroders (founded 1804), which sold its investment banking operations to Citigroup of the USA; Robert Fleming & Co., 127 years old when it fell into the arms of Chase Manhattan bank in 2000; and Cazenove (established 1823), which has merged its investment banking operations into those of J. P. Morgan of the USA.

8. The Texas-based company, then America's seventh-biggest, collapsed into bankruptcy in 2001 with debts of $16 billion in the wake of a massive accounting fraud; it had reported revenues of $101 billion the year before. The scope of the subsequent investigations took in allegations of bribery of tax officials, of a web of complex transactions that kept debt off the books and enriched top executives, and of falsely inflating profits. Top executives at Enron were convicted on charges ranging from fraud to conspiracy to insider trading. Arthur Andersen, the company's auditor, was convicted on charges of obstructing justice, following allegations that its employees had shredded documents relating to Enron.

9. The Sarbanes-Oxley Act came into force in 2002 as a result of the Enron case and a number of other corporate scandals in the USA. Its provisions were grouped into eleven multi-section categories and were mainly concerned with far-reaching reporting and accountability requirements, and a stronger framework for identifying and punishing wrongdoing.

10. At the end of 2008, over half of the UK banking sector's assets was managed by foreign institutions. International Financial Services London.

11. Market information. As of 2009 salaries and bonuses in the different financial centres are not disclosed.

12. Bank of Credit and Commerce International was founded in 1972 and based in London but registered offshore. It spent most of its nineteen-year existence trying to evade regulation as it built up a global operation with $20 billion of assets. In 1991, however, it was forced into liquidation following the discovery that it had disguised losses and was insolvent. Shortly afterwards, BCCI and its chiefs were charged with fraud, money laundering and larceny. Claims against the company from creditors and depositors totalled around $16 billion and liquidation proceedings to recover the money stretched well into the next decade. A legal action was

launched against the Bank of England over regulatory negligence, though the case was dropped in 2005.

13. The newspaper proprietor, whose publishing empire included the Mirror Group in London and the *New York Daily News*, plundered the occupational pension funds of his employees to help prop up his indebted companies. He was found dead in 1991.

14. The insurance market was hit by billion-dollar losses at the end of the 1980s and start of the 1990s as a result of natural and man-made disasters and a rash of asbestos and pollution-related claims. Lloyd's 'names', the people who underwrite losses on insurance policies, alleged they had been recruited on false information; many of them were bankrupted.

15. In a 2005 survey of the world's cities, London came sixth on the measure of GDP and, at $53,000, its GDP per head was ahead of any other European centre. PricewaterhouseCoopers – findings based on data from the United Nations, World Bank and OECD.

16. United Nations data reported in the Arts Council response to Digital Britain Report, March 2009.

17. The Great Depression is the most studied period of economic history. By coincidence one of the important recent studies, *Essays on the Great Depression*, was written by Ben S. Bernanke, who as chairman of the Federal Reserve Board has had a key role in trying to ward off another depression.

Chapter Three – The Celtic tiger: from boom to bust … to recovery

1. In 1990 Ireland's gross domestic product stood at $48 billion and its gross per capita national income at $12,500. By 2000 those figures had risen to $96 billion and $22,000 respectively. In 2007 GDP was $256 billion and average earnings $51,000. As the global recession took hold in 2008 and GDP growth was running below minus 2 per cent, its gross per capita national income was down to $49,500, but that was still $2,000 ahead, for example, of the USA and gave Ireland a ranking of eleventh, on this measure, out of 220 countries. At 10.37 per cent, the rate of annualized economic growth between 1990 and 2007 was the highest in the European Union and among the highest in the world. United Nations.

2. Irish GDP stood at $1.9 billion in 1960. CIA World Factbook; World Bank World Development Indicators Database.

3. Trinity College is over 400 years old, founded in 1592 under the reign of Queen Elizabeth I as 'mother of a university'. Its alumni include Samuel Beckett, Oscar Wilde and Jonathan Swift, author of *Gulliver's Travels*.

4. 4.03 births per woman in 1965. World Development Indicators Database.

5. Irish Central Statistics Office (CSO) censuses. The population had been 2.96 million in 1951.

6. The writer was a regular visitor to Davy Byrnes and developed a friendship with the teetotal proprietor (Dublin Tourism). The pub is immortalized in Joyce's epic novel, *Ulysses*: 'He entered Davy Byrnes. Moral pub. He doesn't chat. Stands a drink now and then. But in a leap year once in four. Cashed a cheque for me once.'

7. United Nations statistics put the Irish population at 4.3 million in 2007. In the same year, according to FAS, the Irish training and development authority, immigrants made up 11 per cent of the workforce.

8. CB Richard Ellis, property consultants, 2009.

9. CSO.

10. At the beginning of 2004, Ireland was attracting some 60,000 immigrants a year; in 2006–7, the total at peaked at well over 100,000 (both figures including returning Irish citizens), with people from the ten new EU accession states accounting for nearly half of the inflow. A 2006 census found that nearly 3 per cent of the population was made up of people from the 'EU10', including Poland, the Czech Republic and Hungary. The net migration rate in 2007 was around 70,000; in the UK (with a population fifteen times the size of Ireland's) it was 237,000. CSO; UK Office for National Statistics.

11. See, for example, 'What difference has membership made?', eumatters.ie, the Department of Foreign Affairs in Ireland. See also *Irish Economic Development in International Perspective: A Tale of Three Covers*, a report by John Bradley at Irish think-tank the Economic and Social Research Institute.

12. In 1986, around 1.6 million Irish citizens were under the age of 25 and unemployment was running at 17.2 per cent. CSO; World Development Indicators Database.

13. Recognizing that the country's future lay in science and technology, Ireland set about building the home-grown skills base needed to fulfil that aim. In 2003, according to European Commission statistics, it had sixteen science and engineering graduates per thousand of population,

contrasting with an average of under seven per thousand across the fifteen European Union member states (ahead of the EU expansion in 2004).

14. Between 1989 and 1999, Ireland received EU funding of more than €10 billion ($15 billion) for investment in infrastructure. Irish government.

15. Irish national income per head in 1987 was only $9,000. World Development Indicators Database.

16. Desmond O'Malley had been expelled from Fianna Fáil early in 1985 for 'conduct unbecoming' over his sympathy for a government measure to liberalize the sale of contraceptives. He announced the formation of the Progressive Democrats later that year, recruiting, among others, Mary Harney from Fianna Fáil, and his party won fourteen seats in the 1987 election and 12 per cent of the popular vote. But the Progressive Democrats were not able to maintain that momentum and in 2009 they were wound up.

17. This watershed moment in Irish politics is referred to as the 'Tallaght Strategy', after a speech given by Alan Dukes to the Chamber of Commerce in Tallaght (a town eight miles outside Dublin) on 2 September 1987. In the address, he pledged not to oppose the government as long as it followed a low-tax, cost-cutting policy. Any other course of action, he said, 'would amount simply to a cynical exploitation of short-term political opportunities for a political advantage which would inevitably prove to be equally short-lived' (Fine Gael). Alan Dukes stood down from the leadership after disappointing performances by his party at the 1989 general election and the 1990 presidential election.

18. American Community Survey, US Census Bureau, 2005.

19. A United Nations survey in 2002 showed a drug-offending rate of 190 per 100,000 people. A European Commission study in the previous year found that almost 30 per cent of Dublin teenagers had taken illegal drugs. A survey by Ireland's National Advisory Committee on Drugs, for 2006–7, found that 24 per cent of people aged between 15 and 64 had taken illegal drugs at some point in their lives; for 2006–7 alone, the figure was 7.2 per cent, although 15.4 per cent of people aged 15 to 24 used illegal drugs in this period.

20. The Irish property boom was widely reported around the world – see for example Irish Property Owners Are Rolling in Green, *The Washington Post*, 2 September 2006 – and it was clear even during the boom that it

would come to an end at some stage. But most commentators predicted that the market would achieve a soft landing. The surprise was not that property prices had risen too much but the savage nature of the correction.

Continental Europe
Chapter Four – Traffic management in Copenhagen: the car-free paradise

1. Average temperatures in Copenhagen range from minus two degrees centigrade in January and February to 22 degrees in July and August.
2. In 'Are pedestrians invisible in the planning process?', a paper prepared in 1997 by Lars Gemzøe of Gehl Architects in Copenhagen, the point is made that the Danish capital is unique among cities in measuring and recording not just motorized traffic but the numbers, flow and behaviour of pedestrians. Findings such as this one are the result of work carried out in 1968, 1986 and 1995 by researchers from the School of Architecture at the Royal Danish Academy of Fine Arts, and for further reading on many of the developments, statistics and analyses covered in this chapter, see the book *Public Spaces, Public Life*, written by Jan Gehl and Lars Gemzøe and published by the Danish Architectural Press.
3. In a paper written in 1989, 'A changing street life in a changing society', Jan Gehl of Gehl Architects reported that the tripling of pedestrianized space by 1986 had been matched by a tripling in the number of people sitting or standing in the area on a summer's day.
4. Each phase of the pedestrianization process has involved the gradual removal of 2 to 3 per cent of the parking space so that people can grow accustomed to a change in their travel habits from car to public transport or bicycles. 'The form and use of public space', a paper presented by Jan Gehl to the European Transport Conference at Loughborough University in the UK in 1998.
5. Lars Gemzoe, 'Are pedestrians invisible in the planning process?'
6. 'The form and use of public space'. Findings based on research from the City of Copenhagen and the School of Architecture at the Royal Danish Academy of Fine Arts.
7. In 2008, Copenhagen came first in an index of the world's 'most liveable cities' produced by the lifestyle magazine *Monocle*. The criteria for the award include such quality-of-life factors as atmosphere, design, environmental credentials and low crime rates.

8. Interviewed by Tim Walker at the office of Gehl Architects, Copenhagen, 2005.

9. *The Bike Account 2006*, an annual report for the City of Copenhagen.

10. Jan Gehl's practice has been involved in either projects or design consultations in Europe, North America, Australia, Japan, Singapore and Saudi Arabia. His work with Transport for London, commissioned in 2004, looked at ways of changing the emphasis from motor vehicles to other forms of transport. In the New York project, from 2007–9, he has reimagined the city's streets as places for pedestrians and cyclists.

11. Established as a town in the twelfth century, nearly half of Copenhagen's buildings were destroyed in a great fire in 1728, so that much of the original medieval architecture no longer remains.

12. *Public Spaces, Public Life.*

13. Article published online, December 2008.

14. See note 8.

Chapter Five – Zurich drug rehabilitation: teaching the world to kick the habit

1. From 2001 to 2008, Zurich topped an annual survey by William M. Mercer, the consultancy, comparing 215 cities worldwide on the measure of quality of life. Criteria for the rankings included safety and political and economic stability. Also in 2008, a survey by UBS, the bank, found that net incomes in Zurich were the highest in a comparison of seventy-three international cities.

2. Dr André Seidenberg's article for *General Practitioner*, published on 4 January 1999 under the title 'What tells us Switzerland's drug policy?', provides an insight into Zurich's drug culture between Needle Park and the Four Pillars, as well as into the success of the treatment programme. Dr Seidenberg is the president of APAC-Suisse and a member of the board of FIAPAC. He is a Research Fellow of the Institut für Hausarztmedizin und Versorgungsforschung, University of Zurich.

3. Carlos Nordt and Rudolf Stohler, 'Incidence of heroin use in Zurich, Switzerland: a treatment case register analysis', *The Lancet* (3 June 2006), vol. 367, no. 9525.

4. New South Wales' 'opioid treatment programme' has mainly involved the replacement therapy of methadone and, since 2001, buprenorphine. In July 2006, the NSW government reported that the number of regular heroin users in the state had dropped by 58 per cent between 1999 and 2002, from 48,200 to 19,900.

5. *Situation Suisse: Rapport de Situation 2000*, findings from the Swiss Federal Office of Police. Offences involving the consumption of marijuana jumped from 15,734 in 1998 to 21,492 in 2000 at the same time as heroin use was going the other way with offences down from 15,870 to 11,721.

6. In 2002, Switzerland ranked fifth-highest in the world for drug offences as a proportion of population, with reported cases of 49,200 out of seven million people (or 0.7 per cent), although this number had dropped to 47,000 by 2006. United Nations Office on Drugs and Crime; Swiss Federal Statistical Office.

7. Noting the scale of the problem, the Cannabis Report for the Swiss Federal Commission for Drugs Issues in 1999 said that the equivalent of 250 hectares of land, including private gardens and balconies, was being used for the cultivation of cannabis. Some three tonnes of hemp products and 317,000 hemp plants had been impounded in 1997. 'It can be assumed,' the report added, 'that Switzerland has become a hemp-exporting country', with most of the crop destined for the illegal market of drugs rather than the legal one of textile production.

8. In the Swiss national referendum in November 2008, 63 per cent of voters rejected decriminalization of cannabis, while 68 per cent registered their approval of prescription heroin. BBC.

9. The 'randomized injecting opioid treatment trial' (RIOTT), a trial project involving 'entrenched heroin addicts who have repeatedly been found to fail to benefit from existing treatments', began in 2005 and split users into three categories: one group was administered with oral methadone; another with injected methadone; and the third with unadulterated injected heroin. In a final report in 2009, the co-ordinators of the pilot scheme, intended as the basis for a national rollout, reported that the most dramatic improvements had been achieved in the third group: after six months, three-quarters had substantially reduced their use of street heroin and one in five were 'totally abstinent' in buying from dealers. Meanwhile, again in the prescription-heroin group, clients who had been spending an average of just over £300 a week on drugs before entering RIOTT had brought this down to under £50 on average after six months, and a total of 1,731 crimes committed in the month before going into treatment had fallen to 547 six months later. Action on Addiction and the National Addiction Centre, King's Health Partners.

10. Though Switzerland had started to take a harder line on drugs in 1991 when the Federal Office of Public Health advocated a twin-track approach of harm reduction and 'repression', the treatment side had not evolved far enough to prevent the drugs scene moving on when the police launched their offensive on Platzspitz the following year. Following a national referendum in 1994, the Four Pillar programme was ratified and Zurich used the new provisions to extend its heroin-prescription programme. Parallel to this, it also cracked down on offenders by detaining and deporting foreigners and 'repatriating' people from outside the canton. While health professionals criticized the element of coercion, the view of the authorities was that Zurich residents accounted for a low proportion of offenders. Swiss crime statistics for 1994 showed that 36 per cent of all drugs offences were committed by non-nationals. Nicholas Dorn, Jorgen Jepsen and Ernesto Ugo Savona, *European Drug Policies and Enforcement* (Macmillan, 1996); 'Drug treatment in Switzerland: harm reduction, decentralization and community response', a paper written by H. K. Klingemann in 1996 with the support of the Swiss Federal Office of Public Health.
11. US Department of Justice.
12. Swiss Federal Statistical Office. The vast majority of immigrants are from Italy, Germany, Turkey and the states of the former Yugoslavia.
13. Swiss Federal Statistical Office.

Chapter Six – The Mittelstand: Germany's industrial powerhouse
1. The value of Germany's exports in 2006 was $1.3 trillion, ahead of China, the USA and Japan. Meanwhile its population, as measured in 2008, was the sixteenth-highest in the world at eighty-two million; China's population stood at 1.3 billion, the USA at 304 million and Japan 127 million. CIA World Factbook; World Bank World Development Indicators Database.
2. In a ranking of 196 countries by annual GDP growth in 2005, France, for example, came 177th with a rate of 1.19 per cent and the Netherlands 178th at 1.13 per cent. Source: World Development Indicators Database.
3. More than two million German companies are family businesses. Institut für Mittelstandsforschung (IfM).
4. In 2007–8 German small and medium-sized enterprises (SMEs), defined as having anything up to 499 employees, accounted for 3.5 million businesses in the industrial economy, or 99.7 per cent of all German

companies in this sector. They employed twenty-one million people, representing 70 per cent of the total. IfM.

5. On one measure, a survey by the US Bureau of Labor Statistics, the average hourly labour cost among all employees in German manufacturing was around $50 in 2007, placing the country second in the world behind Norway. To put that statistic into context, the figure for US manufacturing was $31 and Japan $24.

6. Hermann Simon, the chairman and chief executive of a strategy consultancy called Simon-Kucher and Partners, and a visiting professor at Harvard and London Business School, followed up *Hidden Champions: Lessons from 500 of the World's Best Unknown Companies* (Harvard Business School Press, 1996) with another book on the same theme, *Hidden Champions of the 21st Century: Success Strategies of Unknown World Market Leaders* (Springer, 2009).

7. Webasto.

8. Under allied rule in the aftermath of the Second World War, West Germany burst out of an economic straitjacket when, under the direction of finance minister Ludwig Erhard, price controls were abolished and the over-inflated reichsmark was replaced with a new currency, the deutschmark. At a stroke, aided by the slashing of the country's high taxes a year later, the economy began its march to recovery because it was now worth making food and other goods, while employees worked harder because their wages had some value and they could spend their money in shops that were suddenly fully stocked. The GDP per capita in West Germany was $2,834 in 1948; by 1954 it had almost doubled to $5,247. Ardo Hansson, 'The importance of being earnest: early stages of the West German Wirtschaftswunder', working paper, 1991; *The World Economy: Historical Statistics*, compiled by Angus Maddison (OECD, 2003).

9. In 1990, Germany's year-on-year GDP growth rate stood at 5.7 per cent; by 1993, that figure had dipped into negative territory at minus 0.8 per cent. An unemployment rate of 6 per cent in 1990 was up to 8 per cent by 1994. International Monetary Fund.

10. The IfM reports that around 71,000 family businesses in Germany need to manage their succession each year, and of these roughly half are likely to be kept in the family. Some 21 per cent, the IfM estimates, will be sold, 17 per cent will be the subject of a takeover by the firm's managers and 8 per cent will close for the lack of any successor.

11. A new business start-up rate of 1.5 million in 2003 had declined to 1.2 million in 2005 and 800,000 by 2008. KFW Bankengruppe, the Federal Republic-owned bank.

Chapter Seven – IKEA: style at a price the world can afford
  1. Ikea.
  2. Partly as a result of Sweden's neutrality in the Second World War, which left its industry and infrastructure intact, the country embarked on a sustained period of economic expansion from the 1940s, recording the seventh-highest GDP per capita in the world in 1950 and the fifth-highest by 1960. During this period, the government introduced a system of collective but flexible bargaining between employers and unions, under which many workers took their share in Sweden's prosperity by electing for shorter working hours. However, the country also became the home of 'big government' and high taxes in the 1950s, determining to safeguard the well-being of all its citizens through the goals of wage restraint, full employment and a massively expanded welfare system. Its tax take rose from 21 to nearly 29 per cent of GDP during the course of the decade, and then on past 50 per cent over the next three decades. Ikea, like its home country, proclaims 'social equality' as one of its values. World Bank World Development Indicators Database; CIA World Factbook; OECD; N. F. R. Krafts and Gianni Toniolo, *Economic Growth in Europe since 1945* (Cambridge University Press, 1996); Ikea.
  3. From the 1950s onwards, more young Swedish couples were able to set up home and start families because the 'big state' concept, apart from working towards full employment through measures such as retraining allowances for workers who were made redundant, encouraged more women into jobs. With stronger financial provision being made for maternity leave and childcare arrangements, Sweden became more of a country of dual breadwinners, so a steady rise in the proportion of all women employed in the labour force, from 30 to 40 per cent between 1950 and 1970, ran in parallel with an increase in the birth rate – from 2.21 to 2.32 between 1950 and 1960. The Lund University School of Economics and Management, Sweden; *Sweden: Demographic History*, a report by Watson Wyatt, the consultancy; the World Resources Institute; World Development Indicators Database; CIA World Factbook.

4. This estimate was mentioned in Elen Lewis, *Great Ikea! A Brand for All the People* (Cyan Books, 2005).

5. Ikea.

6. The farm was called Elmtaryd and the village Agunnaryd.

7. Ikea.

8. As of 2009, the president and chief executive of Ikea is Anders Dahlwig, but ultimate control still rests with the Kamprad family through the Stichting Ingka Foundation, the Netherlands-registered parent company.

9. In the early days, Ikea, and in particular its low-cost business model, was stifled by an agreement between established Swedish retailers and furniture manufacturers that restricted newcomers seeking to enter the market. Ultimately, a supplier boycott on deliveries to Ikea had the dual effect of persuading the company to bring design and production in-house and then to start sourcing components more cheaply overseas. Peter Maskell, Heikki Eskelinen, Ingjaldur Hannibalsson, Anders Malmberg and Eirik Vatne, *Competitiveness, Localised Learning and Regional Development* (Routledge, 1998); Ikea.

10. Unicef; World Wildlife Fund; Ikea.

11. Described by Ingvar Kamprad as his 'greatest mistake', details emerged in 1994 of a friendship with the pro-Nazi Swedish politician Per Engdahl during the 1940s and early 1950s – prompting a letter of apology to all of Ikea's employees in which he lamented the stupidity of youth. 'Ikea always was a disaster to assemble', *Sunday Times*, 13 February 2005; 'Sweden's answer to Sam Walton', *BusinessWeek* magazine, 14 November 2005.

12. Apart from working to combat child labour, the Ikea Social Initiative programme runs a scholarship scheme under which students from Eastern Europe study sustainable forestry at the Swedish University of Agricultural Science. Ikea.

13. Peter, Jonas and Mathias.

North America
Chapter Eight – New York philanthropy: the most generous people on earth

1. A report in November 2006 from the Charities Aid Foundation (CAF) in Britain, *International Comparisons of Charitable Giving*, reviewed donations by individuals in a selection of countries whose wealth covered over half of the total global economy. Drawing on data for 2005 from the World Bank's World Development Indicators Database, it found that

Americans led the way as givers, contributing 1.67 per cent of the country's GDP to charity – a proportion that was more than twice as high as the next two nations in the league table: the UK at 0.73 per cent and Canada at 0.72 per cent. Germany and France gave 0.22 and 0.14 per cent respectively.

2. James Smithson, a scientist, named his nephew as beneficiary of his will but stipulated that if he were to die without heirs, the estate should go 'to the United States of America, to found at Washington, under the name of the Smithsonian Institution, an establishment for the increase and diffusion of knowledge among men'; the nephew died in 1835 with no heirs. The funds amounted to $500,000 and, although the reasons for Smithson's bequest remain obscure, the institution has lived up to his vision. It now comprises nineteen museums and 145 affiliate museums – housing collections whose subjects range from African art to American history and aerospace to natural history – and nine research centres whose interests include astronomy, the environment, marine ecosystems and the conservation of threatened species and habitats. Its museums attracted twenty-five million visitors in 2008. Smithsonian Institution.

3. Victims of economic hardship, the Carnegie family left their home town of Dunfermline in 1848 when Andrew was 13 and settled in Pennsylvania. In 1865, using the connections, funds and knowledge he had acquired working on the state railroad, he began to forge the steel empire that he would sell thirty-six years later to John Pierpont Morgan (of investment bank fame) for $480 million. Ranked by *Forbes* magazine in 2007 as the second-wealthiest person (behind his contemporary, the industrialist John D. Rockefeller) in history – a calculation based on the net worth of an individual as a proportion of the GDP of the country they lived in – Andrew Carnegie was anxious to be parted from his wealth and ended up giving away $350 million. But although he stated in his 1889 essay *Gospel of Wealth* (available now as a Penguin Classic) that 'the man who dies rich dies disgraced', he added: 'One of the serious obstacles to the improvement of our race is indiscriminate charity. It were better for mankind that the millions of the rich were thrown into the sea than so spent as to encourage the slothful, the drunken, the unworthy.' Instead, his aim was to help people help themselves through education and research, and his legacy was to include 2,500 public libraries, the Carnegie Institution of Science, Carnegie Mellon University (specializing in scientific and technological research), the

concert venue Carnegie Hall and, in his home country, the Carnegie Trust for the Universities of Scotland. The Carnegie Corporation of New York.

4. The Bill & Melinda Gates Foundation has some $39 billion of assets and has given away more than $27 billion since its inception in 1994. The Foundation Center; *BusinessWeek* magazine.

5. A Giving USA report showed that Americans, both private and corporate, gave $308 billion in 2008. This was down 2 per cent on the previous year as the financial downturn took hold, but still represented 2.2 per cent of US GDP.

6. This figure represents the average annual charitable contribution of Italians over a seven-year period to 2002. Johns Hopkins University.

7. Independent Sector, a coalition of America's charities and philanthropic organizations, carried out a survey of more than 4,000 adults in 2001. Entitled *Giving and Volunteering in the United States*, the report found that 89 per cent of households give, with the average annual donation being $1,620.

8. In 2006, on a global measure of the highest top rates of income tax, the USA came forty-first with 35 per cent, behind all but a handful of the world's developed nations (World Bank World Development Indicators Database). In its 2006 *International Comparisons* report, the CAF noted: 'Giving tends to represent a lower proportion of GDP in countries with higher levels of taxation.'

9. A CAF study in 2005 found that faith-based organizations in Britain accounted for 10 per cent of the 500 largest charities' income.

10. George Soros has made philanthropic gifts of more than $2 billion. *BusinessWeek* magazine.

11. One of the driving forces in the creation of the Museum of Modern Art in 1929 was Abby Aldrich Rockefeller, a New York socialite and wife of John D. Rockefeller. Three generations of the family have sat on the board of trustees for the museum, which now features 630,000 square feet of new and designed space and houses more than 150,000 artworks and 300,000 books. MoMA.

12. Formed in 1972 by eight members of the Greenwich Village community, Visiting Neighbors now has 400 dedicated volunteers spending time with 1,000 older people each year. The stated aim of the scheme is to 'help seniors maintain their independence, by connecting them to someone who cares'.

13. According to Independent Sector's *Nonprofit Almanac*, some 80 million American adults (or 26.7 per cent of the population) claimed in a survey for 2006 that they had done volunteering through an organization.
14. Johns Hopkins University.
15. First published in 1970, *The Gift Relationship: From Human Blood to Social Policy* was reprinted and updated in 1997 by the New Press.
16. Devised in 1895, although construction of the centrepiece building on Fifth Avenue was not completed until 1911, the New York Public Library came into being as an amalgamation of the city's existing Astor and Lenox libraries, which had fallen into financial difficulty, and Samuel Tilden's $2.4 million bequest to 'establish and maintain a free library and reading room'. Now used by more than fifteen million people each year, the NYPL is the hub of a network of eighty-seven libraries throughout the city, with collections totalling 6.6 million items. The origins of those 'branches' go back to 1901 and a $5.2 million donation from Andrew Carnegie. New York Public Library.
17. Henry Clay Frick was a nineteenth-century coal baron whose business interests became closely entwined with those of Andrew Carnegie in providing the power for the burgeoning steel business. He became chairman of the Carnegie Company in 1889, when the founder stood down from day-to-day management, but in 1892 he provoked the 'Homestead Strike' with a proposal to cut wages because of depressed business conditions. The dispute, exacerbated by Frick's decision to recruit strike-breakers, escalated into a battle in which ten people were killed. Frick retired from business in 1901 with the sale of Carnegie to J. P. Morgan and concentrated on building up his collection of fine art. In 1910 he bought land on Fifth Avenue and 70th Street to build a mansion that would house his paintings and, so legend has it – his relationship with his former business partner soured – 'make Carnegie's place look like a miner's shack'. On his death in 1919, he bequeathed the house, the art works and an endowment of $15 million for the creation of a public gallery. The permanent Frick Collection now consists of more than 1,100 works of art from the Renaissance to the late nineteenth century. The Frick Collection.
18. The most notable blow dealt to the image of giving in 2009 came with the conviction of Bernard Madoff, the fraudulent investment manager who cheated clients of billions of dollars. Prominent among the victims of Madoff, a Jewish-American and self-styled philanthropist, were a

number of Jewish foundations who had invested their endowments with him.

19. *The Bottom Billion: Why the Poorest Countries are Failing and What Can be Done About It* (Oxford University Press, 2007).

20. Local residents Joshua David and Robert Hammond formed Friends of the High Line in 1999 to campaign for its preservation and reuse as public open space, at a time when it had been threatened with demolition. Eventually the New York City government was persuaded to commit $50 million to the project and construction began in 2006, with the first section being opened to the public in 2009. The High Line.

Chapter Nine – Main Street America: core values for the world

1. Main Street also became shorthand for the population and real economy of the whole country in 2008 when, as the banking crisis was sweeping through the financial industry, the question was asked of when the Wall Street disease would spread to Main Street.

2. Montana sits in the north-west of the USA, bordering Canada and with the Rocky Mountains running down the western side of the state. It has an estimated population of around 970,000. US Census Bureau, 2008.

3. US Census Bureau, 2008.

4. The Directorate General for Regional Policy in the European Union produced some research on this in 2009, providing comparisons of labour mobility between the USA and the member countries of the EU – in terms of the number of working-age people in 2005–6 who had changed their region of residence during the previous year. It found that 2 per cent of working-age Americans (around three million) had moved region or state, against 0.96 per cent of Europeans, and stripping out the effect of language and cultural barriers, 0.82 per cent of Europeans moved within their own country. In the USA, there are comparatively strong disincentives to long-term joblessness, including a twenty-six-week limit on benefit payments (though the ceiling may be higher at times of recession) and a tax on unemployment income once it has risen above $2,400 – an allowance that was introduced in 2009 to soften the impact of the financial crisis (US Department of Labor, US Internal Revenue Service).

5. Although it owed its existence to the railroad, was named after the president of the Northern Pacific, Frederick Billings, and came to be known as the 'magic city' for the explosive growth in the trackside

population – around 10,000 people had settled there eighteen years after the founding of the town in 1882 – the enduring strength of Billings has been its diversity and openness to outsiders. In the early twentieth century, for example, Mexicans and Russo-Germans arrived to work on irrigated land in the Yellowstone Valley where sugar beet was growing and a sugar refinery had been built in 1906. A livestock industry then evolved from animals fed on beet pulp. Meanwhile, Billings was also growing fatter on the development of natural resources such as coal, oil and gas. In 2000, 43 per cent of its residents hailed from outside the state. Montana State University-Billings Library; David J. Wishart, *Encyclopedia of the Great Plains* (Center for Great Plains Studies, 2004).

6. The population of Butte in 2007 was estimated to be 32,000; at its high point in 1920 the city was host to 42,000 people, compared to 15,000 in the same year in Billings. Butte's story goes back to 1864 with the first discovery of gold. But it was when it struck copper, needed for a new form of energy called electricity, in 1880 that the boom took off and the population soared, bolstered by workers from China and all over Europe. However, copper production peaked in 1917 and underground mining began a long decline in the 1950s. In 2000, 27 per cent of Butte's residents were born outside the state. Butte Silver-Bow Public Archives; US Census Bureau.

7. 'Pork' politics, whose origins date back to the days before the American Civil War when slaves were rewarded with big barrels of salt pork which they were then left to fight over, is now defined as 'appropriations secured by Congressmen for local projects' – or taxpayer-funded projects that benefit only a few. One take on the subject was provided by the journalist Alistair Cooke in *Letter from America*, a weekly radio show that ran for fifty-eight years on the BBC. In a broadcast in 2003, he recounted how elected representatives returning to their home towns to tell constituents of the part they had played in framing important legislation would be met with the reply, 'Where's the pork?' – in other words, 'What have you done for me?' Come an election time for Congress, Cooke continued, and that question would reverberate in their minds, and so it was at the end of 2003 when an Omnibus Bill was passed authorizing the spending of $23 billion on thousands of local projects, including a $50 million request in one constituency to have an indoor rainforest built as a tourist attraction. More recently, President Obama announced that the age of 'just pork coming out of Congress'

was over, only to be criticized for just that sin with his own administration's 'stimulus' spending on areas such as health, education and infrastructure.

8. In 'Bowling alone: America's declining social capital', his January 1995 essay for the quarterly *Journal of Democracy* (published by Johns Hopkins University Press), Robert Putnam argued that not only were Americans no longer sitting on local civic organizations; they were not even talking to each other – a trend he attributed to factors such as political distrust, greater female participation in the workforce and the more insular outlook wrought by time spent in front of televisions or on the computer. As an analogy for this shift towards individualism, he noted that while more Americans were going bowling than ever before, membership in bowling leagues had declined by more than 40 per cent over a ten-year period. His book, *Bowling Alone: The Collapse and Revival of American Community* (Simon & Schuster, 2000), elaborated on the theme and posed the question of how US citizens could reconnect.

9. In 2006, 2.1 million people were employed in the agriculture, forestry and fishing sector, against three million in 2000 and nearly fourteen million in 1910. Between 1910 and 2008, the number of farms declined from over six million to 2.2 million. US Bureau of Labor Statistics; National Agricultural Statistics Service; US Department of Agriculture.

10. In the US Census Bureau's 2004 American Housing Survey, it was found that out of a total of seventy-two million owner-occupied homes in the USA, three million sat behind walls and gates in security-conscious communities.

11. Billings came third in a survey by the men's magazine *BestLife* in 2008, based on factors such as employment, personal safety and quality of education.

Chapter Ten – Harvard: the world's top university

1. Figure for the year to June 2008. In the previous year, Harvard's annual income had been $3.2 billion, and the year before that $3 billion. (Office of the Controller, Harvard University.) The title of 'world's richest university' is a factor of the size of an institution's endowment – the value of its invested funds (see below) – and on this measure Harvard's $26 billion endowment in June 2009 was far in excess of any other US university, with the second-ranked Yale posting a figure of $16 billion. (National Association of College and University Business Officers,

Washington DC.) On a global scale, to illustrate the funding gap between the top American colleges and the rest, Cambridge and Oxford reported endowments of $8 billion and $5 billion respectively in 2007.

2. Harvard's endowment in 2009 represented a sharp drop on the $37 billion recorded a year before. The return on its investments was minus 27.3 per cent as the global financial crisis took its toll, and particularly badly hit was the university's real estate portfolio, whose value plummeted by 50 per cent. (Harvard Management Company.) Unlike, say, in the UK, many American universities are private and so rely on donations from organizations or individuals, particularly alumni, to fund such needs as professorships, scholarships or a degree of financial assistance for students. In 2008, the disbursal of endowment funds accounted for 34 per cent of Harvard's annual income. (Office of the Controller, Harvard.)

3. In Shanghai Jiao Tong University's Academic Ranking of World Universities 2008, Harvard came first in a league table of 500 institutions worldwide. In the top twenty, every university was American with the exception of Cambridge (ranked fourth), Oxford (tenth) and Tokyo University (nineteenth). The grading criteria are based not just on current academic performance but also highly cited research work and scientific articles, and the number of alumni and staff who win Nobel Prizes or other major international awards. This approach has been criticized, among other things, for being too biased towards science. However, a rival league table, the UK-based Times Higher Education-QS World University Rankings, also ranked Harvard first in 2008 and the criteria here are different, being far more weighted towards peer review by academics around the world.

4. The origins of the American university system lie in the seventeenth-century Puritan settlements in New England, home to four 'Ivy League' institutions including Harvard and Yale. (John Harvard, the university's first benefactor, was himself a clergyman.) Higher education at this time was informed by religious instruction and this sense of mission persisted into the second half of the nineteenth century, with an emphasis on teaching the classics of Latin and Greek – rather than the more scientific disciplines that an industrializing nation might require. George W. Marsden, *The Soul of the American University: From Protestant Establishment to Established Nonbelief* (Oxford University Press, 1994); Edward H. Cotton, *The Life of Charles W. Eliot* (Kessinger, 2008; originally published, 1926).

5. Having already written of American higher education that 'we are fighting a wilderness, physical and moral', Eliot, himself a scientist, used his inaugural address on assuming the presidency of Harvard to set out the basis of his academic revolution: 'This university recognizes no real antagonism between literature and science, and consents to no such narrow alternatives as mathematics or classics, science or metaphysics. We would have them all and at their best.' During his tenure, the law and medical schools were revitalized, and the graduate schools of business, dental medicine and arts and sciences were established. Meanwhile, compulsory chapel was abolished and Eliot's model was soon being copied nationwide. Harvard's agglomeration of schools has since been expanded to take in such practical disciplines as engineering and government. *The Life of Charles W. Eliot*; Harvard.

6. As the local professional community became more willing to offer financial support because they saw value in the modern curriculum, so the size of Harvard's endowment under Eliot's tenure rose from $2 million to $22 million. Harvard.

7. See Jerome Karabel, *The Chosen: The Hidden History of Admission and Exclusion at Harvard, Yale and Princeton* (Mariner Books, 2005). See also, Malka A. Older, 'Preparatory schools and the admissions process', *The Harvard Crimson*, the university's daily newspaper, 24 January 1996.

8. Harvard now has 13,600 graduate and professional students; there are 6,700 undergraduates at the university. Harvard.

9. The *Financial Times* newspaper in London compiles an annual league table of business schools called the 'Global MBA Rankings'. In 2009, Wharton shared top billing with the London Business School, and Harvard was third.

10. US News & World Report, 2008.

11. Joseph Nye was dean of the John F. Kennedy School of Government between 1995 and 2004 and before that had served in government security agencies. His concept of 'soft power' advocated the ideas of 'co-option and attraction' – diplomacy, communication, free trade, foreign assistance – rather than a reliance on the hard currency of economic and military might. His approach has been advocated in a number of books, including: *Bound to Lead: The Changing Nature of American Power* (Basic Books, 1990) and *Soft Power: The Means to Success in World Politics* (Public Affairs, 2004). Joseph Nye also coined the expression 'smart power', a mix of hard and soft in American foreign policy, which has

been in vogue under President Obama's Secretary of State, Hillary
Clinton.

12. A system introduced by James Bryant Conant, president of Harvard
between 1933 and 1953. Harvard.

13. Lawrence Summers was appointed by President Obama as director of the
US National Economic Council in 2009. Previously he had served as
Secretary of the Treasury in the Clinton administration and as chief
economist of the World Bank. The catalyst for his departure from
Harvard was a speech he gave in 2005 at a National Bureau of Economic
Research conference on Diversifying the Science & Engineering
Workforce. Addressing the subject of women's representation in tenured
positions at top universities, he used the phrase 'issues of intrinsic
aptitude' – a remark that provoked intense criticism and exacerbated a
reputation for controversy first stirred in 2001 when he had made highly
publicized criticisms of Cornel West, a black civil rights activist and
professor of African-American studies at Harvard, over issues including
grade inflation. Office of the President, Harvard; 'At odds with Harvard
president, black-studies stars eye Princeton', *New York Times*, December
2001.

14. Harvard Management Company.

15. China, India and Dubai had no representation in the top 100 of the
Shanghai Jiao Tong University world rankings, though China did
account for 6 per cent of the top 500; India's share here was 0.4 per cent.

16. There were no Latin American universities in the Shanghai top 100, with
Brazil claiming 1.2 per cent representation in the top 500, and Argentina
and Mexico 0.2 per cent each.

17. The Swiss Federal Institute of Technology came twenty-fourth in the
Shanghai rankings. The next-highest continental European institution in
the league table was the University Pierre et Marie Curie in Paris, placed
forty-second.

18. US Department of Education; Consumer Credit Counseling Service,
San Francisco.

19. Harvard.

20. Andrew Hamilton, formerly provost of Yale, took over the vice-
chancellorship of Oxford from New Zealand's John Hood at the start of
the academic year in 2009.

21. Alison Richard was at Yale from 1972 to 2003, including a spell as
provost.

Chapter Eleven – Whistler: North America's top ski-resort

1. The name 'London Mountain' was coined in the 1860s when the British Navy was conducting a survey of the wilderness that now houses the resort. But it came to be known as 'Whistler' because of the high-pitched warning calls of the hoary marmots, members of the squirrel family, who inhabited the mountains. Whistler Museum & Archives (WMA).

2. Whistler Blackcomb claims a permanent population of 10,000 people and visitor numbers of around two million a year. In 2009 it was ranked the second-best skiing resort in North America in a reader survey conducted by *Ski Magazine.*

3. WMA. The businessmen, led by Franz Wilhelmsen, formed the Garibaldi Olympic Development Association at the start of the decade, naming the scheme after the provincial park in which Whistler was located and using as their base the fishing resort around Alta Lake. In 1962 they established a company called Garibaldi Lifts and work began on developing a ski area; a narrow road from Vancouver was completed in 1965.

4. The 1968 Winter Olympics was awarded to Grenoble, France, and a bid for the 1976 games also failed because Montreal was staging the Summer Olympics that year and the authorities would not allow both events to be staged in the same country.

5. When Fortress Mountain Resorts of Alberta opened a rival operation on the neighbouring Blackcomb Mountain, a game ensued of 'anything you can do, I can do better', with the companies competing to offer the fastest chair lifts and the highest serviced vertical drops. That crown was claimed by Blackcomb in 1985, with its 'mile high' Seventh Heaven T-Bar, and in 1986 the mountain's assets were bought by Intrawest, which went on to merge the operation with Whistler in 1998. Resort Municipality of Whistler; WMA.

6. In 2006 Intrawest was sold to Fortress Investment, a hedge fund group whose co-founder was named by *Forbes* magazine in December 2008 as one of America's biggest billionaire losers of the year as his company's shares fell by 89 per cent. Fortress has struggled to pay back the $1.7 billion loan taken out to fund the Intrawest deal (*Vancouver Sun*), and in 2009 the Vancouver government had to step in with the financing needed to complete construction of the Olympic village (Associated Press).

7. In 2009, Canada came fourth on the United Nations Human Development Index, which ranks all countries according to the measures of life expectancy, education and standard of living.

8. In 2008, Vancouver was eighth in *Monocle* magazine's annual survey of 'the world's most liveable cities'.

9. Apart from the issue of carbon emissions in resorts, the World Wildlife Fund, among others, has raised concerns about the loss of biodiversity when forests are destroyed to make way for new ski facilities.

10. The environmental group Greenpeace has warned that by the 2020s the average ski season could be up to 16 per cent shorter because of global warming.

Middle East
Chapter Twelve – Property development in Dubai: the bumpy desert boom

1. The Burj Al Arab. The hotel is over 1,000 feet tall and was constructed on a man-made island in the 1990s in the shape of a sail. It is located about 300 feet from the beach of Jumeirah and is connected to the mainland by a curved bridge. The seven-star designation is self-proclaimed and the owner, Jumeirah Hotels & Resorts, markets attractions such as a fleet of Rolls-Royces, 'butlers on call round the clock' and 'dining under the sea'.

2. Dubai carried out its first census in 1968, at which time the population was measured at 59,000. It is estimated to have been 20,000 in 1950.

3. In 2006, the oil sector's contribution (between 200,000 and 250,000 barrels per day) to Dubai's GDP was 5.1 per cent, down from 5.4 per cent the previous year. Dubai's share of the overall $130 billion GDP of the seven-state United Arab Emirates was 28 per cent, or $37 billion. In 2005, the UAE's annual GDP growth rate was running at 8.5 per cent and, for comparative purposes, the GDP of the country in 1995 stood at $42 billion. Dubai Chamber of Commerce; World Bank World Development Indicators Database; CIA World Factbook.

4. The three-prong project of Palm Jumeirah, Palm Jebel Ali and Palm Deira, on which construction began in 2001 to bring a new wave of luxury hotels, villas, theme parks and beaches to Dubai.

5. In 2008, the native population was around 158,000 out of a total of 1.6 million. Underlining the skewed balance of the emirate's people, and the type of work they were doing, some 77 per cent of the population was male. Government of Dubai Statistical Centre.

6. The Government of Dubai Statistical Centre, 2005.

7. There are more than sixty international and private schools in the emirate teaching the UK curriculum. Two are named Winchester and Westminster after the historic English schools. www.dubaifaqs.com

8. Human Rights Watch, the campaigning non-governmental organization, released findings such as this in March 2006 under the title 'UAE: address abuses of migrant workers'. They came as a prelude to a report published later that year, *Building Towers, Cheating Workers*, which alleged, among other things, that wages and passports were routinely withheld from construction employees as 'security' to stop them quitting.

9. See note 8 above.

10. As with the other states of the UAE, there is no elected government in Dubai, although in 1996 the UAE's Federal National Council, which reviews federal draft laws, introduced partial elections of members drawing on the votes of 6,689 people out of the emirates' native population of 800,000 (Gulf News). There are restrictions on freedom of speech in the media and among the population.

11. Under the UAE's constitution, Islam is the official religion, but there is a relatively high level of religious tolerance in Dubai and a comparatively relaxed attitude to drink, dress sense and foreign culture. More recently, though, stories have circulated of local concerns becoming anxious that the emirate is in danger of losing its identity.

12. Dubai International – the seventeenth-busiest airport in the world for overall passenger traffic, on 2009 figures, and the sixth-busiest for international passenger traffic. Airports Council International, the industry association.

13. Dubai World Central-Al Maktoum International, which will be, the emirate proclaims, the 'world's largest passenger and cargo hub'.

14. Jebel Ali Port – 'the world's largest man-made harbour'.

15. Foreign direct investment in Dubai in 2006 increased by 13.4 per cent on the year to $11.6 billion, with the British topping the league of investors at $4 billion. Dubai Statistical Centre.

16. Dubai Healthcare City – a tax-free zone in which all treatment areas of the medical sector, including a Wellness Community, are clustered.

17. Dubai Media City – another tax-free zone housing all aspects of the industry from printing and publishing to the internet, marketing, music and film. The first tower went up in the centre in 2005 and under current plans there will be at least eighty-four.

18. Launched in 2004, the Dubai International Financial Centre was ranked twenty-fourth in the world four years later in the Global Financial Centres Index compiled for the City of London Corporation by International Financial Services London.

19. The watchdog role is played by the Dubai Financial Services Authority, which supervises trading licences and oversees companies offering fund management, banking services and share dealing.

20. As a so-called 'free' zone for the import and re-export of goods, with an attitude to port regulation and tariffs often criticized as laissez-faire, Dubai has long been held to be vulnerable to gun running, drug smuggling and people trafficking for slavery and prostitution – with the problem coming back to the fore in recent years due to the convulsions in the Middle East. See Christopher Davidson,'Dubai: the security dimension of the region's premier free port', *Middle East Policy*, 2008, the quarterly journal of the Middle East Policy Council, the Washington-based non-profit organization.

21. See Dan Stoenescu, 'Globalizing prostitution in the Middle East', American Center for International Policy Studies, a think-tank. The article highlights particular trafficking routes from Eastern Europe and Africa.

22. Among others, Frederic Launay, director of the World Wildlife Fund's office in the United Arab Emirates, has highlighted the environmental costs of the Palm Islands project. See 'Dubai's man-made islands anger environmentalists', Reuters interview, 2005.

Africa
Chapter Thirteen – Mobile telephony: changing the face of a continent

1. The Information Society and Development (ISAD) Conference was hosted by the South African government and attended by ministers and senior officials of the world's developing countries and the Group of Seven industrialized nations. It was convened in 1996 to address the threat of a digital divide between rich and poor. Also involved at ISAD was the International Telecommunication Union (ITU), an arm of the United Nations whose stated role is to 'connect the world'.

2. ITU, 2008. Between 2001 and 2006, there was a 51 per cent growth in mobile penetration in Africa. Between 2005 and 2007, mobile subscription growth stood at 39 per cent a year. In 1994 there were 0.06 mobile phones per person; by 2008 that figure was 0.33.

3. ITU. Across the African continent, there were around 300 million phone subscriptions in 2008. The figure for the same year in the USA, according to GFK/NOP research, was 271 million.

4. A World Bank report, *Africa Development Indicators 2007*, showed that average economic growth in Africa between 1960 and 1995 averaged less than 1 per cent a year; by 2005 and 2006 this had risen to 5.4 per cent. Separate research carried out in 2005 by Leonard Waverman, professor of economics at the London Business School, suggested that a 10 per cent increase in a developing country's mobile penetration added 0.6 percentage points to economic growth.

5. MTN's annual results for 2008 recorded a growth in subscribers of 48 per cent, over the previous year, to 91 million, and revenue up 40 per cent to $14 billion.

6. ITU, 2006.

7. MTM management presentation, Sandton, South Africa, March 2009.

8. ITU, 2006.

9. Wizzit was founded by Brian Richardson and Charles Rowlinson. It had an estimated 250,000 customers in South Africa at the end of 2008.

10. *The Africa Mobile Fact Book 2008* (Blycroft Publishing) predicts that mobile subscriptions in Africa will have climbed to 561 million by 2012, 53.5 per cent of the total.

11. World Bank, *Africa Development Indicators 2007*.

12. Sandra Lawson and Raluca Dragusana, 'Building the world: mapping infrastructure demand', Goldman Sachs Global Economics Paper no. 166, 24 April 2008.

India

Chapter Fourteen – The slums of Mumbai: much more than Slumdog Millionaire

1. 'An intelligent mind in a disobedient body' was the description applied to people with cerebral palsy by Mithu Alur, whose own daughter was diagnosed with the condition in the 1960s. Finding that there were no proper educational facilities for families in her position, she trained as a special needs teacher and then took her case for dedicated schools to Indira Gandhi, then India's prime minister. The first centre for special education opened in Mumbai in 1973 and they now operate across sixteen states, catering for multiple disabilities and autism as well as cerebral palsy. National Resource Centre for Inclusion at the Spastics Society of India.

2. A National Census in 2001 put the population of the Mumbai metropolitan area at 17.6 million. In 2005, the population was estimated to be 19.4 million. World Gazetteer.

3. Indian Bank was the first to open an ATM. By 2009, there were five cash machines in Dharavi.

4. Slum Rehabilitation Authority – Dharavi Redevelopment Project.

5. The redevelopment plan was accepted by the state government in 2007 and immediately became mired in controversy as residents raised concerns over the quality of the new accommodation and the proposal, at the time, to grant free re-housing only to people who could prove they had been living in Dharavi since before 1995 – an estimated 57,000 families. Concessions were then made on the size of the new homes and the cut-off point was changed to 1 January 2000. Still, though, officials found that only a minority of families in some of the five sections would be eligible, and in July 2009 a government-appointed committee noted that residents would be crammed into just 47 per cent of the current area under the redevelopment proposals. At the time of writing, towards the end of 2009, the project remained bogged down. *The Times of India*; New Delhi Television; BBC.

Chapter Fifteen – The high-tech industries of Bangalore: turning disadvantage to triumph

1. Estimates for the size of Bangalore's population vary widely, from 5.3 million to eight million, with the figures at the top end being attributable to an expansion of the municipal administration's jurisdiction in January 2007 – to create a Greater Bangalore. The 6.5 million figure is used here because it represents a median value and is a better point of comparison when trying to gauge the rate of expansion.

2. Behind Mumbai and Delhi.

3. In 1991, according to a Census of India survey, Bangalore's population was 4.1 million; by 2001 it had grown 37 per cent to 5.7 million.

4. The World Business Council for Sustainable Development reported economic growth of 9 per cent for 2006–7, and in the following year Indicus Analytics, the Indian economics research firm, put the figure at 10.3 per cent. *The Times of India* reported in 2007 that Bangalore was home to more than 10,000 dollar millionaires. In 2008, the Indian government's Central Statistical Organisation reported, the average per

capita income (earnings) across India was 33,000 rupees, equating to around $6,900; Bangalore puts the average earnings of its own citizens at 50,000 rupees.

5. Wipro, according to the company's own narrative, started out in the 1940s as a vegetable-oil trader before diversifying into consumer goods and then, at the start of the 1980s, into making computers. It is now one of India's biggest companies and a global information technology conglomerate and was one of the pioneers of offshore development centres, or outsourcing. To illustrate the turbo-charged nature of Wipro's growth, it announced revenues of $5 billion for the financial year 2008–9, a rise of nearly 30 per cent on the previous year and a jump of around tenfold on the figure for 2000–1.

6. In 2009 a survey by Transparency International, the anti-corruption organization, ranked Karnataka, where Bangalore is the capital city, the fourth worst offender among Indian states in terms of the corruption of officials.

7. In a survey by the Indian Institute of Management (IIM) of 167 hi-tech and electronics firms in 2006, 49 per cent responded that availability of power was a constraint to doing business in Bangalore, and 50 per cent said transport was a problem.

8. In 2008 the World Business Council for Sustainable Development commented on the declining air quality in Bangalore that had resulted from a 12.6 per cent annual rate of increase in the use of motor vehicles between 1985 and 2006. Compounding the problem was the failure of both the road infrastructure and the public transport system to keep pace with the city's growth.

9. In 2009, government data recorded a literacy rate in Bangalore of 83.9 per cent.

10. Mathew J. Manimala, 'Evolution of the Bangalore ICT cluster: the "crystal growth" model', *Industry and Higher Education*, vol. 20, no. 4 (2006).

11. Bangalore City Development Plan, 2007.

12. See Basant Rakesh, 'Bangalore cluster: evolution, growth and challenges', IIM working paper, 2006.

13. Founder, in 1868, of the Tata conglomerate, which now operates in around 80 countries and has interests in steel, cars, IT, communications, energy and consumer products. It reported group revenues of $71 billion in 2008–9.

14. The Indian Institute of Science and the Indian Institute of Technology, in West Bengal, both featured in the Academic Ranking of World Universities (2008) compiled by the Shanghai Jiao Tong University.

15. Bangalore University has 300,000 students in total, making it one of the largest in the world.

16. See 'America's loss is the world's gain', an American publication released in 2009 by Duke and Berkeley universities, Harvard Law School and the Kauffman Foundation. A survey of more than 1,000 Indian and Chinese immigrants who had returned home found that 54 per cent of the Indian sample had gone back to work in the IT industry.

17. Of Bangalore's population in 2001, according to the Census of India, around a third comprised immigrants either from elsewhere in Karnataka or from other Indian states. Inward migration accounted for 46 per cent of the population growth between 1991 and 2001.

18. The 2001 Census showed that 79 per cent of Bangalore's population were Hindus, 13 per cent Muslims and 6 per cent Christians.

19. The altitude of the city is not the only problem; the river is also around sixty miles away. The Bangalore Water Supply and Sewerage Board has reported that not enough water is piped to meet demand and, further, that 30 per cent of the supply is lost to leaks and pilfering.

20. The Namma Metro is due to be completed by 2011.

China

Chapter Sixteen – The municipality of Shanghai: driving the emerging financial capital

1. China's economic boom has been explosive, its GDP rising by 520 per cent from $354 billion in 1990 to $2.2 trillion in 2005, and its GDP per capita climbing 450 per cent from $312 to $1,720. However, the Shanghai story has been still more dramatic, its GDP of around $10 billion in 1990 mushrooming by over 1,000 per cent to $114 billion by 2005, and the per capita figure putting on 770 per cent in moving from $869 to $7,600. Beijing's GDP in 2005 was $85 billion and its per capita $5,500. Shanghai Municipal Statistics Bureau; Beijing Municipal Bureau of Statistics; World Bank World Development Indicators Database; CIA World Factbook.

2. The beginnings of the economic 'occupation' and expansion of Shanghai came with the conclusion of the Opium War (1839–42), a campaign fought, and lost, by China to stop sales of the drug, which was being

imported by the British East India Company. Occupied militarily in 1842, Shanghai became the subject of a forced British concession under the Treaty of Nanjing in the same year and French, American and Japanese concessions followed. Each of these foreign powers governed their territory and could trade freely with whomever they wanted; Chinese law did not apply. Although the 'fishing town' of Shanghai, located on the country's eastern coast on the Yangtze River delta, was home only to an estimated 500 people, a far larger population lived nearby where the Yangtze met the sea – an area in which trade had flourished as goods were transported upriver. This was part of the story behind Shanghai's surging growth, with the population estimated to have reached one million by 1880 and four million by 1935. Kenneth Pomeranz and Steven Topik, *The World that Trade Created: Society, Culture and the World Economy, 1400 to the Present* (M. E. Sharpe, 2006); Kerrie MacPherson, University of Hong Kong, 'Shanghai's history: back to the future', *Harvard Asia Pacific Review*, 2002.

3. The Bund, loosely translated as a raised or embanked quay, was the heart of the old British concession. Its growing network of wharves on the Huangpu River, which flows into the Yangtze, served the trading companies and was complemented by a construction boom of high-rise buildings at the turn of the twentieth century as financial institutions, hotels and retail outlets followed the money. Chinese Ministry of Culture.

4. An economic reformer whose policies often clashed with the ideology of his Maoist colleagues, Deng Xiaoping was the de facto leader of China between 1978 and 1989, outmanoeuvring other members of the Communist Party and wielding the most influence in the government, while never holding the official title of premier. Under the Four Modernizations project, Deng was instrumental in establishing a series of special economic zones from 1980 onwards, with Shenzen featuring in the first wave of five areas. The purpose of the SEZs was to stimulate exports and attract foreign capital through measures such as tax breaks, and to this end power was devolved to the municipal governments in raising money from the markets, deciding which industries most deserved investment and upgrading the infrastructure. Shanghai was late to the party, partly because of its fiscal contribution to the national economy and partly because its political leaders at the time did not have the appetite to take on the risks involved in a move away from

centralized planning. But Deng's visit in 1992, in which he reasserted the importance of his ideas after officially retiring from politics in the wake of the 1989 Tiananmen Square massacre, provided the spark that brought economic liberalization to Shanghai. Peter T. Y. Cheung, Jae Ho Chung and Zhimin Lin, *Provincial Strategies of Economic Reform in Post-Mao China* (M. E. Sharpe, 1998); the government of the People's Republic of China, 2000.

5. Between 1991 and 1994 direct foreign investment in Shanghai, expressed as a percentage of the city's GDP, rose from 5 to 17 per cent. Investment in infrastructure over the same period nearly doubled from just over 6 per cent to 12 per cent. The hub of the activity was the specially designated New Area of Pudong, whose GDP of under $1 billion in 1990 had soared to over $25 billion by 2005 and where foreign direct investment of $10 billion stood at $75 billion by 1996. Starting more or less from scratch, investment in infrastructure and fixed assets was close to $9 billion for 1998, while investment in property development was over $1.5 billion in the same year and climbed past $4 billion in 2004. Shanghai Municipal Statistics Bureau; Shanghai Pudong New Area Statistical Bureau.

6. Shanghai had a population of 18.9 million in 2008; Beijing's population was seventeen million. Shanghai Demographic Survey; Beijing Municipal Bureau of Statistics.

7. In 1990, 120,000 students were enrolled in the city's institutes of higher education; by 2005 the total was around 450,000. Shanghai Municipal Statistics Bureau.

8. Mao Zedong's Cultural Revolution officially ran from 1966 to 1969, although the resulting political convulsions persisted until Mao's death in 1976, and the enduring influence of the revolution could still be seen in Tiananmen Square twenty years later. A restatement of 'actual socialism' in the face of 'liberal bourgeois' elements,the revolution involved a purge of people perceived as dissidents, and estimates of the eventual death toll have ranged from 500,000 to three million. Shanghai's municipal government was among the victims of the centrist putsch when, in the 'January storm' of 1967, its leaders were overthrown by a coalition of workers who themselves had responded to a Maoist call for a 'seizure of power by proletarian revolutionaries'. An experiment called the Shanghai Commune followed, although that was disbanded almost immediately on Mao Zedong's instructions. Maurice

J. Meisner, *Mao Zedong: A Political and Intellectual Portrait* (Polity Press, 2007).

9. Shanghai Municipal Statistics Bureau.

10. Chen Liangyu was found to have accepted bribes worth $34,000 and to have taken part in frauds in which more than $3.5 billion was diverted into the pockets of himself and his associates. BBC.

11. In 2008, according to the Shanghai Population and Family Planning Commission, more than 20 per cent of Shanghai's locally resident population, or three million people, were aged 60 or over.

12. In 2008, sixteen years on from the reopening of the Shanghai stock market, the authorities finally let foreign companies float on the exchange for the first time. Also being whittled away gradually was the dual system of 'A' and 'B' shares', which had restricted the ability of multinationals to take stakes in Chinese companies listed on the Shanghai Stock Exchange by only allowing them to trade in the foreign currency-denominated 'B' stock. One of the conditions of China's admission to the World Trade Organization in 2001 was that it became more open to foreign companies as well as foreign money, and since then there has been a progressive relaxing of the maximum stake that overseas groups can hold in Chinese businesses and joint ventures. Meanwhile, wholly owned foreign enterprises, a feature of the special economic zones, are now permitted to sell to the domestic market; previously, they could only manufacture goods for export. However, progress has not been uniform across business sectors. Foreign banks, for example, had been restricted to foreign-currency operations until new rules introduced in 2006 allowed them to offer retail services and business carried out in yuan – but only through joint ventures or wholly owned Chinese subsidiaries.

Chapter Seventeen – The Hong Kong Jockey Club: much more than gambling

1. The club paid HK$13 billion (US$1.7 billion) in taxes in 2007–8. Hong Kong Jockey Club.

2. The World Bank and the International Monetary Fund ranked Hong Kong seventh in the world in 2008 for its estimated US$44,000 GDP per capita at purchasing power parity. PPP is a measure that attempts to give more meaning to country comparisons by making adjustments for the local cost of living.

3. The life expectancy was measured at 81.6 years in 2005. Source: World Bank World Development Indicators Database.

4. On 2009 estimates, the infant mortality rate was 2.92 deaths per 1,000 live births. CIA World Factbook.

5. It contributes over HK$1 billion a year to charity. Hong Kong Jockey Club.

6. 'The maximum penalty for betting with illegal bookmakers is a fine of $30,000 and 9 months imprisonment,' the Jockey Club warns on its website. 'Bet only with the HKJC.'

7. CIA World Factbook.

8. Macau opened up its locally controlled casino industry to foreign competition in 2001 and GDP increased by more than 50 per cent from that point to US$14.2 billion in 2006. The population in 2008 stood at just over 545,000, against 448,000 in 2001. World Development Indicators Database; CIA World Factbook.

9. The Macao Judiciary Police reported 12,921 'crime cases' in 2007 (2,393 per 100,000 of population), up 19 per cent on the year before, when a figure of 10,158 itself represented a 6.4 per cent increase. Overall crime in Hong Kong in 2007, as recorded by the Hong Kong Police Force, stood at 80,796, or 1,167 offences per 100,000 of population.

10. To two a week between September and July.

11. The Hong Kong government sets great store by its commitment to the fair treatment of workers, saying that it applies forty-one international conventions on labour rights. Among these regulations is an employment code that governs the payment of wages and termination of contracts and provides statutory protection on severance pay, as well as outlawing anti-union discrimination. All Hong Kong residents have the right and freedom to form and join trade unions. (Hong Kong Labour Department.) A Bill for the introduction of a minimum wage was put before the Hong Kong parliament in July 2009 and it is anticipated that this will come into force in late 2010 or early 2011 (Hong Kong Employment Law Update).

12. Hong Kong's GDP was measured at US$190 billion in 2006, against US$176 billlion in 1997. World Development Indicators Database; CIA World Factbook.

13. Hong Kong has a zero-tolerance attitude, with even 'soft drugs' such as cannabis being subject to heavy fines and long prison sentences for trafficking, manufacturing and possession. The Dangerous Drugs Ordinance.

14. The Index of Economic Freedom, 2009. Singapore's public spending rate is 14.4 per cent.

15. CIA World Factbook.
16. The fertility rate for Shanghai in 2008 was 0.7 babies per mother. Shanghai Municipal Statistics Bureau.
17. Findings for 2008.

Japan
Chapter Eighteen – Public safety in Tokyo: the world's safest giant city
1. National Census, 2005.
2. In Tokyo itself, as opposed to the surrounding conurbation, 228,805 offences were reported to the police in 2007 out of a total estimated population of 12.8 million, or an average of one per fifty-six people. The total figure for murders, caused by intent or other violent assaults rather than negligence, was 138, equating to around one per 100,000 of population. The figure for rapes was 247, or just under two per 100,000, and for burglaries it was 13,145 (down from 31,426 in 2003), or around one per 1,000. Across the whole Japanese population of 127 million, reported murders of 1,309 and rapes of 1,948 in 2006 showed a broadly similar offending rate. Tokyo Metropolitan Government, *Tokyo Statistical Yearbook*; Japanese Statistics Bureau, *Japan Statistical Yearbook 2008*.
3. In the 2005 census, there were around 350,000 foreign residents in Tokyo.
4. National Police Agency (NPA).
5. Japan's crime statistics for 2006 showed 8,636 cases of extortion, 209 gambling offences and 11,723 incidents of indecency.
6. NPA.
7. The earthquake that struck the country's sixth-largest city in January 1995 left more than 5,000 people dead, 400,000 injured and 200,000 buildings destroyed. It was reported that local yazuka had been much quicker on the scene in distributing emergency supplies than official relief support, although it was also noted by the *New York Times* in June of the same year that they were well placed for a share of the demolition and reconstruction work.
8. Japan International Cooperation Agency.
9. Japanese Statistics Bureau.
10. As of the last census, there were two million foreign residents in Japan in 2005, including 635,000 Koreans and 508,000 Chinese. According to crime statistics from the NPA for that year, 47,685 offences were committed by foreigners, up from 40,615 in 2003.

11. Twelve people died and 5,000 were left with damaged health after the sarin attack by the Aum Shinrikyo cult in March 1995. BBC.

Australia
Chapter Nineteen – The great sporting nation: how Australia trains the world
1. At the 1976 Olympics, the Australian squad won five medals overall – one silver and four bronze. The total at Munich in the previous games had been seventeen, including eight gold medals.
2. In the 1980 Moscow Olympics, the tally was nine medals, including two golds. By 1984 in Los Angeles, the first games after the creation of the Australian Institute of Sport (AIS), the total was up to twenty-four with four gold medals. In Sydney 2000 the Australian team won fifty-eight medals, of which sixteen were gold, and in Athens 2004 there were seventeen golds in an overall forty-nine medals.
3. In Beijing 2008 the Australians won forty-six medals, fourteen of them gold.
4. Much of the credit for the performance of the Great Britain swimming team in Beijing – six medals and twenty-one finalists – has been attributed to the intensive training techniques introduced by Australian Bill Sweetenham, a former coach at the AIS who went on to become national performance director for British Swimming from 2000 to 2007. Meanwhile Shane Sutton, from New South Wales, helped British Cycling to its tally of fourteen medals in Beijing in his role as head coach.
5. Concerns about the direction of Australian sport were first brought into focus in 1973 when the government commissioned sports scientist Professor John Bloomfield to devise a new strategy. His 1974 report, *The Role, Scope and Development of Recreation in Australia*, recommended the creation of a national sports institute along the lines of elite establishments that Professor Bloomfield had studied in Europe. In the following year a separate research project, *The Coles Report*, commissioned to look into the feasibility of the Bloomfield plan, backed the idea of a national institute. The poor performance at Montreal added weight to these recommendations, but the growing sense of urgency was not matched politically until 1980 when Bob Ellicott, the minister for home affairs and environment, backed the creation of what was to become the AIS. (See also www.ausport.gov.au/ais/history.)

6. Australian Institute of Sport.

7. Juan Antonio Samaranch paid this compliment at the closing ceremony for Sydney 2000 but went on to say the same thing about Beijing 2008.

8. Interview with BBC Sport, September 2000.

9. The Sydney Organizing Committee of the Olympic Games reported that 92.7 per cent of the 5.7 million tickets allocated had been sold, while the International Olympic Committee said that a global television audience of more than 3.7 billion people had watched the games.

10. www.sydneyolympicpark.com.au

11. According to findings from the US music magazine *Billboard*, based on ticket revenues from November 2007 to November 2008.

12. ANZ stands for the Australia and New Zealand Banking Group.

13. See 'The 2004 Olympic legacy that London must avoid' (February 2009), www.thisislondon.co.uk/standard. See also 'Abandoned, derelict, covered in graffiti' (July 2008), www.xpatathens.com.

14. In 2004, the Greek Embassy in Washington reported that the Athens games had cost an estimated €8.9 billion, equating to US$11.2 billion at the time and A$15.8 billion. Figures for the cost of the Beijing games vary from US$40 billion upwards.

15. Australian Bureau of Statistics, 2008.

16. ABS.

17. Australia's National Health and Medical Research Council received A$617 million in the government's 2008–9 budget.

18. 'Obesity in Australia: a need for urgent action', National Preventative Health Taskforce, Technical Report no. 1, 2008.

Global

Chapter Twenty – The International Baccalaureate: schooling the brightest kids

1. The International Baccalaureate Organisation (IBO). In 2009, 3,322 programmes were being taught in 2,734 schools around the world, with North America accounting for 1,349 of the schools (the USA, 1,039) and 1,516 of the programmes, and the Europe/Middle-East region another 127 schools and 915 programmes. However, highlighting the IB's explosive growth in the developing world, the Asia Pacific has in 2009 538 programmes, with the 'top ten' largest IB countries now including the 65 schools in India and the 44 in China (against 39 in tenth-placed Germany).

2. First published by Carus Publishing Company in 1987.

3. The League of Nations, forerunner to the United Nations, was established in the aftermath of the First World War as a mediation forum for representatives of forty-two states (that total was to rise to a maximum of fifty-eight, though membership levels were always volatile and plagued by withdrawals) to head off any fresh conflicts. Based in Geneva, partly because of Switzerland's neutrality in the First World War, the League had a permanent 'civil service' staff of around 500 drawn from all over the world, and employed hundreds of others in Geneva in agencies such as the International Labour Organisation and the Health Organization (now the World Health Organization). Undermined at first by America's non-participation and then by its failures at resolution in conflicts such as Japan-Manchuria and Italy-Abyssinia, as well as the German annexing of Austria, the League lost its authority and finally gave way to the UN after the Second World War. Rumki Basu, *The United Nations: Structure and Functions of an International Organisation* (Sterling Publishers, 1993); the United Nations Office at Geneva; League of Nations Archives.

4. Set up in 1919 by Edward A. Filene, an American businessman and philanthropist, the Twentieth Century Fund, now called the Century Foundation, describes itself as a non-partisan foundation dedicated to researching and improving public policy.

5. Chartered in Michigan in 1936 by the family behind the famous car company, the Ford Foundation says its rationale is to award grants where they can help 'build knowledge' and 'promote international co-operation'.

6. The vision of Kurt Hahn, a German educationalist, was that if young people from around the world could be brought together, grounded in their own cultures but still impressionable enough to learn from each other, then this would help to avoid the misunderstandings that lead to conflict. Born in 1886 into a Jewish family in Berlin, he was educated at Oxford University from 1910 to 1914 and then took a posting in the Foreign Office in Berlin, where he tried to work towards a negotiated end to the First World War. In 1920 he set up the Salem School in southern Germany with the aim of teaching students 'moral independence' and the physical fitness that he believed would help foster mental fitness. Forced out of Germany in 1933 after criticizing Nazi education values, he returned to the UK and settled in Scotland, setting up Gordonstoun School a year later. Among the pupils there was the future Prince Philip, who would go on to complement Hahn's Outward

Bound Trust with the Duke of Edinburgh Award Scheme. The catalyst for the creation of the United World Colleges (UWC) movement came in 1956 when Hahn was invited to speak to the Nato Defence College in Paris and noted the co-operation among people who had been enemies eleven years earlier. Sources: UWC; 'Genius of Experimental Education in the Twentieth Century', an essay by Charles Stetson at the US Fund for Leadership Training – part of the www.kurthahn.org archives.

7. The first UWC was set up in Wales in 1962. Influenced by his own experience of conflict, Lord Mountbatten – a Second World War naval commander (whom Alec Peterson had served under) and Prince Philip's uncle – became the UWC's first president in 1967 and played a big part in the opening of the second college, in Singapore, in 1971. He passed on the presidency to his great-nephew Prince Charles in 1978, and Queen Noor and Nelson Mandela became joint presidents in 1995. Nelson Mandela's family has been educated at the Waterford Kamhlaba UWC in Swaziland. Sources: Ernest Stabler, *Innovators in Education* (University of Alberta Press 1987); 'Genius of Experimental Education'; IBO.

8. The IB North America was established in 1977.

Index